Detention Reviews in Canada

Detention Reviews in Canada

A practical handbook on
law, procedure and practice
for lawyers, immigration
consultants and law students

RAJ NAPAL, L.L.B. (HONS)

Copyright © 2019 Raj Napal

19 20 21 22 23 5 4 3 2 1
Printed and manufactured in Canada

Thank you for buying this book and for not copying, scanning, or distributing any part of it without permission. By respecting the spirit as well as the letter of copyright, you support authors and publishers, allowing them to continue to create and distribute the books you value.

Excerpts from this publication may be reproduced under licence from Access Copyright, or with the express written permission of Brush Education Inc., or under licence from a collective management organization in your territory. All rights are otherwise reserved, and no part of this publication may be reproduced, stored in a retrieval system, or transmitted in any form or by any means, electronic, mechanical, photocopying, digital copying, scanning, recording, or otherwise, except as specifically authorized.

Brush Education Inc.
www.brusheducation.ca
contact@brusheducation.ca

Editing: Peter Enman
Proofreading: Shauna Babiuk
Cover design: Dean Pickup; Cover image: © Lightfieldstudiosprod from Dreamstime.com
Interior design: Carol Dragich, Dragich Design

The forms showed on pages 247–250 are used with permission of the Immigration and Refugee Board of Canada.

All character names in the book, as in the case study of Alfred Blake, are fictional to protect the identities of the individuals who were involved in the actual case. Therefore, if the names have any resemblance to actual persons living or dead, it is entirely coincidental and beyond the intent of either the author or the publisher.

Library and Archives Canada Cataloguing in Publication

Title: Detention reviews in Canada : a practical handbook on law, procedure and practice for lawyers, law students and immigration consultants / Raj Napal.

Names: Napal, Raj, 1956- author.

Identifiers: Canadiana (print) 2019011827X | Canadiana (ebook) 20190118296 | ISBN 9781550598179 (softcover) | ISBN 9781550598186 (PDF) | ISBN 9781550598193 (Kindle) | ISBN 9781550598209 (EPUB)

Subjects: LCSH: Emigration and immigration law—Canada—Handbooks, manuals, etc. | LCSH: Detention of persons—Canada—Handbooks, manuals, etc. | LCGFT: Handbooks and manuals.

Classification: LCC KE4454 .N37 2019 | LCC KF4483.I5 .N37 2019 kfmod | DDC 342.7108/2—dc23

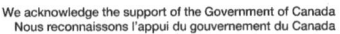

Contents

Preface IX
Acknowledgements XI
Introduction XIII

1 Summary of the Law and Procedure on Arrest and Detention 1
    Arrest 1
    Detention 3
    Conclusions 10

2 Case Study of Alfred Blake: The Initial Interview 12
    Commentary 13

3 First Stage Preparation 16
    A Note on the UCI and the GCMS 17
    The Detention Review Transcript 17
    Retainer Agreements and Waivers 19

4 The 48-Hour Detention Review Transcript 22
    Questions to Consider 31

5 Extract from the Interview of Alfred Blake at the Holding Centre ... 33
    Commentary 37
    Credibility 38
    Ethical Issues 38

6 The Importance of the Bondsperson(s) 40
    Checklist of Essential Elements in the Bondsperson's Affidavit ... 40

	Counsel's Interview of Gill St. John	44
	Review Questions	48
	Affidavit of Gill St. John	49
	Review Questions	52
7	Advocacy in the Immigration Division	53
	Examination in Chief	53
	Cross-Examination (XX)	59
	Re-Examination	62
	Oral Advocacy	64
8	Sample Oral Submissions at the Detention Review Hearing of Alfred Blake	69
	Commentary	71
9	It All Comes Together: The 7-Day Detention Review Transcript	72
	Review Questions	87
10	Danger Ground for Detention	89
	Youth Convictions and Charges that Are Withdrawn	90
	Plans for Release	91
11	Identity Ground for Detention	94
	A Typical Example: The Case of Tariq Mustafa	94
12	Detention of Children	98
13	Release	102
	Extract from ENF 8 Current to May 15, 2017	102
14	Appeals	107
15	The Impecunious Detainee without a Bondsperson or Residence	111
	Provincial Legal Aid	115
	Voluntary Organizations and Legal Clinics	115
16	Recent Developments	117
	The External Audit 2017/2018 on Detention Reviews: The Laird Report	121

    Recommendations for Amendments 137
    Comments 140

17 The Amended Chairperson's Guidelines (effective April 1, 2019) 142
    A Robust and Meaningful Review 142
    Procedural Fairness and Natural Justice 143
    2. Grounds for Detention 143
    3. Release and Alternatives to Detention 145
    4. Minors 149
    5. Vulnerable Persons 150
    7. Conducting the Detention Review – Robust Hearing 150
    8. Sufficiency of Reasons for Decision 153
    Conclusion 153

Glossary of Terms, Acronyms and Initialisms 155

Appendices 158
    A Immigration and Refugee Protection Act, sections 54–61 159
    B Immigration and Refugee Protection Regulations, sections 244–250 166
    C Immigration Division Rules 172
    D Chairperson's Guidelines on Detention 192
    E Chairperson's Guidelines on Vulnerable Persons 216
    F Precedents and Templates 226
    G Important Resources on Detention 251

About the Author 253

Preface

When I first practised immigration law in 1996 and for several years thereafter, I was confused about how all these complex immigration laws and regulations fit together, and how to apply them. In those days, the governing statute was the *Immigration Act 1976*. Although there were good practitioner books on immigration law, they failed to outline the procedural steps necessary to maximize the chance of achieving a successful result in an actual case. With the implementation of the *Immigration and Refugee Protection Act* and Regulations in 2002, the law became even more complex.

I am prepared to admit that during that initial foray through the jungle of immigration law, I made mistakes, which I believe I would not have made if I'd had practical guides or handbooks dealing with the various areas of my immigration practice.

From the late 1990s onward, I drifted toward the advocacy part of immigration practice, appearing in all the divisions of the IRB (Immigration and Refugee Board of Canada) and in the Federal Court. I did more appellate work, and this enhanced both my practical and academic knowledge of immigration law. Since August 2016, I have taught students at Ashton College the immigration diploma course, which is the foundation course in the licensed immigration consultant program. During that time, and having taught hundreds of students, I discovered that these students did not know the practical "how-to" of immigration law. Like me at the start of my practice, they were confused. A standard book such as Waldman's *Canadian Immigration & Refugee Law Practice*, although an excellent resource, could not help them understand the fundamental procedural and substantive steps they must take in an immigration matter. Another excellent text, by Fournier-Ruggles, *Canadian Immigration and Refugee Law for Legal Professionals*, will help students understand the subject but does not explain how a practitioner can manoeuvre through an actual case. This is where I think this handbook fills a gap.

During the classes at Ashton College, the students and I had lively discussions about the need for a practical guide with an in-depth case study. They urged me to use my classroom notes to create a practical handbook. It was out of these discussions that the idea was born that handbooks on various areas of immigration law ought to be written, each of which will contain one or more case studies that will guide the reader in applying the law and understanding the procedural and practical aspects involved in that area of law.

Each handbook should be a one-stop resource that provides the relevant law, procedural rules, practical processes, tactics and resolution of ethical issues that can arise, along with precedents—a handbook that an immigration practitioner, student or reader can use as a reference and guide for cases in that area of law.

I faced the challenge boldly, and this first handbook, in the area of detention reviews, was an intensive and laborious enterprise. After reviewing this handbook on detention reviews, readers can tell me whether it is useful. If it is, I will continue the challenge when I write the next series of handbooks on other important areas of immigration practice.

Raj Napal
Barrister and Solicitor
Instructor at Ashton College
September 4, 2019

Acknowledgements

I am grateful to my publishers, Brush Education, their staff and all the persons associated with that company who worked on this book. I am especially thankful to their managing editor, Laura Seidlitz, for publishing this first handbook. Without her confidence in me, this book would have languished on my bookshelf and just been an aide to my Ashton College students. It would not have been available to the larger audience of immigration lawyers, consultants, students and general readers to help them understand this challenging and complex area of law. Only time will tell whether it is of value and can be regarded as a one-stop resource for practitioners doing detention review work in Canada.

My friend and colleague, Susan von Achten, encouraged me to keep on writing, and when at times my writing energy ebbed, she spurred me forward. I am also indebted both as a father and a writer to my children, Helena and Joshua, who kept a watchful eye on me to make sure I was not slack but on track toward completing this book.

I thank the director of Ashton College, Ron McKay, who gave me the freedom as an instructor to develop some of the course materials. I am also indebted to Zainab Bukhari and Lynn Truong for their assistance. The students at Ashton College, with their searching questions, thirst for hands-on practical knowledge and our lively discussions, fueled my desire to create a handbook that would satisfy their needs and be of benefit to other legal professionals.

Without the encouragement of Brush Education, Ashton College and their students, this handbook may not have been born. I am deeply grateful to all of them for giving me this unique opportunity.

Introduction

This handbook starts off with a summary of the law on detention reviews in chapter 1. It is necessary for the reader to be familiar with the law in order to understand the practical detention review processes as we plow our way through the case study of detainee Alfred Blake in chapters 2 through 9.

In chapter 2, we look at the lawyer's initial telephone intake interview with Gill St. John, the girlfriend of Alfred Blake. Counsel must know what questions to ask at this interview. As we go through chapter 3, there are discussions about the preliminary steps you must take in every case, such as drafting a suitable retainer agreement. There is a lively discussion on retainers and waivers, with an examination of some of the ethical issues that can arise in immigration practice. A properly drafted retainer can be critical in avoiding client complaints to the practitioner's regulatory body, so this subject is treated in some depth. We also look at the contact information forms that must be completed and the routine correspondence with the Immigration Division requesting the key documents that counsel must obtain in every detention review case, such as the detention review transcript or audio tape.

In chapter 4, we examine the detention review transcript of the first 48-hour review, where Alfred represented himself. The ground for detention was flight risk, and Alfred failed to put forward a release plan that would lessen the flight risk concern. When we read the transcript, we will see the defects, in both Alfred's presentation of his case and the release plan, that led to his continued detention. Those defects provide the platform and focus for the probing questions that counsel must ask Alfred at the holding centre in chapter 5. An essential component of success in these cases is to develop a proper strategy, bearing in mind throughout the necessity for an effective presentation and release plan that will persuade the member of the Immigration Division to release the detainee. There is an in-depth discussion in chapter 6 of how to draft the affidavits of the bondspersons so that they contain all the information that will persuade the member to find the bondspersons suitable and appropriate. Chapter 7 provides a useful refresher on the rules of questioning of witnesses, evidence and oral advocacy that are essential skills when engaging in advocacy at the IRB.

In chapter 8, I provide an example of the oral submissions that counsel for Blake will deliver at the end of the 7-day detention review hearing.

Chapter 9, "It All Comes Together," shows how the thorough preparation outlined in this handbook has paid off when we examine the 7-day detention review transcript. We see how the tactics, evidence and tight release plan presented by counsel have persuaded the member to release Alfred.

In chapters 10 and 11, there are brief and focused discussions on the other grounds of detention: danger to the public and identity issues. The problems inherent in the detention of children and vulnerable persons are discussed in chapter 12. In chapter 13, we examine the important solvency assessments of the bondsperson by the Canada Border Services Agency (CBSA) after there has been a release order. This is a topic that is not given enough attention, despite its critical importance. If the CBSA makes a negative solvency finding, the detainee will not be released, irrespective of the member's decision ordering release.

After a member makes a detention order, the representative must know the test for a judicial review challenge to the Federal Court in order to properly advise the detainee whether he or she has a reasonable prospect of appealing that decision. (*Representative* means an immigration lawyer or consultant who is paid for representing the detainee. It can also include a person—a friend or the member of a voluntary organization—who is representing the detainee without a fee.) Chapter 14 deals with appeals and the test of reasonableness that must be applied. Although immigration consultants are not allowed to practise in the Federal Court, the knowledge gained from this chapter will enable the consultant to do a preliminary assessment of the merits of the challenge prior to seeking advice from an experienced Federal Court lawyer.

This handbook would not be complete if we ignored the vast number of detainees who do not have the funds to retain counsel. Usually, these impecunious detainees know no one in Canada and they have nowhere to live. In chapter 15, we discuss the resources that these unfortunate immigrants can access for assistance.

Finally, in chapter 16, we look at some of the recent developments involving detention reviews. Every practitioner in this area of law must read the Laird Report, an audit that was commissioned in September 2017 and released in July 2018. It involved a comprehensive investigation of the detention of immigrants throughout Canada and provides well-reasoned criticisms of the flaws in the detention review system—flaws and defects that led to the unjust and inequitable long-term detention of many immigrants. It made some much-needed recommendations, all of which must be implemented in order to provide fundamental justice to detainees.

On April 1, 2019, the Chairperson's Guidelines on Detention were amended to implement some of the recommendations in the Laird Report. These guidelines must be followed by members of the Immigration Division throughout Canada. The amendments update the guidelines that had been in force since June 5, 2013. The new amendments are very important, and in chapter 17, I have highlighted some essential portions of them that representatives must know when acting for detainees at detention reviews.

I explain in the glossary at the end of chapter 17 the meaning of various terms and acronyms mentioned in the book. The appendices in this handbook provide important materials that must be considered in every detention review case. Appendix A contains the relevant sections of the *Immigration and Refugee Protection Act* (IRPA). Appendix B sets out the Immigration and Refugee Protection Regulations (IRPR), which further define the mandated factors that members must consider when deciding whether to detain or release an immigrant. Appendix C provides the rules of the Immigration Division, which all legal professionals and other representatives must know when appearing before that tribunal. Appendix D contains the recently amended Chairperson's Guidelines on Detention that came into effect on April 1, 2019. Appendix E presents further guidelines from the Chairperson that provide insight into the treatment of vulnerable persons, including children and the mentally ill, at detention reviews. Appendix F provides a set of sample templates to help legal professionals and general readers draft some of the important documents that are necessary in every detention review case. Finally, Appendix G provides useful links to the immigration manuals on detention, enforcement and solvency. Links to the Laird Report and a study of the plight of children in detention are also included, as well as a link to the previous Chairperson's Guidelines on Detention that had been in force since June 5, 2013, until replaced by the new guidelines in April 2019. I have included this link so that readers can compare it with the newly amended guidelines. The June 2013 guidelines are also useful as they refer to a list of helpful cases on detention.

I hope this handbook proves useful to legal professionals, students and readers who intend to do detention review work in the Immigration Division.

CHAPTER 1

Summary of the Law and Procedure on Arrest and Detention

Arrest

Before we embark on an examination of the case study of Alfred Blake, we will examine the law of arrest and detention under the *Immigration and Refugee Protection Act* (IRPA) and its Regulations. Under section 55 of IRPA (see appendix A), an immigrant, whether a foreign national or a permanent resident, can be arrested with or without warrant if an officer (referring to a Canada Border Services Agency [CBSA] officer) has reasonable grounds to believe that the person is inadmissible and either a danger to the public or unlikely to appear for an examination, admissibility hearing or any immigration proceedings that could lead to the person's removal from Canada. Additionally, arrest and detention may be necessary where the officer is not satisfied as to the identity of the foreign national during the course of any procedure under IRPA. I have set out some of the fact scenarios that could lead to either a foreign national or permanent resident being arrested under section 55.

The case of Julie Mandala

Julie arrived in Canada from Ghana on a visitor visa on January 30, 2018. Her visitor visa was for three months so she could visit relatives in Toronto. She decides that life is good in Canada, and she does not want to go back to live in her home on the outskirts of Accra, where there is poverty and disease. She stays on in Canada, making no attempt to seek an extension of her visitor visa. She moves out of Toronto and rents a cheap basement apartment for cash in Shelburne, a town north of Toronto. She obtains a cash paying job in a convenience store in the town. She is not on the immigration radar screen as she is paid cash, and she pays cash for all her expenses. She does not file tax returns. However, after Julie has lived in this apartment for six months, the tenant upstairs, Betty, gets into an argument with her. Betty makes a complaint to the police alleging that Julie threatened her. The police attend Julie's basement suite, and when they do a CPIC (Canadian Police Information Centre) check, they discover that Julie is a foreign national. They then refer the matter to the CBSA, who with their comprehensive database will identify Julie as a visitor to Canada. But her UCI (Unique Client Identifier) immigration number shows that she failed to leave Canada after her authorized stay here. The wheels are now put into motion when she is arrested by the CBSA for breach of section 29 of IRPA, staying in Canada beyond the period of her authorization to remain here. Irrespective of whether she is charged by the police with uttering threats, she is now under the lens of the CBSA. If she is not charged by the police for uttering threats or she is charged but released by the police, the CBSA has the power to detain her under section 55 of IRPA. In this case, it would be primarily for flight risk concerns. This is the ground for detention in the Alfred Blake case study, which we will examine in chapter 2.

There are other fact scenarios that will lead to arrest and detention under IRPA. The examples below represent some of these situations, but it is not an exhaustive list:

- Breaking the conditions of a work permit: for example, the foreign national does not leave Canada after the period of work authorization here.
- Breaking the conditions of a student permit: for example, the foreign national does not leave Canada after the period of their student permit here.
- A PR (permanent resident) is convicted of a serious criminal offence here and becomes criminally inadmissible in Canada for serious criminality. In these circumstances, the PR's permanent residence is revoked and the PR may be arrested and detained.
- A failed refugee claimant does not leave Canada pursuant to a removal order. This individual, if apprehended by the CBSA, is liable to arrest and detention.
- A PR loses their permanent residence in Canada for failing to satisfy the 730-day residence requirement in the period of 5 years since the issuance of their PR card. The PR is issued a removal order and does not leave Canada. If apprehended by the CBSA, they are liable to arrest and detention.

Detention

Once a PR or foreign national is arrested and detained, section 56 of IRPA enables a CBSA officer to release the person before he or she appears at a detention review hearing in the Immigration Division (ID) if the reasons for detention no longer exist. The officer may also impose conditions such as a cash deposit or performance guarantee to ensure the immigrant attends for removal or at an immigration proceeding.

Detention reviews in the Immigration Division: Time frames

Section 57 of IRPA (see appendix A) sets out a timeline for mandated statutory reviews in the Immigration Division.

The **first review** must take place within *48 hours* of the date and time of the immigrant's arrest and detention. During the review process, the member of the Immigration Division will examine whether the grounds for detention are made out. There are three main grounds for detention: (1) that the immigrant is likely to fail to appear for removal or an immigration proceeding such as an admissibility hearing; (2) that the immigrant is a danger to the public; and (3) that there are issues with respect to the identity of the immigrant. The onus is on the CBSA to prove one or more of these grounds for detention. If the member of the ID is satisfied that one or more of the grounds for detention are made out, the member must look at a list of factors to decide whether the immigrant should be released, usually on conditions.

If the immigrant's detention continues after the 48-hour review, there is a **second review** that must take place within *7 days* of the 48-hour review.

If detention continues after the 7-day review, there is a **third review** that must take place within *30 days* of the 7-day review. *Thereafter reviews are held every 30 days.*

Detention review time frames for designated foreign nationals

Designated foreign nationals are defined as foreign nationals who entered Canada as part of a human smuggling and trafficking enterprise. For example, in 2010, large numbers of Sri Lankans entered Canadian waters on a boat, the *Sun Sea*, through a human smuggling enterprise. All the foreign nationals on the *Sun Sea* became designated foreign nationals after their apprehension by the CBSA. The rights of designated foreign nationals are severely restricted under IRPA. In relation to detention review time frames, their first review is *after 14 days and then after every 6 months.* One can argue that such a severe time frame is harsh given that these foreign nationals are usually victims of persecution in their country of origin. Should their entry into Canada through a human smuggling enterprise wherein they are the victims render them liable to such inhuman treatment by the Canadian authorities here?

Inadmissible on grounds of security, violating human or international rights, serious criminality, criminality or organized criminality

Under section 58(1)(c) of IRPA, if there is a suspicion that the immigrant is inadmissible on one or more of the above grounds, they can be detained pending the conclusion of the steps taken by the Minister to investigate this suspicion.

Detention review procedures

As you will learn from the case study of Alfred Blake, there are specific procedures that govern a detention review, as set out below:

- It is a public hearing.
- The member will record the hearing by audio tape. The Immigration Division will transcribe the tape of the review hearing upon request by counsel for the immigrant or Minister's counsel. In most cases, the ID will transcribe the audio tape even if there are no such requests. This is because the ID is mandated with the task of reviewing previous detention reviews, as the member must give reasons if they make a decision that is contrary to a previous detention decision. However, if there have been no requests by either party for the detention review transcripts, the member is entitled to review the previous review by listening to the audio tape. Sometimes, counsel for the immigrant may request the audio tape as opposed to insisting that it be transcribed, especially if the detention review hearing is imminent and the ID cannot provide the transcription before the date of the review hearing.
- The hearing is adversarial, so that there are two parties, one of which will argue for detention and the other for release. The proponent for detention is the CBSA represented by counsel, who is called either a Hearings Officer or Minister's counsel. The advocate for release is the immigrant's counsel or, if the detainee is self-represented, the detainee. There is also the member of the Immigration Division, who will adjudicate and decide whether the immigrant should be released or detained.
- The onus and burden of proof that the grounds for detention have been satisfied are on the Minister, but it is arguable that the onus and burden can shift to the detainee when they are adducing evidence of alternatives to detention to prove that they are not a flight risk or a danger to the public or on identity grounds. The standard of proof is the civil standard of a balance of probabilities. Is it more probable or not that the Minister has established the grounds of detention?

- The hearing is usually conducted in the correctional centre or holding centre where the immigrant is detained. Sometimes, if the correctional centre where the immigrant is detained is a great distance from the location of the ID in that city, teleconference links are set up between the ID location and the correctional centre so the immigrant can participate in the review hearing by video.
- Strict adherence to the rules of evidence is not enforced. The immigrant is entitled to provide testimony at the hearing and if represented by counsel, will be examined in chief by his counsel and cross-examined by Minister's counsel (see chapter 7 on advocacy).
- New procedures were established in 2017 in Toronto whereby the bondsperson can only be interviewed by Minister's counsel in the hearing room, in the presence of the panel member, the detainee and his counsel, as opposed to the previous practice when Minister's counsel interviewed the bondsperson outside the hearing room. This procedure was introduced in order to make the process more open and accountable. There were cases where, after Minister's counsel interviewed the bondsperson outside the hearing room, there would be criticism of the biased interpretation of what the bondsperson had said to Minister's counsel. As of April 1, 2019, this procedure applies to all detention reviews in Canada through the new Chairperson's Guidelines.
- Documentary evidence will be provided by Minister's counsel before the hearing to support the grounds for detention. Similarly, the immigrant's counsel will provide documentary evidence that supports release. The ID rules mandate that documentary disclosure be provided to the opposing party and the ID at least 5 days before the commencement of the hearing in the case of 30-day reviews. In the case of a 48-hour or 7-day review, the disclosure should be provided as soon as possible before the commencement of the hearing (see appendix C for the ID Rules).
- At the end of the hearing, after all the evidence has been adduced, counsel for the immigrant and the CBSA will be invited to make submissions. After this, the member will provide the reasons for the decision, whether it is that the immigrant will be detained or released.

Factors the ID must consider under the flight risk, danger to the public and identity grounds (see appendix B)

The member of the ID cannot make a finding that any of the three grounds for detention are established without first considering the factors set out under the regulations (*Immigration and Refugee Protection Regulations* [IRPR], SOR/2002-227) that are relevant to the particular ground for detention.

The IRPR 245 factors apply to the flight risk ground for detention.

The IRPR 246 factors apply to the danger to the public ground for detention.

The IRPR 247 factors apply to the identification ground for detention.

The matters set out in these regulations are mandatory factors that must be considered by the ID before deciding whether the ground for detention has been established (see appendix B for the factors set out in these regulations).

REGULATION 245: FLIGHT RISK

Paragraphs (b) to (d) help the member of the ID assess the risk of the immigrant failing to appear for removal and other immigration proceedings by looking at the immigrant's previous compliance with removal orders and attendance for reporting and at immigration proceedings. Evidence of such compliance and attendance would make the immigrant seem less of a flight risk.

On the other hand, factors such as the immigrant being a fugitive from justice in his or her foreign country of residence would make the flight risk concerns greater. Also, the immigrant being involved in human smuggling and trafficking, along with the coercion that can be exerted onto the immigrant by the organization not to comply with our immigration laws, would increase the flight risk concerns. The immigrant's previous non-attendance for removal or attempted escape from custody would also heighten the flight risk concerns (see paragraphs [a], [e] and [f]).

The extent of the immigrant's ties to the community in Canada can act in two ways. Those ties could reinforce the immigrant's compliance with the immigration laws or their intensity could deter the immigrant from doing anything that would cause them to have to leave Canada (see paragraph [g]).

The member of the ID must have regard to these statutory factors, but on a case by case basis, there may be other facts that overcome or intensify a flight risk concern.

REGULATION 246: DANGER TO THE PUBLIC

A "danger to the public" opinion by the Minister under IRPA would be a strong factor. These opinions are only issued where there has been a detailed analysis of the immigrant's criminal activity, including whether the crimes the immigrant committed are violent and whether there are any indications of recidivism, that makes it seem likely that the immigrant poses a danger to the public. There are also cases where the immigrant poses a danger to the security of Canada, which would be a strong factor in establishing the danger to public ground under regulation 246. The danger opinions are usually submitted by the Minister in order to justify removal of the immigrant to their home country even though the country conditions there may pose a risk of persecution and harm to them. In the typical case, the immigrant becomes a permanent resident through a successful refugee claim but then loses their PR status by virtue of a finding of serious criminality and liable to removal. In other cases, the danger opinion is rendered when there are grounds to believe the immigrant is a member of a criminal organization or gang or has threatened or is a threat to Canadian security (see paragraphs [a] and [b]). The law and case law on danger opinions can be complex, and a detailed examination of it is outside the scope of this handbook.

The commission of offences involving people smuggling and human trafficking would be a strong factor in finding that the immigrant poses a danger to the public. Convictions in Canada of offences involving sexual or violent offences or trafficking, importing/exporting and production of illicit drugs are also factors to be considered in assessing the danger ground (see paragraphs [c]–[e]).

Interestingly, where the alleged commission of these offences occurs outside Canada, there is no requirement that a conviction is recorded against the immigrant. It is sufficient that these allegations are the subject of pending charges. It is arguable that it is unjust for an immigrant to be deemed a danger to the public when there has been no finding of guilt by the criminal courts in the foreign country where these alleged offences occurred (see paragraphs [f] and [g]).

In chapter 10, we will delve into some of the case law on the danger ground in order to extract the exact meaning of danger to the public in the current jurisprudence.

REGULATION 247: IDENTITY NOT ESTABLISHED

Some immigrants are arrested and detained on this ground when the CBSA or the IRCC (Immigration, Refugees and Citizenship Canada) cannot establish their identity from reliable sources, such as a passport, national identification card, birth certificate, electoral card or other identity document. This regulation stipulates that the assessment of whether the immigrant will be detained will depend on several factors:

- Has the foreign national cooperated with the CBSA and IRCC by providing all the necessary documents that will prove the foreign national's identity? Or has the foreign national deliberately obstructed the government in the process of investigating and establishing their identity?
- Has the foreign national destroyed genuine identity documents and used fraudulent identity documents to deliberately conceal who he or she is?
- Has the foreign national provided contradictory evidence to the IRCC and CBSA that is inconsistent with other identity documents in the government's files?
- Can a refugee claimant provide genuine identity documents from their country of origin without divulging their personal information to the government of the country where they face persecution?

There have been several cases where a foreign national is detained for a lengthy period because the foreign national has made it difficult for the CBSA to obtain travel documents from the national's country of origin to facilitate the person's removal from Canada. The Federal Court has said where the foreign national has deliberately obstructed their removal from Canada through lack of cooperation in providing documents to the CBSA that will establish their identity, the foreign national can expect their detention to continue. On the other hand, where the foreign national's identity has not been established through the negligence and lack of diligence by the CBSA in failing to instigate or follow through on an investigation into their identity, that can be a factor that may favour release.

After the member examines the factors in the regulations and is satisfied that the immigrant poses a flight risk or danger to the public or there are identity issues, the member must examine the factors set out under regulation 248.

REGULATION 248: OTHER FACTORS

The factors in this regulation were codified from the principles of law and guidance set out in the leading authority of *Sahin v. Canada*, [1995] 1 FC 214.

The member of the ID at a detention review must consider the reason for detention, the length of detention and any elements that can forecast how long the detention will likely continue.

If the period of detention, or likely continued detention, will be lengthy, the member must consider all potential alternatives to detention so that the immigrant can be released with appropriate conditions.

An analysis of the case law makes it obvious that finding answers as to the length of likely detention can be difficult. Consider the example below:

> A, who is a foreign national, has not been able to establish his identity. The CBSA needs reliable evidence of identity to engage the processes necessary to obtain a travel document so he can be removed to his country of origin. A fails to provide that evidence. In this situation, the immigrant is likely to be detained pending the completion of the identity investigation by the CBSA because he cannot be removed to his country of nationality/residence until that investigation is complete. But the question that the ID must wrestle with is, how long will the detention continue until A's identity is established?

Another aspect of the regulation 248 factors will be an examination and a balancing of which party has exercised due diligence in the investigation that is central to the ground for detention. Any unexplained lack of diligence by the CBSA could weigh in favour of the immigrant's release. On the other hand, the immigrant's lack of diligence and failure to cooperate with the CBSA may result in the immigrant's continued detention.

Detention of children

A more detailed discussion of this topic will be found in chapter 12. For now, there are some important principles to note governing the detention of children under IRPA and the IRPR. Section 60 of IRPA sets out the guiding principle "that a minor child shall be detained only as a measure of last resort, taking into account the other applicable grounds and criteria including the best interests of the child."

Special considerations are engaged when dealing with the detention of a child. Regulation 249 of the IRPR lists six factors that must be considered whenever the member is grappling with the issue of the detention of a child. I will list them in question form below:

- Are alternative facilities available in local child care agencies or child protection services for the care and protection of the child? If such facilities are available, then the child must be accommodated in these facilities as opposed to a holding centre.
- What is the anticipated length of detention? If the period of detention is likely to be long, it may lead to the immediate release of the child into the care of his parents. But there are difficult issues if the parent is being detained.
- Is there a risk of continued control by the human smugglers or traffickers who brought the child to Canada? Consideration must be given to ensure the cessation of any contact by the child with these smugglers and a complete separation between the child and these individuals or organizations.
- What is the type of detention facility envisaged and what are the conditions of detention? The facility must be appropriate for housing the child and not pose any threat of being akin to a jail, holding centre or other repressive form of incarceration.
- Will the child be segregated from adult detainees who are not the child's parents or legal guardians of the detained child? All steps must be taken to ensure that there is such separation in order to prevent adults from abusing or otherwise molesting the child.
- Are there services in the detention facility, such as education, counselling and recreation? If not, the facility may be deemed not suitable to accommodate the child.

Detention of vulnerable persons

I have reproduced, at appendix E, the Chairperson's Guidelines on Vulnerable Persons. The representative must give special attention and consideration to detainees who are vulnerable by reason of mental illness or who are particularly vulnerable through trauma they have experienced. For example, a female detainee who has been the victim of abuse and rape by men in her country of origin may feel harassed and frightened in a male-dominated environment at a detention review hearing where the panel member and Minister's counsel are men. The IRB must consider a detention review setting where, perhaps, the panel member and Minister's counsel are female. Furthermore, the panel member and Minister's counsel, being aware of the vulnerability of the detainee, may be obliged to create and adopt a more relaxed, informal and friendly setting so that the detainee does not feel intimidated. The content and manner of questioning of the detainee from the panel member, Minister's counsel and the detainee's own counsel must be sensitive to the detainee's trauma and not inflame wounds that are healing.

The guidelines stress that where a representative believes that his or her client is potentially vulnerable, the registry of the division of the IRB must be alerted to the immigrant's condition. If the detainee is not represented, the Immigration Division or Minister's counsel must be alive to any behaviour from the detainee that may indicate vulnerability issues. Finally, if the issue is the inability of the vulnerable person to understand the proceedings, a designated representative should be appointed to act as a channel of communication for the immigrant when he or she gives instructions to counsel or, if unrepresented, when addressing the division.

Conclusions

There are three steps that must be undertaken by the ID in every detention review case.

First, has the CBSA established that there are reasonable grounds to believe that the immigrant is a flight risk or danger to the public or is there an identity concern? This threshold test of "reasonable grounds" is lower than proof on a balance of probabilities but more than mere suspicion. If that test is satisfied, then the immigrant will be arrested and detained subject to the discretion of the CBSA officer to release the immigrant on appropriate conditions.

Second, if the CBSA officer continues the immigrant's detention, the member of the ID at the detention review hearing must be satisfied that the CBSA has proven the ground(s) for detention on a balance of probabilities. In making that assessment, the member must look at the prescribed mandatory factors under regulations 245–247 of the IRPR and any other relevant factors.

Third, if the ID member is so satisfied, the member must look at the prescribed mandatory factors under regulation 248 of the IRPR to determine issues relating to the length of likely detention and alternatives to detention such as release on appropriate conditions. When the immigrant puts forward a release plan that will persuade the member to release him or her, it is arguable that the onus and burden of proof shift to the detainee to prove that he or she should be released.

CHAPTER 2

Case Study of Alfred Blake: The Initial Interview

In most cases, a member of the public, perhaps the father, mother, girlfriend, wife or friend of the detainee, will contact you by phone. This will be your first opportunity to gather the essential information you will need to prepare the case. Below, I have set out an extract from one of my preliminary telephone interviews so you know the basic questions you should ask.

Here, the girlfriend of the detainee, Gill, called me on the morning of Tuesday, May 1, 2018, to find out what she could do to help her boyfriend, who was detained by the CBSA.

GILL:	I got your number from someone. My boyfriend, Alfred, was arrested by these immigration cops, and he is in their holding centre. Can you help me?
COUNSEL:	When was he arrested?
GILL:	Yesterday morning.
COUNSEL:	Do you know what he was arrested for?
GILL:	He told me it was because he was speeding, but later he told me it was because he was illegal in Canada.
COUNSEL:	What do you know about Alfred's immigration history? When did he come to Canada? How did he become illegal here?
GILL:	He came to work here from Jamaica. I thought he was okay to leave the farm where he was working in Hamilton, as he told

	me he would find a job at a farm in a neighbouring town near Orangeville when he came to live with me.
COUNSEL:	So, he is illegal here?
GILL:	I guess.
COUNSEL:	Where is he being detained?
GILL:	Rexdale Holding Centre. Can you get him out?
COUNSEL:	Not right now. There will be a detention review hearing tomorrow morning when a member of the Immigration Division will decide whether to release him. You should contact the officer who is dealing with his case and tell the officer you'll give a money guarantee and a cash deposit to make sure he appears for any immigration proceedings. If they continue to detain him, you can contact me, and we will prepare for the next detention review hearing 7 days after the 48-hour review tomorrow.
GILL:	Right now, Tony and I are too upset to do anything for him.
GILL:	However, I'm prepared to pay you some money to go to the detention review hearing tomorrow and get him out. But Tony and I do not want to get involved in that process.
COUNSEL:	I am not prepared to do that, as I won't be prepared for that hearing and must see him at the holding centre to take instructions from him. I must also get key documents and prepare materials to submit to the Immigration Division. I cannot do that in the next 24 hours. Let's see how the land lies after that first detention review hearing. If you want to call me after this hearing, we can discuss the matter further. Thanks.

Commentary

From appendix A, and section 57 of IRPA, it will be clear to you that after the detainee's arrest by the CBSA, there is a strict timetable for reviews you must follow under IRPA. The first review is within 48 hours after arrest. The second review, if they still detain the person, takes place 7 days after the 48-hour review. If they still detain the person after that, the subsequent detention review will take place 30 days after the 7-day review. If still detained, further reviews will take place every 30 days thereafter.

As we go through this handbook, you will find you must take detailed instructions from the detainee and must gather important documents for use at the detention review hearing. It is impossible to do all this preparatory work in less than 24 hours. It is possible that during this rushed preparation, you will miss important documents and make factual errors. This may compromise the detainee and lead to their continued detention. You should not expose the detainee to that kind of risk.

Once you present a plan that is rushed and not properly thought out because of the imminence of the 48-hour review hearing, the plan sticks after the member continues to detain your client. You have created a situation where you now must devise further plans of release to persuade the member to release your client at a subsequent review. These plans may not be persuasive because of the rushed, ill-considered first release plan. These detention reviews are tape recorded, and usually, the members of the Immigration Division prepare transcripts of the reviews. The case law has established that each review is a rehearing. The members must consider these previous reviews, and if they make a different decision, the members must explain the reason for their departure from a previous ruling (see appendix D, article 1.1.8 of the Chairperson's Guidelines on Detention). Members in subsequent reviews will look at the release plan presented in earlier reviews, which may influence them from considering the new release plan you have prepared in the subsequent review. My motto is "better get it right the first time around." But under article 1.1.8 of the new guidelines, members must consider the evidence and arguments afresh at each detention review and come to their own determinations.

Can you accept at face value everything Gill told you? Are there more facts you are not aware of concerning Alfred's status and immigration history? Perhaps he is the subject of a removal order and a Canada-wide arrest warrant. Did he arrive in Canada at a port of entry? Or did he cross into Canada illegally from the US, having travelled to the US from Jamaica?

The list of possible factual uncertainties is endless, as you cannot rely on the accuracy of what Gill said. She may think she is telling you the truth, but she herself may not know the full facts about Alfred's immigration history. The following are some typical factual situations I've encountered during my lengthy practice of immigration law:

- The detainee and their relatives are not sure of the facts and are making up some facts, which they assume are correct but are not.
- They are not aware of the full facts themselves.
- Some of the facts are true, but the rest are inaccurate.

You deal with facts and must investigate the credibility of your client or his relatives or friends. In most cases, your detainee client will give evidence at the detention review hearing, and Minister's counsel and the member of the ID will ask the detainee searching questions. You want the evidence to be credible. How do you enhance Alfred's credibility?

You must be familiar with all the facts and allegations from the IRCC and the CBSA, well before the detention review hearing. It is that knowledge that will enable you to extract the proper facts from your client. But how can you do this if you learn the facts for the first time from Minister's counsel when you appear at the first detention review? Everything now collapses, as the facts as received from the client and his relatives or Gill are different from the facts in the IRCC and CBSA file that Minister's counsel is reading.

After this interview with Gill, she calls you back after the 48-hour review, telling you that Alfred is still detained. She also says she could not help Alfred, as she feared posting bond would affect her student loan. Gill tells you that her brother, Tony, who lives with her, is confused about the process involved and does not want to have anything to do with it. She says Alfred relied on two guys he didn't know to act as bondspersons. However, the member did not accept these bondspersons, and the member detained him after the 48-hour review. Gill informs you that the next review hearing will be on Wednesday, May 9, 2018.

After you explain the detention review process to her and the kind of bondspersons that the Immigration Division will accept, she tells you she will help, and she will persuade Tony to post bond. Now you can start preparing for the upcoming detention review in seven days.

In the next chapter, we will examine the core documents and inquiries you must make as part of your initial preparation for the upcoming detention review hearing.

CHAPTER 3

First Stage Preparation

There are two documents you must prepare as soon as the client retains you to do the detention review: the retainer agreement between you and the client and the Counsel Contact Form. They are both in appendix F. In that appendix, I have included both a lawyer retainer agreement and a Regulated Canadian Immigration Consultant (RCIC) retainer agreement, approved by the Immigration Consultants of Canada Regulatory Council (ICCRC). The written retainer agreement is important, as it will protect you in various ways. We will discuss this in greater detail later in this chapter.

The retainer will help your client understand the scope of your services and provide your hourly rate and an estimate of fees for the work you must do. The Counsel Contact Form is a recognized form used by the Immigration and Refugee Board (IRB) that allows the IRCC, the Immigration Division (ID) and the Canada Border Services Agency (CBSA) to communicate with you as Alfred's authorized representative. The *Immigration and Refugee Protection Act* (IRPA) and the Regulations (IRPR) regulate who can represent an immigrant for compensation. These are immigration lawyers in good standing with their law society or RCICs who are licensed by their professional body, the ICCRC. In Ontario, paralegal licensees can only do advocacy work in the divisions of the IRB. No other persons can represent an immigrant, but a non-licensed representative can do so if they are not receiving any compensation from the detainee for representing him or her.

The first thing you must do after Alfred has signed your retainer agreement is to correspond with the ID, referencing the client's unique client identifier number, known as a UCI # (also known as a Client ID #), indicating that you represent Alfred through the Counsel Contact Form that you will provide the ID when making a request for your client's previous detention review transcript or the audio tape. Appendix F includes a sample of correspondence with the Immigration Division. Under the new Chairperson's Guidelines, a request ought to be made to both the ID and the CBSA for all the documents that the Minister intends to rely upon at the review hearing, including exculpatory materials. Should these documents not be provided prior to the review hearing, counsel can object to the documents being admitted in the proceedings. See appendix F, template 6 for a precedent.

A Note on the UCI and the GCMS

Every immigrant's history and activities are recorded and tracked in a computerized platform called the Global Case Management System (GCMS). Immigration officers, CBSA officers and other immigration personnel must input all an immigrant's activities and events into the system referenced by the immigrant's UCI. It is important to be familiar with the GCMS because it will enable you to understand the immigration history of a foreign national or permanent resident (PR) such as a refused temporary resident visa (TRV) application or the expiry of a visitor visa, student permit or work permit. With a PR, it could include details of an admissibility hearing when the PR became subject to a removal order due to serious criminality.

There is an erroneous conception by inexperienced immigration legal professionals that either there is no database that contains information about immigrants or that any such database is inaccurate or incomplete. This leads to the mistaken belief that an immigrant can hide things about their immigration activities or history. The immigrant's true status and any breaches of IRPA are an open book to the IRCC and the CBSA through the GCMS notes. In fact, if there was sufficient time, you would request the GCMS notes of your client in order to understand the core facts about your client's immigration history. This would enable you to prepare properly for the detention review hearing. However, it takes 30 days to obtain these GCMS notes, which given Alfred's imminent detention review hearing, would not give you enough time to secure them. You must find another way to get to the core facts of Alfred's immigration history, and that is through you obtaining from the ID the 48-hour detention review transcript or the audio tape. Additionally, you could request the client's GCMS notes directly from the CBSA.

The Detention Review Transcript

We know Alfred had a detention review hearing before a member of the ID 48 hours after his arrest by the CBSA as mandated under IRPA. The hearing is tape recorded (it is usually transcribed within two days, but sometimes it can take longer), and at the hearing, the CBSA is represented by Minister's counsel. Sometimes this representative is also called the "Case Presenting Officer," or "Hearings Officer," who will outline both Alfred's immigration history and the grounds for detention. At appendix D, the Chairperson's Guidelines on Detention (CGD) provide comprehensive case law and a commentary by the Chairperson on the various grounds for detention. In any event, these grounds are clearly set out in IRPA and the IRPR (also reproduced at appendices A and B). The three most common grounds for detention are (1) that the foreign national poses a flight risk, namely, that the detainee will not appear for either or both the inadmissibility hearing or for removal from Canada, if released; (2) that the immigrant poses a danger to the public; and (3) that the identity of the immigrant has not been established. Any one of these grounds, if proven on a balance of probabilities by Minister's counsel, will be sufficient to cause your client to be detained.

There will be "no surprises" at the 7-day detention review hearing after you read the 48-hour detention review transcript or (if the transcript is not ready in time) listen to the audio tape of the hearing. Then, for the first time, you will know the facts about your client's immigration history. You will be aware of the grounds for detention that led to your client's detention. You will know whether your client at that detention review presented a release plan and what kind of plan it was. If the ID has rejected the proposed plan, the detention review transcript or audio tape will tell you why. Before reading the detention review transcript or listening to the tape, you will have received hearsay and probably inaccurate information from Gill at the initial telephone interview with her, and from Alfred when you went to see him at the holding centre to have him sign your retainer. Now you will know the true facts. Instead of speculating or theorizing on a lot of hearsay information or rumour, and building castles in the air, you'll have the hard facts, and with a proper analysis of the evidence that supported the grounds for detention, you will be able to use your expertise to build a persuasive release plan.

But we must do a bit of housekeeping first by drafting a suitable retainer agreement for the work involved in a detention review and waivers to deal with solicitor- or consultant-client privilege and confidentiality as well as completing the Counsel Contact Information Form (see appendix F).

In chapter 4, we will examine the detention review transcript you will receive from the ID.

I have skipped the first meeting with Alfred at the holding centre when he will sign your retainer agreement. However, I urge you to go to the holding centre or jail to explain the retainer to the client. It is not ethical to delegate this important function by sending clerks or assistants to the holding centre or jail to do this since it is you, as the lawyer or consultant, whom Alfred has retained. Therefore, it is your duty to explain the retainer to your client. It seems some larger law and consultancy firms do not adhere to this policy in their effort to be overly efficient at the expense of ethics. Remember, at the first interview with Alfred, you will not have the detention review transcript, so the facts will continue to be murky!

Retainer Agreements and Waivers

Scope of the retainer

The retainer agreement is an important document, and if it is drafted properly, it will protect the legal professional from complaints from the client or the applicable regulatory body. The document must define the scope of the retainer. In this retainer, the legal professional will say "he (she) is retained to prepare for and attend a detention review hearing on (date) and use his (her) best endeavours to secure a release but *not in connection with any appeal or any other work.*"

You can be even more specific in detailing the work you must do in a typical detention review case. I do not believe that is necessary, but that is your choice.

Hourly rates, dockets and billing

It is important that the client know the basis upon which fees are charged, irrespective of whether this is a "fixed fee" retainer or an "hourly" retainer. The ICCRC does not seem to insist on the inclusion of hourly rates in its template retainer agreements, but the law societies of the provinces do. I believe in setting out your hourly rates for the work you and any of your staff do. In a typical example, your hourly rate would be $200 per hour and that of your law clerk $75 per hour. It is not fair that a client should be charged $400 for two hours of administrative and clerical work that your clerk is doing on the file. This system saves the client money and makes sense. The hours are charged in increments of 0.1—in other words, 6-minute portions. The hourly rate will provide the justification and support for the fee billing and any fixed fee or estimate of fees in the retainer agreement. But all this can work well only if there are proper dockets where you itemize the time spent on various pieces of work. Computer software such as Amicus Online or Officio will do your time entries on command, and in fact if that phone call with Gill was inputted into counsel's case management software, it would calculate the time automatically, and if requested the bill would be calculated in an instant.

A clause that enables you to charge more than the fixed fee or estimate of fees when certain events occur

If this is a fixed fee retainer, it is important that there be a clause in the retainer agreement that enables you to charge more in the event of complexity or the necessity that more work is required on the file or in the event the review is adjourned to another date or the review hearing continues to the following day. What happens in a case is often uncertain, and if these unpredictable events occur, you need to be able to bill out more than the fixed fee and not find yourself out of pocket. Hence the inclusion of hourly rates is essential even in a fixed fee retainer agreement, as it will justify the actual amount of fees you charge with an itemization of the additional work you had to do on the file. However, it is not wise to regularly bill clients more than the agreed fixed fee or estimated fees. The client will feel you are not honouring your obligations, so make sure the fixed fee or estimate is one you can work with, and do not, under any circumstances, charge substantial amounts over the fixed fee even if the additional work you have done was reasonable. Sometimes it is better to bite the bullet and eat up the excess hours than jeopardize your client's trust in you.

The OUT clause in the retainer agreement
At the beginning of the client–lawyer/consultant relationship, everything may seem rosy, but as in life, it is a truism that things can go wrong. Your client does not cooperate with you, so you cannot advance his best case. His bondsperson(s) are not cooperating with you and miss numerous appointments you arranged with them. This leads to your inability to do a proper intake interview and draft the necessary affidavits, causing serious problems preparing for the detention review. In these circumstances, which I would describe as the breakdown in the client–lawyer/consultant relationship, there must be a clause in the retainer agreement that entitles you to terminate your services and provide the client with a refund from your trust/client account for any work you will no longer do for him. You must never allow your professionalism, competence or credibility to be compromised by a client or the bondsperson(s) involved in the detention review. It is better to terminate the retainer and perhaps lose money on the file than compromise yourself by appearing at the detention review hearing unprepared through this lack of cooperation. It can lead to complaints from the client and the Immigration Division. *Withdraw your services before it is too late for you to extricate yourself from the trap your client and/or bondsperson(s) have created for you* (see sample lawyer and consultant retainer agreements at appendix F).

Waiver of privilege and confidentiality
The rules are clear from the ICCRC and the provincial law societies that a client is entitled to expect all his or her information that is disclosed to the legal professional to be kept confidential and not divulged to any third parties unless the client has expressly consented to such disclosure.

In the case we are dealing with, Gill seems to be working with Alfred to give you information about the detention review that is coming up. But Alfred is the client, NOT Gill. As the case progresses, Gill, as a potential bondsperson for Alfred, will need to receive information from you about Alfred. You, as the legal professional, stand in the middle of this. You must protect yourself by ensuring that Alfred has waived the strict privilege and confidentiality expectation between the two of you so Gill is able to receive information from you. This waiver must be in writing and signed by Alfred. It can be incorporated into the retainer agreement, as you can see from the sample retainer at appendix F.

It is a universal truism that what happens in life is uncertain and unpredictable. Let's provide you with this hypothetical example: Several weeks after Alfred retains you, Alfred and Gill have a big quarrel, and they no longer talk to each other. Alfred has built up an intense hatred of you for irrational reasons. He is trying to find someone else to represent him and decides he will make a complaint against you to the effect that you breached your duty of privilege and confidentiality by telling Gill about his case. If you do not have a signed waiver, you may have problems with the Law Society or the ICCRC. There should, therefore, be a further clause in the waiver that says the waiver can only be later revoked in writing and that any alleged breach can only run from the date of the client's written revocation. It is not likely you will tell Gill anything about Alfred's case on or after the date Alfred revokes the waiver in writing. A waiver is required only in those cases where family members or friends are intimately involved in the client's case, and the waiver thus enables them to become privy to the client's information through the client's consent.

THE DIRECTION FOR PAYMENT OF FEES

Usually the client who is the party to the retainer agreement will pay your fees. However, in a typical detention review case, the client is detained and cannot pay your fees directly and thus nominates another person, in this case Gill, to pay the fees. In these circumstances, it is important that you have a provision in the retainer agreement wherein the client is directing you to accept payment from the third party he or she nominates. This is important because then your dealings with the third party become transparent and will resolve any issue that arises if the client says he or she did not authorize the third party to pay you. As I said earlier, at some point in your career, you will realize that anything you think cannot happen will! So plan for it in advance by dealing with these issues in your retainer agreement.

CHAPTER 4

The 48-Hour Detention Review Transcript

I have reproduced below the 48-hour detention review transcript in Alfred's case, which we will work through in this handbook.

```
1-0007-F1-5-5-DR-02-May-18-BOSWMA-58(1)(b)
```

IMMIGRATION AND REFUGEE BOARD

-IMMIGRATION DIVISION-

Record of a Detention Review held under the
<u>Immigration and Refugee Protection Act</u> concerning

ALFRED BLAKE

HEARING: PUBLIC

HELD AT:	Immigration Holding Centre
DATE:	May 2, 2018
BEFORE:	Gregory Boswell —Member

APPEARANCES:

  Alfred Blake   —Person Concerned
                     Self-Represented

| Mr. Burrows | –Minister's Counsel |
| N/A | –Interpreter |

MEMBER: Good morning.

This is the detention review of Alfred Blake.

Is that you, sir?

PERSON CONCERNED: Yes.

MEMBER: This hearing is now being tape recorded. Today is May 2, 2018. My name is Gregory Boswell, and I am a member of the Immigration Division. I will be presiding over your hearing today.

Representing the Minister today is Mr. Burrows, and I understand you are representing yourself, Mr. Blake? I understand that you do not require an interpreter as your first language is English. Is that correct?

PERSON CONCERNED: Yes, sir.

MEMBER: I understand that there are 2 persons outside, one of whom would like to post a performance bond, and the other a cash bond. Is that correct, Mr. Blake?

PERSON CONCERNED: Yes, sir.

MEMBER: These persons can attend the hearing and tell us about their proposals. Would you like them to do that, Mr. Blake?

MINISTER'S COUNSEL: I'm sorry to interrupt, but I have spoken to these people and invited them to attend the hearing. They have refused to do so, and in fact they left this facility shortly after I walked into the hearing room.

PERSON CONCERNED: They are only casual acquaintances. At least Mr. O'Connor is so I'm not bothered about them attending the hearing if they don't want to.

MEMBER: Very well. Sir, the information I have is that you have been detained by the immigration authorities since April 30, 2018 and that this is your 48-hour review of the reasons for your detention. This is a public hearing. The procedure we shall follow is that, firstly, Minister's counsel will outline your immigration history and the grounds they assert for your continued detention. Secondly, you will be given an opportunity to say whatever you consider necessary in response to Minister's counsel. During the process, Minister's counsel and I may ask you some questions to clarify your evidence. Do you understand?

PERSON CONCERNED: Yes, sir.

MEMBER: Yes, Mr. Burrows.

MINISTER'S COUNSEL: Mr. Blake had been accepted on the farm worker's program where he was employed looking after livestock at a farm in Hamilton. His employer was Fresh Farm Produce Inc—FFP. He received a work permit to work at FFP. I am reading from the GCMS notes. It seems he first came to Hamilton from Jamaica, his country of citizenship and ordinary residence, on May 1, 2014. In accordance with his work permit, he left Canada on February 10, 2015. He received another work permit to work for FFP on May 1, 2015 and left on February 10, 2016 before his work permit expired. However, after he received a work permit to continue work at FFP on June 12, 2017, he did not leave Canada before his work permit expired on February 10, 2018. In fact, CBSA received a call from FFP that Mr. Blake had abandoned his employment at the farm at the beginning of February 2018 and then disappeared. Eventually, on March 1st, 2018, CBSA issued a Canada-wide warrant for Mr. Blake's arrest, and shortly thereafter a CBSA officer issued a removal order against Mr. Blake. This removal order was sent to his last known address in Hamilton. There are some pages missing toward the end of the GCMS notes, which may have dealt with events after the removal order was issued. I will investigate that. In any event, Mr. Blake has breached IRPA in failing to leave Canada before the expiry of his work permit on February 10, 2018. Furthermore, he breached his conditions of employment as outlined in the work permit conditions in ceasing work at the farm and effectively fleeing from the program at the beginning of February 2018. On April 19, 2018, Hamilton police stopped Mr. Blake for speeding. Upon checking the CPIC system, police became aware of the Canada-wide arrest warrant on Mr. Blake. Police alerted the CBSA, giving them Mr. Blake's address in Orangeville, which was apparently on Mr. Blake's driver's licence. The CBSA arrested Mr. Blake at that residence on April 30, 2018 and detained him at the Rexdale Holding Centre until his 48-hour review, which is today. It seems Mr. Blake was staying with his girlfriend, Gill St. John, at her home in Orangeville. I also have a note here that a Tim O'Connor telephoned the CBSA officer earlier this morning indicating that he and a friend could provide a $2,000 bond and $1,000 cash deposit. When the officer attempted to obtain further information, it seems that Mr. O'Connor terminated the call. The officer had the impression that Mr. O'Connor was very nervous during that phone call. The Minister takes the position that Mr. Blake is a flight risk in that he has demonstrated through his actions that he is contemptuous of our immigration laws by breaching IRPA in both leaving FFP in breach of his work permit conditions and failing to leave Canada before the expiry of his work permit. For these reasons, I ask that you continue his detention, sir.

MEMBER: Thank you, Mr. Burrows. Now, Mr. Blake, is there anything you want to tell me about the allegations that Mr. Burrows has made? Do you have any release plan or conditions you want to offer, which might persuade me to consider releasing you?

PERSON CONCERNED: I just couldn't continue to work at FFP. There was a bloke there, a Luke Brown, who was one of the farm hands. He kept wanting to fight me. Every day was hell with this guy, shoveling manure at me and trying to kick me. I complained to the boss, Dick, but Dick did nothing. Then, in the fall of 2017 at a church gathering in Hamilton, I met Gill. It seems that my twin brother, James Blake, knew Tony St. John back in Jamaica. Tony started to talk to me and introduced me to his sister, Gill. Gill and I had a lot in common, and soon after meeting, we dated regularly. She is a super girl, and we fell in love. With this mental case at work and wanting to be with Gill, I left FFP. I went to live with her and Tony at their house in Orangeville. But I was worried about what I'd done, so I wrote a letter to immigration and gave them my new address in Orangeville. Gill and I wanted to be engaged. Our plan was to marry. Gill is a Canadian citizen, you know. She got her citizenship in 2015. She would have sponsored me. She said she would. I'm sorry for what I did, but I don't know what else I could have done with the abuse at work and my deep love for Gill. This is the first time I did this. Before, I always left Canada before my work permit ran out.

MEMBER: Do Gill and Tony know that you fled from FFP, and that you stayed in Canada illegally after your work permit expired?

PERSON CONCERNED: No, sir. I told them that there was a dairy farm in Grand Valley, a town that is near Orangeville, that wanted to hire me. I said I had a good work permit. We just left it at that, sir.

MINISTER'S COUNSEL: So, you lied to them? And why didn't you write a letter to an immigration officer, telling the officer of the abuse at work, seeing that FFP was not doing anything about your situation there?

PERSON CONCERNED: I did lie to Tony and Gill. I didn't write to immigration because I didn't think they could help me.

MEMBER: Is Gill employed, and what about Tony?

PERSON CONCERNED: Gill has a good job at the CIBC bank in Orangeville, and Tony is a self-employed carpenter.

MEMBER: You told Minister's counsel before the hearing started that you had a couple of people who could post a bond and cash as part of your release plan. Can you tell me about them?

PERSON CONCERNED: Tim O'Connor is a friend of mine. He can post bond for $2,000.

MINISTER'S COUNSEL: How do you know Mr. O'Connor?

PERSON CONCERNED: He is the manager of a No Frills store in Hamilton where I used to get my groceries. We chatted with each other when he was in the store.

MINISTER'S COUNSEL: How many times did you chat with him, and how well did you know him?

PERSON CONCERNED: I chatted with him two to three times. We spoke about the weather, women and the work we did. I didn't really know him that well, but we did have a casual friendship.

MINISTER'S COUNSEL: Did you know how much money he made as the manager of the store or whether he was married or had kids?

PERSON CONCERNED: No. I just contacted him yesterday to see whether he could help me. He said he could post a bond for $2,000. He also said he would come to Rexdale this morning. I think he was in the waiting room with his friend Mr. Philpot earlier on.

MEMBER: Have you spoken to Mr. O'Connor, Mr. Burrows?

MINISTER'S COUNSEL: Yes. He told me pretty much what Mr. Blake said. He is a casual acquaintance of Mr. Blake. He knows absolutely nothing about Mr. Blake's immigration history and does not even know what his duties are as a bondsperson. He did not want to disclose his income and assets to me. He is clearly inappropriate as a bondsperson.

MEMBER: Okay. Is there anyone else that you want to put forward?

PERSON CONCERNED: There is James Philpot, who I am told can put up a cash deposit of $1,000.

MEMBER: Do you know Mr. Philpot?

PERSON CONCERNED: No. I was told about him by Mr. O'Connor. He said Mr. Philpot is a close friend of his who can also help.

MINISTER'S COUNSEL: I spoke to Mr. Philpot in the waiting room. He admitted he does not know Mr. Blake and only came to the hearing because Mr. O'Connor asked him to come. My position is that Mr. Philpot is not a suitable bondsperson who can assure you through his cash deposit that Mr. Blake will abide by any conditions of release you impose.

MEMBER: Is there anything further you want to say about why you should be released?

PERSON CONCERNED: No, sir.

MEMBER: Why did you not propose your girlfriend, Gill, as a bondsperson and her brother, perhaps, to provide a cash bond?

PERSON CONCERNED: Gill said she could not do it as it would affect her student loan. Tony said he doesn't know enough about the process to put up a cash deposit. I left it at that.

MEMBER: Do you have a current and unexpired Jamaican passport?

PERSON CONCERNED: It is at home and Gill can bring it here for you.

MEMBER: That will not be necessary at this time. Thank you. Anything further from Minister's counsel?

MINISTER'S COUNSEL: I believe I have outlined the grounds for detention, and it is clear from what we have heard about Mr. Blake's release plan that it is wholly inadequate as the people he proposed are completely inappropriate to ensure that he appears for removal or any future immigration proceedings.

MEMBER: Thank you. We will stand the matter down for 15 minutes while I collect my thoughts before making a decision.

Short Recess

REASONS FOR DECISION

Mr. Blake failed to complete the Farm Workers Program and failed to return to his homeland, Jamaica.

Without any permission from the CBSA, he left the program and went to cohabit with his girlfriend, Gill St. John, in Orangeville. Ms. St. John is originally from Jamaica, but she became a Canadian citizen in 2015.

There was a Canada-wide warrant for Mr. Blake's arrest after the CBSA became aware from his employer that he had fled from the farm in Hamilton where he worked. It seems that Mr. Blake fled from FFP on February 1, 2018. The CBSA also issued a removal order against him, which was sent to his last known residential address. Fortunately, the CBSA became aware of his whereabouts when Mr. Blake was stopped by police for speeding in Orangeville on April 19, 2018. The police checked CPIC and as soon as they knew he was wanted by immigration, they informed the CBSA. The CBSA now knew his residential address from the driver's licence he showed to the police. A few weeks after the police stop, on April 30, 2018, CBSA officers went to his address in Orangeville, and Mr. Blake was arrested on the warrant. The detention review hearing today is the first 48-hour review. I note that Mr. Blake is not represented. Minister's counsel, Mr. Burrows, has explained the facts and the grounds for detaining Mr. Blake. Essentially, Mr. Blake is a flight risk because he left the Farm Workers Program without permission and when he was required to leave Canada on February 10, 2018, he did not do so as he had gone to cohabit with Ms. St. John in a different town. Through his actions, Mr. Blake demonstrated a complete contempt for our immigration laws by breaking IRPA in two ways. Firstly, leaving the Farm Workers Program before he completed the work that he had to do there during the period of his work permit. Secondly, he breached his limited authorization to remain in Canada only until February 10, 2018 by illegally staying in Canada after that date. At the hearing, Mr. Blake told me that he had provided his new residential address in Orangeville to the CBSA. I reviewed the GCMS notes produced by Mr. Burrows, and there is no notation in the notes that such a report was made by Mr. Blake. However, there were some pages missing from the notes—pages 32-37 are missing. Mr. Burrows could not explain the missing GCMS notes, but he undertook to make some enquiries on this issue.

Mr. Blake said that he met Ms. St. John when he attended a Pentecostal church in Hamilton in the fall of 2017. Ms. St.

John attended the church, so she could meet various members of her family who live in Hamilton. Apparently, Ms. St. John's brother, Tony St. John, knew Mr. Blake's twin brother in Jamaica. Mr. Blake and Tony conversed with each other and that is how Mr. Blake became acquainted with Ms. St. John. In any event, a relationship blossomed between Mr. Blake and Ms. St. John. The two dated for several months so that by the beginning of February 2018, Mr. Blake and Ms. St John agreed that he would move into her townhouse in Orangeville. Mr. Blake could not hold back his tears when he expressed the intense love he had for Ms. St. John, which led him to leave the program and not return to Jamaica. Although it seems that a contributing factor to him leaving FFP was the harassment and abuse he received from a fellow employee.

    I note Mr. Blake's love for Ms. St. John and their commitment to each other through their proposed engagement, but that cannot be an excuse for his clear breach of our immigration laws. In my opinion, there are strong and cogent grounds for Mr. Blake's continued detention as he is clearly a flight risk. There are, however, indications in the GCMS notes that since 2014, he had attended the Farm Workers Program on two occasions and returned to Jamaica prior to the expiry of his work permit. But on his third visit in 2017, he did not—he says because of the force of love and the abuse from this fellow employee, Luke Brown. It seems he has the capacity to respect our immigration laws and some of the factors in regulation 245 are favourable to him to warrant release. However, there are other factors here, failing to stay at his job and staying in Canada after he had to go back to Jamaica, that suggest Mr. Blake is a flight risk. I must approach this case carefully before ordering his detention by considering the regulation 248 factors. Mr. Blake has a current passport. Therefore, his removal to Jamaica will not be an issue. I envisage the detention will be short. But under regulation 248, I must still consider possible alternatives to detention that will minimize the flight risk concerns of the Minister through the imposition of appropriate conditions. Incarcerating Mr. Blake must be a matter of last resort if there is a suitable and workable release plan in place. Here, the regulation 248 factors relating to the likely length of detention are not a concern as there should not be any inordinate delay removing Mr. Blake from here to Jamaica, as he has a passport. However, the inquiry does not end at this point as I must consider alternatives to detention under regulation 248.

    I will now examine the release plan proposed by Mr. Blake.

Mr. Blake said his friend, Tim O'Connor, can post a performance bond of $2,000, and somebody called James Philpot can provide a cash bond of $1,000. In the cross-examination of Mr. Blake by Mr. Burrows, Mr. Blake said he only met Tim twice in the last year. When asked about Tim's income, Mr. Blake said he did not know what it was or whether Mr. O'Connor was married or had kids. When questioned about James Philpot, Mr. Blake said he does not know James, but Tim knows James.

I asked Mr. Blake the reason that he did not propose Ms. St. John as a bondsperson given that I have been told by Mr. Blake that she has a good job as a manager at her local branch of the CIBC. Mr. Blake said she did not want to do this as she believed her student loan would be put in jeopardy. I then asked Mr. Blake the same question in connection with Tony, Ms. St John's brother, who lives with them and is apparently a self-employed carpenter. Mr. Blake said Tony was not prepared to do it as he did not know what was involved.

I have concerns about the proposed bondspersons, Mr. O'Connor and Mr. Philpot. It seems to me Mr. Blake knows very little about them, and Mr. Blake's evidence confirms my suspicion that Mr. O'Connor does not really know Mr. Blake and vice versa. He put these names forward in the faint hope that I might be persuaded to allow his release. As I have repeatedly said at previous detention reviews, the ID is tasked with the duty to examine these bondspersons in other cases carefully to ensure that detainees are properly supervised by financially solvent and responsible people who have a proper relationship with the detainee. They must also know what their duties are and what the consequences are to them if the immigrant breaches his conditions of release. They must also be fully aware of the detainee's immigration history. Mr. O'Connor and Mr. Philpot are clearly totally inappropriate based on the criteria of suitability I have outlined.

In these circumstances and especially in view of the weak release plan presented by Mr. Blake that failed to overcome my concerns that if released he will not appear at future immigration proceedings and removal, I order the continued detention of Mr. Blake. The next detention review hearing will be held on Wednesday, May 9, 2018. Just a helpful comment to you, Mr. Blake. I suggest you seek the services of counsel and come to the next detention review with a tight and persuasive release plan, if you want to have a chance of being released. Thanks.

------------REVIEW CONCLUDED-------------

I HEREBY DECLARE THAT THIS IS A TRUE
TRANSCRIPT OF THE RECORDING AND THAT I HAVE
SWORN THE OATH OF SECRECY

_____

Ellen Blanchford—Transcriptionist for Transcribe Inc.
Security # 76647321-0000872322

May 2, 2018

Questions to Consider

Keep the questions below in mind when you consider the transcript and during your interview of Alfred and the proposed bondsperson/cash depositor.

1. What was wrong with the release plan that Alfred presented at the hearing?
2. Now that you know what was wrong with the release plan, how would you prepare a better and tighter release plan?
3. Did you notice any factors here that would be persuasive in arguing that Alfred can obey our immigration laws?
4. Is the fact that Alfred and Gill are engaged and plan to marry a relevant consideration?
5. Are there points here that must be clarified when you interview Alfred?
6. Who would you propose as bondsperson(s)?
7. Are there points here that you must clarify when you interview the proposed bondsperson(s)?
8. Is it important that the bondsperson(s) know Alfred's immigration history? If so, why is that important?
9. What is the relevance, if any, of Alfred's insistence that he provided the CBSA his new residential address when he went to live with Gill?
10. Was Alfred aware of the removal order that was issued against him?
11. What is the significance, if any, of the missing GCMS notes?
12. Was the amount of performance bond and cash bond proposed by Alfred sufficient? If not, what do you think would be an appropriate amount of bond and cash?
13. How relevant is the issue of the solvency of any bondsperson(s) you propose? What evidence would you present on this issue?
14. Is the issue of the strength of the relationship between the bondsperson(s) and the detainee important?

15. Apart from a performance bond and cash bond, are there any other conditions you would propose at the next detention review hearing? If so, why are these additional conditions important?
16. When you interview the bondsperson(s), will you tell them what their duties and responsibilities are? Will they know what will happen to their performance bond and cash bond if Alfred breaches any release plan that is approved by the member?
17. Is the abuse that Alfred experienced by a fellow worker at FFP relevant? If so, how?
18. Was the member's analysis of the factors under regulation 245 adequate or did he miss the factor relating to Alfred's previous compliance with IRPA?
19. Was the member correct in finding that Mr. Blake's detention would be for a short period under regulation 248?
20. Are there any facts in this case that suggest the detention might be lengthy? If you were counsel in this case, would you have explored the issue of length of detention at the hearing? Give reasons for your answer.

CHAPTER 5

Extract from the Interview of Alfred Blake at the Holding Centre

COUNSEL: Hello, Alfred. I hope you are coping with the situation. As I said at our last interview when you signed the retainer agreement, you need to be patient. I will do everything I can to secure your release.

BLAKE: Thank you.

COUNSEL: I have read the 48-hour detention review transcript. There are some things I need to clarify. Are you sure you gave the CBSA your residential address in Orangeville when you moved there?

BLAKE: Yes. I wrote the letter and I mailed it to them.

COUNSEL: Was Gill with you when you wrote or mailed the letter?

BLAKE: No.

COUNSEL: Did Gill and Tony know about you being illegal in Canada?

BLAKE: Initially when I lived with them, all they knew was that I had a valid work permit and I had a job lined up at a dairy farm in Grand Valley. I didn't tell her that I had fled the Farm Workers Program and was illegally in Canada. I was scared that if she knew all that stuff, she would end our relationship. However, on the second phone call after my arrest by the CBSA, I told her the truth about my illegality in Canada.

COUNSEL: When did you speak to Gill?

BLAKE: The first time I spoke to her was from her home when I got arrested, and at that time, I thought it was because I had been stopped by the police for speeding. Later that evening, I told her about my illegal status in Canada. Tony was in on the telephone call, and they were both upset with me. They didn't want to help me.

COUNSEL: Did you tell her why you were arrested by the CBSA?

BLAKE: Yes, I told her everything. She was upset with me, and when I asked her to help me to get out of this detention centre, she said she'd contact a lawyer the following day.

COUNSEL: Yes, she did contact me, and on the first phone call I had with her, she didn't want to help you. It seems from the detention review transcript that you told the member that Gill was not prepared to act as a bondsperson. However, she did call me again when you were detained after the 48-hour review and said she would act as a bondsperson. Did you talk to Gill again before your detention review last Wednesday?

BLAKE: A guy in a suit came to see me after my second phone call with Gill at the detention centre. He explained that I needed a bondsperson and someone who will post cash as a guarantee that I would follow all the conditions of release. He only spent five minutes with me, and I still didn't understand the process. I spoke to Gill again later that night and asked her if she would provide me with a bond. She said no, as she was still paying off her student loan. She was still angry with me for not telling her about my illegal status in Canada. Tony was on the phone call too. He also refused to help as he was still upset with me and didn't understand what was involved. I was frustrated. The following morning, I decided to try other people who could act as bond. The only other person I knew was Tim. He was a casual acquaintance, whom I met at the store where I did my grocery shopping when I worked at FFP. I called him, and he said he could post $2,000 for me and his friend, James, could provide $1,000 cash. I told Tim to come to the hearing the following morning and to bring his friend with him.

COUNSEL: In the detention review transcript, you told the member that Gill did not know about you being illegal here in Canada. Why did you lie about that?

BLAKE:	I just didn't want to get Gill and Tony in trouble. Anyway, they only got the full picture after the phone conversation with Gill in the evening after I was arrested in the morning.
COUNSEL:	Did you know about the removal order that had been made against you?
BLAKE:	No. I'd like to know where they mailed the removal order document as I gave the CBSA my new address in Orangeville.
COUNSEL:	When did you do that and how?
BLAKE:	As I said, I mailed them the change of address as soon as I started living with Gill in Orangeville on the 1st of February 2018.
COUNSEL:	When you were arrested by the CBSA, did they give you a copy of the removal order?
BLAKE:	Yes, I have it.

Blake takes a wad of documents out of a folder sitting on the table and hands it to counsel. Counsel flips through the documents.

COUNSEL:	As I thought, it seems the removal order was issued on March 1, 2018, by a CBSA officer. The address on the correspondence that enclosed the removal order is your residence where you used to work in Hamilton—FFP. It seems the CBSA did not update your new address in their computer system, or if they did, it could be in the missing pages from the GCMS notes.
BLAKE:	Well, it's not my fault they messed up.
COUNSEL:	On top of that, the member of the Immigration Division did not spot this issue. It is certainly something that I will highlight at the forthcoming review hearing. Just so you know, after I explained the detention review process to Gill and Tony, they changed their minds and are prepared to act as bondspersons for you.
BLAKE:	I am so glad they want to help me. When I phoned Gill after being detained by the member, she cried and said she'd do anything to get me out.
COUNSEL:	After reading the review transcript, I'm a bit confused as to the reason you left FFP and stayed on in Canada after your work permit expired. Why did you do that?

BLAKE: The main reason was my deep love for Gill and our wonderful relationship, but the abuse from that character at the FFP kind of pushed me to leave FFP and start a new life with Gill.

COUNSEL: Did you tell Gill or Tony about the abuse you experienced at FFP?

BLAKE: I told Gill all about it and how desperate I was to find a job in Orangeville, so I would not face the agony of this abusive fellow employee.

COUNSEL: Did you report this fellow employee to your boss and immigration?

BLAKE: I told my boss, Dick, about it, but he did nothing. I didn't think it would be any use reporting the abuse to immigration.

COUNSEL: What are your future plans with Gill?

BLAKE: I want to marry her. I discussed it with her before I got arrested, and she agreed to set an engagement date. Now, I don't think she'll want to marry me until I've got out of this hell hole and sort myself out with immigration.

COUNSEL: I'll be asking you some questions at the review hearing. Keep your answers short and to the point. Counsel representing the Minister will likely ask you questions as well. Again, answer the questions. Don't be evasive, and stick to your story. A strong point in your case is that when you had work permits to work here under the Farm Workers Program before, you never left the job, and you left Canada before your permit expired. It was only through compelling and compassionate reasons that you, on this one occasion, failed to obey the conditions of your work permit. These reasons are your committed relationship with Gill and the emotional/physical abuse you experienced at work. This will be the theme we'll run at the next review. Here is a copy of the previous review transcript. Read it carefully and make sure you don't say anything at the forthcoming 7-day review hearing that contradicts what you said at the previous hearing. I want you to admit to the member that you lied at the last detention review hearing when you said that Gill and Tony did not know you were illegal in Canada. That's pretty much it. Leave the rest to me, as I now need to do the paperwork that we will need for the review hearing after I have interviewed Gill and Tony. I will

	do the best I can to get you out, but it is the member at the next review hearing who will decide whether to release you, not me. I cannot give you any guarantees.
BLAKE:	So, what's the point of paying you all this money to represent me?
COUNSEL:	The point, my friend, is that you did a bad job of persuading the member to release you. The plan of release you presented was weak. I don't think anything will be gained by going into it in any detail, but the plan of release I will present to the member will be strong and tight. I explained in the retainer agreement that all I can do is to use my best endeavours to secure your release, and I'm not the decision maker. Furthermore, we don't know who'll preside at the review hearing, and we don't know whether they'll have some bias against you. We simply don't know. We can only hope for a fair-minded member, so please don't think you'll be released. Let's just hope for the best.
BLAKE:	Fair enough.

Commentary

Through a comprehensive analysis of the answers given by Alfred at the interview and a careful reading of the detention review transcript, your plan of action is now ready to be implemented as the following points emerge:

1. The strength of the relationship between Gill, Tony and Alfred as well as the solvency of both Gill and Tony will make them the ideal bondspersons. Gill will post a performance bond and Tony will provide a cash bond.
2. The fact that Alfred can reside with Gill and Tony will ensure maximum supervision of Alfred by them.
3. Alfred has demonstrated his past compliance with previously issued work permits, and if counsel can establish Alfred provided the CBSA with his Orangeville address, it makes the argument that he can comply with conditions of release even more compelling.
4. An exploration of the abuse at work, perhaps, through an investigation of the employers, FFP, may disclose evidence to support Alfred's contention that his employer failed to stop the abusive conduct of Alfred's fellow employee.

5. After the interview of Gill, a concrete engagement date between Alfred and Gill could be established, cementing the ties that Alfred has with Gill and his future brother-in-law, Tony.

Credibility

Alfred will give evidence at the next detention review hearing, from his counsel's own questions (examination in chief), questions from Minister's counsel (cross-examination) and questions from the member (see chapter 7 for the rules on advocacy). It is important that Alfred is properly coached to ensure that you establish and bolster his credibility. As you can see from the extract above, counsel briefly explained the importance of the client being concise and to the point when answering questions. The client was also cautioned not to be evasive. Finally, the client was given a copy of the detention review transcript so that he can read it carefully to ensure there are no contradictions between his testimony at the next review hearing and his testimony at the previous 48-hour review hearing. The member and Minister's counsel will have read the 48-hour detention review transcript or listened to the audio tape prior to the next review hearing, and if Alfred says something different at the next hearing, it will affect his credibility. Therefore, it is important to protect Alfred's credibility from being carelessly shattered by ensuring he reads the transcript to make sure his evidence at the 7-day review hearing is consistent with it.

In actual practice, the coaching part of the exercise would be more detailed, but this brief outline is sufficient to highlight the credibility issues.

Ethical Issues

No guarantees of the result

Both in the retainer agreement—see the samples at appendix F, and in the extract above—counsel must ensure that the client did not enter the retainer agreement because counsel offered a guarantee of a successful result. It is both unethical and dishonest for immigration legal professionals to assure their clients a successful result. In all areas of immigration practice, counsel does not decide the case. In all cases, that decision is made by a third party, whether it be a member of the IRB, an immigration officer, a CBSA officer or a Federal Court judge. It is, therefore, impossible to advise a client of a certain result. The best assurance that counsel can give to the client is as follows:

"I will use my best endeavours to achieve a successful result, but ultimately the decision as to whether you will succeed will be made by someone else, and I cannot predict what that decision will be."

There have been many times when potential clients would tell me that they would only retain me if I could guarantee that they would be successful. I have refused to give them such an assurance and politely declined to be retained if they insisted that I give them such a guarantee of success. However, unscrupulous lawyers and consultants, intent on lining their pockets with their client's money, will do and say anything to their clients to make themselves richer. Fortunately, they are a minority in our profession.

Lowering the client's expectations

The other policy you should consider implementing in your practice is lowering your client's expectation of a successful result. Bolstering their expectation by saying things like, "We really have a great chance of getting you out," or "I'm pretty certain you'll be released," is to be avoided because if the client is not released, the high expectation you've created will be dashed. Through these foolish remarks, you will have created a disgruntled client, who will then not hesitate to make a complaint against you to your regulatory body.

Insist on the truth, not lies

As you can see from the extract above, a subtle ethical issue arose when Alfred said he had lied to the member at the first review hearing by claiming Gill and Tony did not know he was illegal in Canada so as not to cause them problems. On its face, it is a minor point, and one solution is that Alfred persists in this lie at the next review hearing. Another solution is that counsel at the next review hearing clarifies this issue by Alfred admitting that he lied but did so based on a misunderstanding. Gill and Tony did not harbour an illegal immigrant or assist Alfred, as at the time he lived with them, they did not know he was illegal. Alfred only told them of his illegal status after he was arrested and in detention. I prefer to adopt this solution and I encourage you to do so in this sort of situation. It is based on the truth, and I believe as a legal professional, it is your duty to insist on the truth and avoid any form of lies. In one of my recent cases, an issue like this arose. The member appreciated my candour and my client's admission. In fact, it helped me secure my client's release. Honesty and complete candour is always the best policy.

In the next chapter, we will examine the evidentiary matters that must be dealt with in preparing the documentary evidence of our bondspersons, Gill and Tony.

CHAPTER 6

The Importance of the Bondsperson(s)

In almost every detention review case, presenting evidence in the form of affidavits from the bondsperson is critically important. The content of the affidavits must be well structured and contain the essential evidence that will help in securing the detainee's release. In this discussion, reference to a bondsperson includes both the person who will provide the non-deposit performance bond and the person who will provide the cash deposit. (Note that in some cases, there may just be one bondsperson who will provide both the performance bond and the cash.) I have listed these essential elements in the checklist below:

Checklist of Essential Elements in the Bondsperson's Affidavit

1. **Their status.** The bondsperson must be a Canadian citizen or a permanent resident. I know of no cases where the ID would accept a person who only has temporary status as an appropriate bondsperson. Exhibit proof of citizenship such as the bio page of their Canadian passport or citizenship card, or a birth certificate if they are a citizen because of birth in Canada. With permanent residents, exhibit their permanent resident card.
2. **No criminal convictions or pending criminal charges.** The member of the ID should know the bondsperson is of good character and has no criminal convictions or outstanding criminal charges. If they do, explain why the convictions or charges would not bar them from being considered an appropriate bondsperson.

3. **Their relationship to the detainee.** It is important to provide full details of that relationship. The more solid the relationship, with clear indications that the detainee will respect the house rules and discipline of the bondsperson, the greater the likelihood that the bondsperson will appear more compelling and attractive to the member of the ID. Here, the committed common-law relationship between Gill and Alfred, along with the fact that they have known each other since September 2017 and have lived together for the past three months, is a strong positive factor. The daily contact between Tony and Alfred is again a positive factor. A sentence such as "Alfred respects me and will obey the rules of my household" is useful and should be included in the affidavit.

4. **Solvency.** One of the things you need to establish is that your bondsperson has appropriate savings and assets they can liquidate in the event the detainee breaches the conditions of release. However, be careful in your analysis. One of the problems I have seen in assessing the solvency of a bondsperson who is providing a performance bond is the failure of lawyers or consultants to consider ENF 8 of the IRCC (see chapter 13 for a detailed analysis of the solvency rules and a link to the ENF 8 manual at appendix G), which contains detailed information on this solvency assessment. There is nothing more frustrating than to find out, after the release order, that your bondsperson cannot meet the solvency test as set out by ENF 8 and, therefore, that the CBSA cannot release the client. If the bondsperson has savings of $3,000, and she relies on the savings for her living expenses as her income is low, it can pose problems. The rule of thumb is that the amount of the bondsperson's income (less liabilities) and assets (less liabilities) must be at least three times the amount of the performance bond. Similar problems can arise if the bondsperson cannot meet his living expenses as a result of posting the cash deposit. It is, therefore, important to outline the employment of the bondsperson and exhibit their notice of assessment for the past three years to demonstrate their solvency and ability to post bond and provide the cash deposit. You may want to exhibit their recent pay stubs and any letters of employment. Your assessment of the solvency of the bondsperson and whether the CBSA will accept them after a release order by the ID is made ought to be done at the beginning of your preparation for the hearing, certainly before you draft their affidavit, so that no complications arise after release. The CBSA has its own solvency questionnaire and procedure. The worst-case scenario here is that the ID makes a release order but your client cannot be physically released because the bondsperson does not meet the solvency tests.

5. **Knowledge of the detainee's immigration history and illegal status.** The ID member will want to know that the bondsperson is aware of the exact immigration status of the detainee so that the member is satisfied that they know the risks involved in being a bondsperson for the detainee. Here, the fact that Alfred is a flight risk through his abandonment of his employment at FFP and failing to return to Jamaica after his work permit expired are matters that the bondsperson must be aware of.
6. **The amount of the bond/cash deposit and flexibility.** This is one of the most difficult matters to quantify. An assessment must be made of the grounds for detention, how serious these grounds are and how likely the immigrant may be to breach any conditions of release or fail to keep the peace. Here, Alfred poses a flight risk. However, the fact he will reside with his bondspersons means there is a greater degree of supervision.

   The level of income of the bondsperson can also be a factor. A bond of $3,000 and a cash deposit of $2,000 seems enough, but in the affidavits, I want to ensure the ID member knows that imposing a higher amount of bond or cash deposit is possible (so long as, under ENF 8, the bondsperson will meet that higher amount of bond when the CBSA assesses the bondsperson after the release order—see chapter 13). You should include a sentence in the affidavit such as "In the event that the member believes a higher amount of bond or/and cash deposit is required, I am prepared to comply with this." But be cautious and follow the solvency tests in ENF 8. Remember to consider any debts the bondsperson has in assessing the net income or assets that the bondsperson has. Remind your bondsperson to provide full disclosure on these issues so you can do an accurate assessment of their solvency and whether they can meet the ceiling for any increase of the bond or cash deposit the member may decide to impose.
7. **Any compassionate or compelling circumstances that justify release of the detainee.** There are cases where it would be appropriate for the bondsperson to outline some of these compassionate circumstances in the affidavit. In our present case, Alfred told Gill about the abuse and intolerable conditions at FFP, and there is also their committed relationship, which led to this isolated breach of IRPA. It would be important for Gill to outline these matters in her affidavit.
8. **That the bondsperson is aware of the consequences of breach of conditions by the detainee.** In the present case, you need to explain to Gill and Tony the whole detention review process and what the consequences are to them if Alfred breaches any conditions of release. Gill must know she will lose the amount of the bond she posted to the CBSA and Tony will lose the

cash deposit he provided if there is a breach. Gill's student loan will not be affected by posting a bond (although the student loan may affect the calculation of net income when doing the solvency assessment). However, you must make sure that both Gill and Tony are fully aware of their supervisory duties over Alfred and the consequences to them of a breach of the conditions of release by Alfred. Their affidavits must make that clear.

After counsel has provided a copy of the affidavits to Minister's counsel before the detention review hearing, the representative from the CBSA will interview the affiants. It is thus important that you ensure they have read and understand the contents of their affidavits. They must ensure that when Minister's counsel interviews them, their answers are consistent with their affidavits. If Minister's counsel accepts that the bondspersons are appropriate, it will lead Minister's counsel to recommend the release of the detainee. However, you do not know that will happen, so be prepared for either result at the hearing. In some cases, after Minister's counsel interviewed my bondspersons and seemed satisfied with them, he nevertheless opposed release when he appeared before the member.

Fortunately, in late 2017, a new procedure was implemented in Toronto where the bondsperson will be examined by Minister's counsel at the detention review hearing with all parties present. This new procedure was introduced to make the process of assessing the bondsperson more open and to remove the perception of biased interpretation by Minister's counsel of the answers of bondsperson when these interviews were conducted in private.

With this new procedure, or where Minister's counsel insists that the bondsperson be examined at the hearing, there is a special need for affiants to be consistent with the evidence they presented in their affidavit. They must also be able to deal with difficult probing questions from Minister's counsel. You must coach your affiants effectively, and this means going over their affidavits with them. Prepare them so they understand the weak points in their affidavits and guide them as to the answers that would neutralize the searching cross-examination of Minister's counsel.

Please see appendix F for sample affidavits from Gill and Tony. Refer to the checklist above to ensure that these affidavits deal with all the items in that list.

Since the bondsperson's affidavits and evidence at the hearing are important in securing the detainee's release, we will examine the interview of Gill St. John to determine whether counsel extracted all the relevant information necessary to draft her affidavit.

After examining the interview, we will look at the affidavit of Gill St. John to see whether it deals with all the matters in the checklist and whether it is effective and persuasive.

Counsel's Interview of Gill St. John

COUNSEL:	Thank you for seeing me in my office at such short notice.
GILL:	No problem. Do you think we can get Alfred out? He is so depressed being locked up in that hell hole.
COUNSEL:	From my experience, it will depend on us presenting a tight and persuasive release plan that will overcome the flight risk concerns of the CBSA and the member. Let's get working on the information I need to obtain from you so I can prepare a strong affidavit for you.
GILL:	Okay.
COUNSEL:	What is your immigration status in Canada?
GILL:	I am a Canadian citizen and I took the oath in 2015.
COUNSEL:	Could you provide me your citizenship card and the bio page of your Canadian passport? I need to make copies of these documents and attach them as an exhibit to your affidavit.
GILL:	Yes, I only work half a day next Monday. I'll bring them to you then.
COUNSEL:	Excellent. I learned a little about your relationship with Alfred when I read the 48-hour detention review transcript and from what Alfred told me when I visited him at the Rexdale Holding Centre yesterday. As I understand it, you met Alfred at a family gathering at a church in Hamilton last September after you were introduced to him by your brother, Tony. You then dated Alfred for a while, and eventually, at the beginning of February 2018, he came to live with you and your brother at your house in Orangeville.
GILL:	That's right. Alfred and I fell in love, and we planned on forging a lifelong commitment with each other, but everything was ruined when he was arrested by the CBSA.
COUNSEL:	Do you still love him? More importantly, do you intend to marry him, eventually?
GILL:	Yes. Eventually, I do want to marry Alfred. But only if he is released, and we can sort out his immigration problems.
COUNSEL:	That's fair enough. While you lived with him, did you discuss a date for an engagement?
GILL:	Yes. We planned to become engaged in the late summer of 2018.

COUNSEL: If he is released, are you still prepared to do that?

GILL: Yes, definitely.

COUNSEL: What did you know of Alfred's immigration history at the time Alfred lived with you and your brother but before his arrest?

GILL: He told me he had a work permit to work at FFP and that he was not happy working there because of a fellow worker, who was abusive toward him.

COUNSEL: When he came to live with you in Orangeville, did he tell you he'd left FFP?

GILL: I was concerned that the commuting distance to Hamilton from Orangeville was long. That's when he said he'd left FFP and the abuse at work. He also told me he'd arranged to work for a dairy farm in Grand Valley, a neighbouring town.

COUNSEL: What did he tell you about his work permit and whether he could legally work at this dairy farm?

GILL: Very little. I assumed it was okay for him to work at that farm in Grand Valley. Looking back on the situation now, I should have asked him more questions about his status in Canada.

COUNSEL: If we all had hindsight, we'd all do things differently. Don't worry about it. Tell me how you found out about Alfred's arrest by the CBSA.

GILL: On Monday, April 30, I went to work at my branch of the CIBC in Orangeville. I know Tony had left home earlier to go to his carpentry store in town. At about 11.00 a.m., I received a frantic call from Alfred that immigration cops had arrested him for speeding. He said he'd call me later in the evening. He was about to give me more information when I heard loud voices in the background and he suddenly hung up the phone. I was distressed and immediately phoned Tony to tell him what happened.

COUNSEL: Did he call you later in the evening and, if so, what did he tell you?

GILL: Like I told you when I phoned you up last Tuesday, Alfred phoned me and told me he was being detained by immigration because he was illegal in Canada as his work permit had expired and he'd not left Canada. He also said he had left FFP when he was not allowed to do this. Tony was in on the phone call, and we were both distressed and angry that Alfred had lied to us. That's the main reason Tony and I were reluctant to help Alfred out. He betrayed our trust in him.

COUNSEL: I understand that, but now you are both willing to act as bondspersons. Why is that?

GILL: When Alfred lived with us, he respected us and obeyed the rules of our household. He is a good man and deserves a second chance. During my phone call with him, he told me he'd come to Canada on the Farm Workers Program twice before and always went back to Jamaica before his work permit expired. Is that correct?

COUNSEL: Yes. So why do you think he did not go back to Jamaica this time round?

GILL: Because of our intense love for each other but also due to the terrible time he was having with this fellow worker at FFP.

COUNSEL: Do you think you and your brother can supervise Alfred if the member releases him and names you and Tony as bondspersons? And how will you do it?

GILL: I work day shifts—8.30 a.m. to 5.00 p.m.—at the CIBC bank Monday to Friday. Tony has his own carpentry workshop at my home, and he does most of his work there. Occasionally, he pops into his carpentry store in town, usually late in the morning or mid-afternoons. He is only there for a few hours and he can take Alfred with him to the shop. In the evenings and weekends, we are both at home. So there can be 24-hour supervision of Alfred.

COUNSEL: Excellent. How much do you earn at the bank and how long have you worked there?

GILL: I earn $50,000 gross and $38,000 net per year. I have worked there for three years.

COUNSEL: Do you have your notices of assessment for the tax years 2015 to 2017? Do you have any assets?

GILL: I have all my notices and the only asset I have is the house at 20 Becca Drive in Orangeville that I own. My property tax assessment gave it a value of $350,000, but it has a $175,000 mortgage on it. I pay a mortgage of $1,000 per month and $12,000 for the year.

COUNSEL:	Great. When you bring your citizenship card and passport, bring these notices of assessment, a letter of employment, the deed of your property, your tax statement for 2017 and your mortgage document that shows your monthly mortgage payments and a few utility bills to confirm your residence there. Is the property in your name only or does Tony or anyone else have any interest in it?
GILL:	I'll bring these documents. 20 Becca is in my name only. No one else apart from the mortgage company has an interest in it.
COUNSEL:	Good. I need to tell you about your responsibilities as a bondsperson if the member releases Alfred. I'm proposing to put you forward as a bondsperson, who will provide a performance bond of $3,000. You do not need to make any payment to the CBSA, but if Alfred breaches his conditions of release, you will forfeit that $3,000, as you must pay it to the CBSA. I urge you to be flexible in terms of the amount of performance bond you are prepared to give. I don't want Alfred detained because the member thinks he can't increase the amount of your bond.
GILL:	Yes, we can be flexible. But what do I need to do to supervise Alfred properly?
COUNSEL:	You need to make sure you always know his whereabouts. He must keep the peace and be of good behaviour. If he needs to report for an immigration proceeding or for removal, you must make sure he attends. There will probably be a condition that he report to the CBSA at Airport Road in Mississauga once a month or more frequently. You must make sure he reports to the CBSA. If you and Alfred move to another address, you must tell the CBSA about the change of address. Similarly, if Alfred can work legally and finds employment, you must make sure the CBSA is provided the name and address of the employer. That's pretty much it, and Tony will have the same obligations to protect the cash bond he will post. Finally, if you or Tony believe Alfred is about to commit a breach of his conditions of release, you must inform the CBSA immediately. In fact, if you or Tony feel uncomfortable continuing to be bondspersons because, perhaps, Alfred is behaving badly for whatever reason, you can attend the CBSA and withdraw from being a bondsperson.

GILL: I don't think that will happen. Alfred will behave well, obey our rules and comply with all the release conditions. He has too much to lose if he does not. In fact, when he lived with us, we had an 11.00 p.m. curfew during the week when we had to be in bed. I live in a quiet neighbourhood and wanted to do this. Alfred did not complain about the curfew. How will we deal with his immigration issues if the judge releases him?

COUNSEL: I must do a lot of work before the detention review next Wednesday, so let's focus on getting him released first. We can discuss Alfred's general immigration problems later. After I draft your affidavit, Gill, I want you to read it carefully. Tell me if there are any changes you want me to make. Once you agree it is accurate, I will give you a copy of it. Read it so you are very familiar with everything you said. At the hearing under the new Toronto detention procedures, Minister's counsel will have a copy of your affidavit and will also have Tony's affidavit. He will question both of you about the contents of your affidavits. The member may also question you. You must make sure your answers are consistent with your affidavit. It is important that you stick to your affidavit evidence during cross-examination by Minister's counsel or questioning by the member of the division. Do not deviate from what you've said and avoid adding new things, unless it is necessary. Keep your answers short and focused when answering the questions. Do not be evasive. Be forthright in your answers. The same rule applies to Tony, but I'll tell him all this when I see him later today.

GILL: I appreciate all the hard work you are putting into this case, John. Of course, both Tony and I will do everything you say.

COUNSEL: Thanks, and make sure you bring all the documents to my office on Monday at 3.00 p.m. It's good you have a half day at the bank that day. We will also go through the first draft of your affidavit, although I will send it to you by email on Sunday, so you can review it before the meeting. Have a great day.

GILL: Thanks. You too, John.

Review Questions

1. Did counsel extract from Gill all the relevant information from the checklist?

2. Did counsel properly explain the role and responsibilities of Gill as a bondsperson?
3. Did counsel properly explain the consequences to Gill of a breach of the conditions of release by Alfred?
4. Is there any further information you believe counsel should obtain from Gill?
5. Are there other documents that should be exhibited to Gill's affidavit?
6. When reading that interview, did it seem that Gill was anxious to have Alfred back home, without any regard to her supervisory duties or preventing any breach of the proposed conditions of release? How would you deal with this in your submissions to the member of the Immigration Division?
7. Did Gill provide an adequate answer to the issue of her change of heart in now wanting to help Alfred when before she was reluctant to do so?
8. How would you deal with the fact that Gill appeared to have been reckless in failing to inquire into Alfred's immigration status when he lived with her and Tony?
9. Did counsel properly advise Gill how to deal with the cross-examination by Minister's counsel on her affidavit? If not, what else would you have said to Gill?
10. Overall, was counsel's interview of Gill adequate or less than adequate? If you found it was less than adequate, explain why.

Affidavit of Gill St. John

Below is the affidavit of Gill St. John that counsel drafted based on Gill's answers in the interview:

IN THE IMMIGRATION DIVISION

IN THE DETENTION REVIEW HEARING OF ALFRED BLAKE

AFFIDAVIT OF GILL ST. JOHN

(SWORN MAY 7, 2018)

I, Gill St. John of the town of Orangeville in the county of Dufferin **MAKE OATH AND SAY AS FOLLOWS:**

1. I have direct knowledge of the matters to which I hereinafter depose.

2. I am a Canadian citizen and I have no criminal convictions or pending criminal charges against me. I have never had any trouble with the police or the authorities.

   Attached to this my affidavit marked exhibit "1" is a true copy of my citizenship card and the Bio page of my Canadian passport.

3. I have known Alfred Blake (Hereinafter referred to as Alfred) for nine months, having first met Alfred when I attended a church in Hamilton with friends and family sometime in September 2017. I came to know him as my brother, Tony St. John, knew Alfred's twin brother in our country of origin—Jamaica. I liked Alfred and soon we dated regularly. By the end of 2017, we both knew we loved each other and wanted to make a lifelong marital commitment with each other. I invited Alfred to come and live with me and Tony at my house in Orangeville. At the beginning of February 2018, he moved in with me. I asked him about his job at the Fresh Farmers Produce company in Hamilton and mentioned that it would be a long commute from my home to that farm. He told me he had to quit the job as one of his fellow employees was emotionally and physically abusive to him. I was shocked by the nasty behaviour of this fellow worker and could understand Alfred's reluctance to continue working there. He said he had arranged employment at a dairy farm in Grand Valley, which is a town that is a 20-minute drive from Orangeville. I knew there are many farms in that rural town and was pleased with his work plans.

4. During the time Alfred lived with me and Tony, he was always well behaved and obeyed the rules of our household. He contributed to the expenses of our home as he still had some savings. He told me he would contribute more money to our living expenses once he secured the job in Grand Valley. As he is quite skilled at carpentry, Tony, who is a licensed carpenter, gave Alfred occasional jobs to do until he could secure employment at the farm in Grand Valley at the beginning of May 2018. Things were going well with Alfred and me, so much so that we planned to become engaged in the late summer this year.

5. On Monday, April 30, 2018, at about 11.00 a.m., while Tony and I were at work, I received a call from Alfred saying that immigration cops had come to my house and arrested him for speeding a few weeks ago. He told me he would call me in the evening, and he was about to talk more when I heard loud voices in the background, then Alfred hung up. Both Tony and I were distressed about Alfred's arrest and patiently waited for Alfred to call us. Later that evening, he called me and told me that he had been arrested because he was illegal in Canada as he was supposed to go back to Jamaica soon after he came to live with me in Canada but stayed on. During the call, I put Alfred on speaker-phone, so Tony could hear what Alfred was saying. Alfred told us he was being detained at Rexdale Holding Centre and wanted us to help him. Tony and I were upset that Alfred had lied to us, and I told Alfred we could not help him. However, the following morning I called an immigration lawyer, whom one of my friends recommended, to help me

understand what was going on with Alfred. I was reluctant to provide a performance bond at that stage as I was worried about my student loan, even though the lawyer assured me my loan would not be affected by me standing as a bondsperson.

6. When I learned that Alfred's detention had continued after his 48-hour review, I decided to help Alfred as I knew he was a good person and always respected Tony and me, consistently following the rules of our household. I spoke to Tony, and he was also willing to help Alfred.

7. I've worked at the CIBC in Orangeville for the last three years. My gross income is $50,000 a year. After payment of all my statutory expenses, my net income is $38,000 per year. I own a 3-bedroom detached home at 20 Becca Drive in Orangeville. It is worth $350,000. I have a mortgage of $175,000 with annual mortgage payments of $12,000 per year. I can provide a performance bond of $3,000. However, if the member requires a higher bond then I am prepared to abide by such a decision.

Attached to this my affidavit marked exhibit "2" is a true copy of my notice of assessment for 2015-2017, a letter from my employer confirming my employment/income and the deed/mortgage documents of 20 Becca Drive, Orangeville, showing my ownership of the property and the mortgage that is owed on it.

8. Both Tony and I know Alfred's immigration history, and that he breached our immigration laws by fleeing from FFP where he was supposed to work in accordance with his work permit. Alfred also failed to leave Canada when he was required to do so on February 10, 2018 but decided to continue to live in Canada illegally as an overstayer. I understand these are serious breaches of the law. I have assessed the risk involved in being a bondsperson and I am confident that he will not imperil my bond and will appear for removal or any immigration proceedings. Since he has lived with Tony and me, he has shown respect to us and obeyed our rules of the household. I do not believe he will jeopardize the trust we have placed in him.

9. I understand and appreciate the risk I face in being a bondsperson. I am fully aware that my performance bond will become payable if Alfred breaches any conditions of release that the member imposes on him. Both Tony and I will ensure that he is always supervised. I work day shifts and Tony usually works in his carpentry business in his workshop at our home during the day. Only occasionally, he visits his store during the day, and as Alfred is currently assisting Tony, he will be with Tony during the day and will accompany Tony to his store. Furthermore, we live in a quiet neighbourhood and we usually retire to bed at 11.00 p.m. When Alfred lived with us, he obeyed this bedtime household curfew and will continue to do so upon his release. I ask the Immigration Division to impose a condition of residence at my home in Orangeville, so Tony and I can exercise strict control and supervision over Alfred. Furthermore,

I will check any mail to Alfred from the CBSA or the CIC [Citizenship and Immigration Canada] and ensure he complies with any directives in that mail. I intend to drive Alfred to the CBSA office on the dates and times he needs to report to them. Finally, I will make sure he reports for removal and any immigration proceedings, so he complies with his conditions of release.

10. I make this affidavit in support of Alfred's release on appropriate conditions and for no improper purpose.

SWORN BEFORE ME   )
This 7th day of May 2018   )
at the City of Toronto   )

_____   _____
Commissioner for Oaths etc…,   Gill St. John

Review Questions

1. Does this affidavit cover all the points in the checklist?
2. Are there any additional matters that you want to include in the affidavit?
3. Are there any matters in this affidavit that you believe should not be in there? If so, why?
4. What is the purpose of this affidavit, and how will it help you persuade the member to release Alfred?
5. Do you intend to read this affidavit at the hearing, or will you summarize it when you make your oral submissions (see chapter 7 on advocacy)?
6. Do you think it was necessary for Gill to include in her affidavit what Alfred told her about the emotional and physical abuse in his workplace, and if so, why?

In the next chapter, we will engage in a comprehensive discussion of the advocacy skills required in the Immigration Division. In chapter 8, I will also set out the submissions that counsel will orally deliver at the detention review hearing on May 9, 2018, to assist you further in understanding the rules of oral advocacy.

CHAPTER 7

Advocacy in the Immigration Division

In order to present your client's case properly in the ID, you need to have a basic knowledge of the rules governing the questioning of witnesses, whether it be conducting the examination in chief of your own witness or cross-examining opposing witnesses. Your credibility as an advocate will be severely compromised if you do not know how to examine your own witness and are ignorant of the rules that you must follow. We will deal with the rules you must follow when examining your client. Certainly, Minister's counsel will cross-examine the detainee. You must, therefore, know the rules of re-examination so you are able to clarify issues that have arisen or neutralize potentially damaging answers your client has given during the cross-examination by Minister's counsel. An effective re-examination can minimize the damage done to your client's case through a lethal cross-examination. Unless the IRCC/CBSA intends to call witnesses to the detention review hearing, which is rare, cross-examination of witnesses by counsel for the detainee in the ID may not be necessary. However, this handbook would not achieve its purpose if we left that topic out, so we will briefly deal with the basic rules of cross-examination. The advocate must also know the basic rules of evidence, and we will also discuss these. Also important is acquiring the advocacy skills necessary to be persuasive when making oral submissions. We will explore the rules for the delivery of effective and persuasive oral submissions in this chapter. In chapter 8, I will reproduce a written draft of the kind of oral submissions required in Alfred's case.

Examination in Chief

This is also known in the United States as direct examination.

On the face of it, the rules are simple. But, in actual application, adherence to the rules can be difficult, especially when the advocate is caught up in the excitement of the moment and perhaps forgets the rules.

1. No leading questions

You must not ask leading questions. Leading questions are questions framed in such a way that the witness is given (led to) the answer to the question.

Example

The weather is grey and gloomy. Then, there is a slight drizzle. Assume that in this simple fact scenario, the issue of whether it was raining or not is an important fact. The advocate asks the witness:

ADVOCATE: It was raining at the time, wasn't it?

WITNESS: Yes, I agree. It was raining at the time.

This question offends the examination in chief rules because the advocate *has led or provided the answer to the witness*. This is forbidden in our adversarial system because it compromises the integrity of the evidence of the witness. The witness's answer was given in the question by the advocate rather than being based on the witness's independent recollection.

The appropriate way to ask the question is as follows:

ADVOCATE: Was it raining at the time?

WITNESS: Yes, it was raining.

This question is framed in such a way that the witness has no clue as to the answer the advocate wants the witness to give. The question is neutral in that the answer could be "it was raining" or "it was not raining," unlike the question "It was raining at the time, wasn't it?" Here, the advocate is providing, or strongly suggesting, the answer to the question, and *a competent advocate must never do that*. Doing so shows that the advocate is inexperienced and incompetent, or that the advocate is deliberately flouting the rules to advance the case at any cost.

2. The pickup rule

This is a technique used by many advocates where the evidence in chief flows well because the advocate is using the answer of the witness to frame the next question in a non-leading way. I will use the facts in the Alfred Blake case to illustrate this rule.

COUNSEL: When did you commence work at FFP?

BLAKE: I started work there in February 2017.

COUNSEL: Were you still working there prior to your arrest by the CBSA?

BLAKE: No, I'd left FFP at the beginning of February 2018.

COUNSEL:	Were you allowed to do that?
BLAKE:	No. I had to work there until mid-February 2018 when my work permit would have expired.
COUNSEL:	The documents show that you were arrested by the CBSA on April 30, 2018. So you remained in Canada unlawfully? *[One exception to the rule against asking leading questions is that where there are documents that have been admitted into the proceedings, counsel will be permitted to refer to the documents in the examination of their witness.]*
BLAKE:	Yes, I did.
COUNSEL:	Why? *["Why," "when," "how," "which," "was–were," "what" and "where" questions are useful because they are neutral and non-leading.]*
BLAKE:	Because of the abuse from a fellow worker at FFP and my love for Gill.
COUNSEL:	So, the main reason you left FFP was because you fell in love with Gill.
MINISTER'S COUNSEL:	Objection. My friend is asking a leading question. He is suggesting that the main reason Blake left FFP was because of his love for Gill. The witness did not say that.
MEMBER:	I accept this objection. Please refrain from asking leading questions of your own witness, counsel.
COUNSEL:	I will rephrase the question, sir. What was the main reason you left FFP?
BLAKE:	My affection and love for Gill.

If there are undisputed facts in the case, you can confer with Minister's counsel so that you have permission to ask leading questions to elicit these undisputed facts. For example, if identity is not an issue, the detainee's name, date of birth, date of issue or expiry of the work permit and the fact that there was a Canada-wide warrant for the detainee's arrest will probably be admitted facts and with Minister's counsel's consent can be the subject of leading questions.

The pickup rule is well illustrated in the extract below from one of my Immigration Appeal Division cases. The people involved were Bill Smith and Betty Opoku, and the case dealt with the refusal of a spousal sponsorship.

As you will see, the advocate is extracting the evidence from Smith without leading him. The questions and answers are flowing well because the advocate is using the answer of the witness to frame the next question. However, there are some comments made by the advocate in some of the questions that may cause the opponent advocate to raise an objection. These are in italics.

ADVOCATE: Do you know Betty Opoku?

SMITH: Yes, I know her.

ADVOCATE: How do you know her?

SMITH: I met her online.

ADVOCATE: Which online site was this?

SMITH: Harmony.com.

ADVOCATE: What happened after you first met her online?

SMITH: We began chatting there frequently.

ADVOCATE: How often did you chat with her on the harmony.com site?

SMITH: We chatted together almost every day.

ADVOCATE: Is that the only place you chatted with her almost every day?

SMITH: No, after a few months we started exchanging emails.

ADVOCATE: Which email service did you use?

SMITH: We both used yahoo.com.

ADVOCATE: Were online chat and email the only forms of communication you used?

SMITH: No. We also phoned each other occasionally.

ADVOCATE: How old are you?

SMITH: I'm 63.

ADVOCATE: How old is Betty?

SMITH: She is 35.

ADVOCATE: So, there is a 28-year age difference between the two of you? *[Although this appears like a leading question, it is not as it is a conclusion based on facts and not a suggestion.]*

SMITH: Yes.

ADVOCATE: Did you have any opinion about the big age difference between you and Betty? *[Again, this remark is grounded in the facts, so it is permissible, but it could be argued by the opponent that counsel should not render an opinion, and therefore it is not a proper question.]*

SMITH: We loved each other a lot, and we both thought our ages were just a number and it meant nothing to us.

ADVOCATE:	It's plain you are a white man, correct? *[Although a strictly leading suggestion, it is still grounded in fact. A better question would be "What is your race?"]*
SMITH:	Yes.
ADVOCATE:	What colour and race is Betty?
SMITH:	She is black and is an African woman.
ADVOCATE:	So, your race and colour are different. Did that bother either of you? *[It is arguable that the word bother in the question is a suggestion that the race difference could bother them. A better question would be "Did this affect you?"]*
SMITH:	Race and colour means nothing when you are in love.

3. No insinuations or comments in your questions – keep it factual

Objections from your opponent are usually raised when you lose control of yourself in your examination in chief with the tension or excitement bubbling within you, and you inadvertently include opinions and comments in your examination. Avoid these lapses so that you deal only with the facts in the examination. Your thoughts and opinions are irrelevant and inappropriate. These lapses can lead to well-founded objections from your opponent. This will inevitably begin a chain reaction, which can result in the loss of your credibility as a professional advocate. I have committed this sin on more than one occasion in the middle of a delicate examination in chief. *Don't do it.*

4. Relevance

Remember when you are examining your witness that you are supposed to be extracting factual information or evidence that is relevant to the case you are presenting. If that evidence is irrelevant and has nothing to do with your case, omit these irrelevant questions. *If you don't, it will affect your credibility, as you will be seen as an ineffective advocate.*

5. Keep your questions short and concise

Keep your questions short and concise. A long-winded, three-sentence question may on rare occasions be appropriate for a piece of cross-examination but not for an examination in chief. If your questions are too long, it means you may be committing the sins of irrelevancy, uncalled-for comment or insinuations in your questions. In the examples I have given you, all the questions are short and concise—less than 15 words. *Keep to that habit.*

6. Hearsay

The hearsay rule is there to exclude what others have said to your witness. This kind of declaration is excluded from being considered by the panel member because it is not under oath, cannot be tested through cross-examination and is thus regarded as unreliable. If the declarant will later be a witness in the proceedings, it is admissible. In some situations, the court or tribunal will admit hearsay evidence, subject to an assessment of the weight to be given to that piece of untested evidence. In my experience, the immigration advocate must steer clear of attempting to elicit hearsay evidence, as the divisions of the IRB attach little weight to it.

However, there are circumstances that will allow the admission of hearsay—for example, when it is necessary and reliable. The exceptions to the hearsay rule are complex. Any immigration consultant who wants to specialize in oral advocacy in the divisions of the IRB must have a good working knowledge of the rules of evidence. It is recommended that they have a good book on evidence for easy reference during the case. Pick up a simple and concise handbook on this subject. A useful text is *The Portable Guide to Evidence*, 5th edition, by Michael Doherty.

7. Agreement that certain facts are not in dispute, enabling you to lead the witness on these uncontested facts

As discussed earlier, there will be situations where you and your opponent can agree that certain basic facts like time, date and location are not in dispute. In these circumstances, you can lead. One word of caution: do not seek this agreement if it affects the perceived truthfulness and independence of the evidence. Where and how Betty Opoku and Bill Smith met may not be in dispute, but see how the two different passages below read:

"You met Betty online, right?"

"Yes."

As opposed to the witness, without any prompting, saying, "I met Betty online."

8. The bar on opinion evidence

Most of your witnesses are lay persons. Such witnesses can only give evidence of the facts. They cannot render an opinion. However, some questions may seem to be eliciting an opinion but in the final analysis are not. For example, it is permissible to ask, "Do you believe Betty loves you?" Strictly speaking, it is eliciting an opinion, but it is an opinion concerning the affairs of humans and the emotions of love. Therefore, it would not prompt an objection from your opponent, especially if you followed it up with the question, "How do you know she loves you?" "She told me she did." Betty will be also giving evidence at the appeal hearing by teleconference, so that remark from Betty is not hearsay. However, consider the question, "Alfred, do you know how the machinery used at FFP is constructed?"

This is an attempt to elicit opinion evidence that assumes that Alfred has expert knowledge of how the machines used at FFP are made and is thus inadmissible opinion evidence.

9. The bar on legal opinions

You cannot ask questions of your lay witness about the law. The issue of what the law is, and how it ought to be interpreted, is a matter for you to make submissions on at the end of the case when all the evidence has been adduced. Consider this question: "Did you breach IRPA when you fled from FFP?" You might get an objection from your opponent because that is an attempt by you to elicit opinion evidence from your witness about some of the ultimate legal issues in the case.

Cross-Examination (XX)

The golden rule

You must know the answer to every question you ask a witness in XX. This is to ensure there is damage control in connection with your case. I will amplify on this concept as we discuss some examples in this chapter.

In XX, you will invariably and ONLY ask leading questions so as to effectively extract the information you want from the opponent's witness and to avoid the open-ended type of questions used in examination in chief, which will invite unknown and possibly dangerous answers.

Elements of a competent cross-examination

1. *Work out in advance the story the witness will tell under XX, which will assist the client's case.* In order to do this, the advocate must know what the weaknesses and strengths in the client's case are and what information in the GCMS notes will be helpful to bring out from the opponent's witness during XX.
2. *Read the papers in the case, including the GCMS notes, the respondent's record and the applicant/appellant's materials carefully before the hearing* in order to extract the information from these documents that will help the client's case, bearing in mind the purpose and strategy outlined in paragraph 1 above.
3. *Organize the questions* so that the answers provide a logical series of answers that tells a compelling and persuasive story that helps your client.
4. *Don't ask questions that have the potential to damage your client's case.*
5. *Be persistent.* If the witness attempts to evade the questions or provide answers that are deliberately intended to hurt the client, you must have the courage to doggedly pursue and discredit the testimony of the witness. If you cannot do this, stop the XX.

6. *Frame the question so as to trap the witness into answering the question in the way that you want.* A lot of advocates will tag the question with, "Is that correct," "Is it right," "From the material before you at page . . ., paragraph . . ., it is clear, is it not, that my client did . . . ." More experienced advocates will use a question intonation to avoid too many tag lines. If a witness is evasive on a matter that is clear on the face of the documents, pin the witness down by saying, "Please read page . . ., paragraph . . ., carefully. After you tell me you are satisfied that you understand these notes, I will ask you some questions." In this example, you are forcing the witness to consider the evidence and instilling fear in the witness that any lies or exaggeration they proffer will be obvious unless they answer the question in accordance with the GCMS notes—so that the answer is truthful!
7. *Be brief and focused.* Stop the XX immediately once you have the answers that will support your submissions.
8. *Stick to one answer per question.* Long-winded questions with lots of facts will confuse both the witness and the panel member.
9. *Listen to the answers.* This means understanding whether the answer helps you and being decisive as to whether it is necessary to continue the XX. Do not be caught up in the excitement of the situation by continuing a XX that may ultimately damage your client's case.
10. *Don't quarrel with the witness.* Be polite, courteous and professional. Be like a poker player: if the answer of the witness hurts you, don't show it.
11. A useful tactic is to *ask a question in a different way* after a while on a topic that is very relevant to your case where the witness in chief gave a damaging answer.
12. *Don't ask questions that will elicit the same answer given by the witness in chief.* It does not help you, as you are causing the witness to repeat testimony that is damaging to your case. The evidence becomes more important in the mind of the trier of fact when the damaging evidence is repeated through your ill-considered questions.
13. *Don't permit the witness to explain anything* unless the panel member orders you to allow the witness to explain. Most answers should be "Yes," "No" or "Don't know."
14. *Avoid one question too many.* There you are in a trance, building this fantastic castle in your XX when you recklessly ask that one question too many that causes your castle to fall to pieces.

This section on cross-examination is necessarily brief because an RCIC or an immigration lawyer, practising in the divisions of the IRB, has few cases where effective cross-examination is necessary, unlike a trial lawyer, for whom XX is part and parcel of everyday court work. In most cases, you will rely on the contents of the GCMS notes/respondent's case record as the basis for your submissions. It is usually inadvisable to summon a CBSA/Immigration officer for XX because of the inherent danger that the CBSA/Immigration officer might explain the notes in such a way that does not help your client. So why take the risk?

Note that the rules I discussed under examination in chief—relevance, hearsay, the bars on opinion and legal opinion evidence—are applicable to cross-examination as well.

Example of cross-examination techniques

In order to understand effective XX, I have reproduced below an extract from the GCMS notes in the Alfred Blake case. For the purpose of this exercise, the CBSA officer will attend the detention review hearing to give evidence. You need special knowledge and training to properly understand GCMS notes, so for this exercise, I have made the notes more intelligible and less technical.

Enter Can 05/01/14 from Jam to FWP in Hamilton with Fresh Farm Produce Inc. (FFP) leaves within PAS on 02/10/15.

Enter Can 05/01/15 from Jam to FWP in Hamilton with FFP leaves within PAS on 02/10/16.

Enter Can 06/12/17 from Jam to FWP in Hamilton and FFP expires 02/10/18. No record of departure to Jam.

02/15/18: Address change info received, AB lives at 100 Williams Street, Orangeville no address changes registered so it is unconfirmed.

03/01/18: Issue Removal Order and CW warrant on AB at FFP.

04/30/18: CW warrant executed. AB arrested, in detention at RHC.

05/02/18: Detained after 48-hour DR.

In order to assist the readers in their XX, the abbreviations in the extract are as follows:

Can: Canada
Jam: Jamaica
FWP: Farm Workers Program
FFP: Fresh Farm Produce Inc.
PAS: Period of authorized stay
AB: Alfred Blake
CW warrant: Canada-wide warrant for the arrest of AB
RHC: Rexdale Holding Centre in Etobicoke, Toronto
DR: Detention review

The cross-examination might proceed in this way:

ADVOCATE: On May 1, 2014, Mr. Blake came to Canada legally on a work permit to work for FFP, is that correct?

CBSA OFFICER: Yes, sir.

ADVOCATE: And he left before the expiry of his authorized stay in Canada on February 10, 2015?

CBSA OFFICER: Yes, sir.

ADVOCATE: Mr. Blake made a further legal trip in May 2015 to Canada to work for FFP in the Farm Workers Program, correct?

CBSA OFFICER: Yes, sir.

ADVOCATE: And he left Canada when he was required to do so before the expiry of his authorized stay on February 10, 2016?

CBSA OFFICER: Yes, sir.

ADVOCATE: So, you'd agree that in connection with no less than two trips to Canada in 2014 and 2015, Mr. Blake complied with the immigration laws of Canada by leaving before the expiry of his work permits?

CBSA OFFICER: Yes, sir.

ADVOCATE: In connection with these two trips, he complied fully with his work permit conditions by working for FFP until he had to leave Canada when his work permit expired?

CBSA OFFICER: Yes, sir.

In the example above, you controlled the witness by your concise and clear leading questions, and you successfully extracted the story of an immigrant who has *broadly* complied with IRPA and IRPR. You will use this evidence in your submissions. You have just highlighted and emphasized an important component of your case!

Hint: There are further facts in the GCMS extract that will be useful to you in closing arguments, but you must get the right answers from the witness. How will you do it?

Re-Examination

The rule
You cannot ask any questions in re-examination of your witness unless the matter you are asking about arose out of answers given by the witness from cross-examination by opposing counsel.

ADVOCACY IN THE IMMIGRATION DIVISION • 63

Caution: Think carefully before you decide to re-examine *and do so only if you are sure that the damaging evidence that came out of XX can be neutralized through your re-examination.* The danger is that the re-examination may hurt your case even more, and you must avoid doing this.

Examples of re-examination

Let's go to the Bill Smith and Betty Opoku case for a moment. Assume that in the narrative that was enclosed with the spousal sponsorship application, there was the following statement from Betty:

"We like the same kind of fruit."

At the Appeal Division, Minister's counsel cross-examines Betty during the telephone conference as follows:

MINISTER'S COUNSEL:	So, you say you like the same fruits in your narrative, correct?
BETTY:	Yes.
MINISTER'S COUNSEL:	But there is a statement from Bill Smith that he doesn't like sweet potatoes, correct?
BETTY:	Yes.
MINISTER'S COUNSEL:	So, there is an inconsistency as it seems you and Bill don't like the same fruit?
BETTY:	I suppose so. *[She is getting tired of the extensive XX from Minister's counsel and is on her last legs!]*

The re-examination might then proceed as follows:

IMMIGRATION CONSULTANT:	Do you regard sweet potatoes to be in the same category as fruits?
BETTY:	No. A sweet potato is a vegetable and not a fruit. *[She just realized her mistake under cross-examination, which the consultant helped her explain and clarify.]*

Clearly, a sweet potato is a vegetable and **not** a fruit. You've just neutralized the apparent inconsistency between the statements of Bill and Betty!

Below is an example of an effective re-examination in the Alfred Blake detention review case.

Minister's counsel cross-examines Alfred Blake as follows:

MINISTER'S COUNSEL:	When you gave evidence in chief, you agreed that you lied to the member at the last detention review when you said Gill and Tony did not know that you were illegal in Canada?

BLAKE: Yes, but I lied so as not to get them in trouble.

Re-examination by Blake's counsel:

COUNSEL: When you were living with Gill and Tony, did they know you were illegal in Canada?

BLAKE: No, they only found this out after I was arrested and detained.

COUNSEL: Thinking about it now, do you think Gill and Tony would have got into trouble if at the last hearing you had explained how and when they found out you were illegal?

BLAKE: Definitely not. I was foolish to have lied.

COUNSEL: Thank you.

Counsel, through this piece of re-examination, has effectively neutralized this lie so that it has lost the capacity of undermining Alfred's credibility.

Practice tip

Take these notes to an appeal at the Immigration Appeal Division or to a detention review hearing at the Immigration Division (which is usually open to the public—although at the Immigration Division, you should accompany a mentor consultant or lawyer who is doing the review hearing) and focus on the advocate's questions so you obtain a sense of how questions are framed and the rules of questioning that advocates must be mindful of when they are in the midst of an examination in chief or cross-examination or in re-examination. You will learn a lot.

Oral Advocacy

Structure and sequence

STATEMENT OF THE CASE

You should always begin your argument with a clear and persuasive statement explaining the essence of your case. This statement should be confident, succinct and, to the extent possible, slanted in favour of your version of the case. For example, in the Alfred Blake case, when attempting to secure the release of your client, you could say, "This is a case about an immigrant who through love made a misjudgment, which led to a breach of IRPA. However, as I hope to demonstrate, Alfred has consistently abided by our immigration laws, and because of the strict plan of release presented, he ought to be released and forgiven for this one transgression." *(This is just one possible example out of many. Use your own original preliminary remark.)*

"ROAD MAP"

At the beginning of your address, narrow down and identify the main issues you will discuss. Make sure you set out for the member the topics that will form the basis of your submissions and that they follow a logical order.

If you present the topics of your oral argument in outline form, you will not miss the important points that you must convey to the member. When you follow the road map, the member will appreciate it, as your factual presentation and arguments will not be muddled and disorganized. The road map gives the tribunal a general picture and outline of the substantial arguments that will follow.

Memorize your road map. The most successful advocates memorize their road map and maintain eye contact with the tribunal throughout. This is the best way to make a good first impression demonstrating you are confident and prepared for the hearing.

FACTS

Briefly outline the relevant facts of your case in accordance with your road map, taking care to highlight those points that support your position. Keep your submissions short (no more than 10–15 minutes—longer only if the case is complex) and focus on the critical elements of your case. Be forewarned that the member might interrupt you in midstream with questions. If the member does this, answer the questions and then proceed with your argument.

ORDER OF ARGUMENT

Begin the body of your argument by discussing the first issue in your road map. Make your argument and then proceed directly to your second issue and the third issue. There is no need to pause or to solicit questions. The member may interrupt you with questions. Answer the questions directly, but do not lose your place in your argument. Avoid repetition.

CONCLUSION

When you have finished your argument, end with a clear statement of what you are asking the member to do. For example, "I respectfully ask you, sir (or madam), to release Alfred Blake with the conditions that I have previously outlined."

Preparing your oral argument

- Know your arguments completely. In planning your presentation, make sure to highlight and make an outline of the merits and theme of your case. But anticipate all the problems/difficulties in your case and deal with them in your submissions. Be prepared to respond to questions you believe the member may ask, and try to deal with issues that you anticipate opposing counsel may raise in his or her arguments.

- Ensure the member knows that you know the law on detention and release. Refer to important sections of IRPA and the IRPR that are applicable. Cite a few of the major cases on the subject that support your arguments. In appendices A and B, I have reproduced all the relevant sections of IRPA and the IRPR on detentions. The CGD, reproduced in appendix D, is also helpful, as it provides a useful digest of important detention review cases.
- Focus on the most important arguments in your case. They should constitute your entire argument. *Oral arguments are brief, so you should deal with only the most important (and convincing) arguments available to you.* Do not attempt to argue all the points, as some of them will be minor and not strong, so be selective in highlighting the important points that will help you to persuade the member to release your client. *Avoid repetition, as your points will not be made stronger by doing this. It will certainly irritate the member and wear out the member's patience.*
- Always focus on why your side is right, rather than on why the other side is wrong. Doing it the other way around creates the impression that your opponent's case is strong and, therefore, you need to dodge their bullets. It weakens your advocacy. When crafting your argument, put yourself in the position of the tribunal. *Look for the weaknesses in your argument, anticipate the questions that the tribunal might ask and plan responses that strengthen your position.*
- "Know when to hold 'em, know when to fold 'em, know when to walk away, know when to run . . . ." *Knowing when to make concessions, without weakening the core of your argument, is an important skill of oral advocacy.* If you and your opponent's cases did not both have strengths and weaknesses, and all was favourable to your side, there might not have been a full hearing, as it would have been decided through the consent of Minister's counsel that the detainee should be released. In a contested detention review case, there are always strong points for detention that will be highlighted by Minister's counsel and points for release that you will emphasize. The trick is for you to neutralize and weaken the apparent strong points for detention in your opponent's case when preparing your submissions. It is acceptable to stand firm in respectful disagreements with the member, and you can admit a weakness in your case if it doesn't undermine the core basis of your argument for release.
- *Do not write out an entire speech* that you intend to deliver to the ID. Instead, it is a good idea to make a brief outline through the road map we discussed to help you remember the key arguments and issues of your case and to note key theories and how they tie up to your argument and

cases. Try to limit your outline to one sheet of paper. *Use key words and phrases to jog your memory.* While you should certainly have some idea of what your argument sounds like—what words you will use beyond your outline is up to you—reading a speech is not persuasive. Reading their submissions is one of the most common mistakes made by inexperienced advocates. Approach your submissions in a conversational style, but with formal language and not in the form of a lecture to the member.

Additional points to consider

- Immigration lawyers and consultants often refer to the adjudicator who sits in the Immigration Division, Immigration Appeal Division and the Refugee Protection Division as a "Member" or "Panel Member." Sometimes the advocate may refer to them as the tribunal or the Division Member. Always refer to them as either "Sir" or "Madam/Ma'am," depending on gender. They are not judges, and some of them may not even be lawyers. They are civil servants. It is, therefore, inappropriate to refer to them as "Your Honour" or "Your Worship" or "Justice."
- Try not to use abbreviations or acronyms in your address. If you do, make sure you identify on the record what the abbreviation means—for example, "Sir, I am referring to the GCMS notes, that is the Global Case Management System." Once you have described what the abbreviation is, you can use the abbreviation in your submissions.
- Similarly, when you cite cases, do a full cite for the ID and the record—for example, "I refer you, sir, to the case of *Sahin v. Canada*, decided in 1994 in the Federal Court and reported at volume 1 of the 1995 Federal Court Reports, at page 214." This not only looks professional but also preserves the integrity of the record, especially in the event of a judicial review of the detention review decision to the Federal Court.

Etiquette and style

- Dress appropriately, as it demonstrates that you respect yourself as an advocate and that you respect the tribunal. For men, wear a suit. For women, wear a dress or conservative clothes. You must appear professional and neat and avoid any clothing that is flashy, showy, tasteless or crude.
- Do not fiddle with pens, pencils or other objects while you make your submissions. Do not gesticulate with your hands. A useful tip is to keep your hands either clasped behind your back or at your front-waist or keep your arms at your side. Mannerisms such as fiddling with pens or

gesticulating with your hands not only shows you are nervous but also distracts the member.
- Be aware that at any time during your argument, the member may interrupt you with questions. It is vital you answer the question fully when the member asks it. Do not tell the member that you will answer that question later. Go to where the member leads you, even if that means not following the order of arguments that you originally planned. The danger of memorizing the whole of your submissions is that it creates an obstacle and mental block that prevents you being flexible, especially when the member asks questions.
- If you do not understand the question the member asks you, seek clarification from the member. It is better to do this than to answer a question the member did not ask.
- Approach your oral argument as a conversation with, not a lecture to, the member. But use formal language. Avoid contractions such as I'll, won't or don't. Say the correct long form words—I will, I will not, I do not. It sounds more professional. Engage in an exchange of ideas with the member and respond to his or her concerns. Don't read a speech to the member.
- If the member asks a "yes" or "no" question, answer first with "yes" or "no"—then, if it is necessary, elaborate. For example, reply with "Yes, sir, in fact . . .," or "No, sir, rather . . .."
- *Never speak over a member.* When the member starts talking, you should stop talking immediately, even if he or she has interrupted you in mid-sentence (or even mid-word).
- It is acceptable to stand firm and disagree with the member, but you should be respectful. You can say, "I respectfully disagree because . . .." But if you disagree, you must be able to support your position with a well-reasoned argument.
- Unless the case is complicated with many issues that must be addressed, your oral submissions should not exceed 15 minutes. Condensing your submission will make it not only concise but also more focused. Too many advocates believe that wordiness and long submissions are more thorough. They are not. They become boring and will soon lose the listener's attention.
- When you finish your oral submissions, thank the member and sit down: "Thank you, sir. These are all my submissions in this matter."

In the next chapter, we will look at the draft of the oral submissions of Mr. Blake's counsel at the detention review hearing.

CHAPTER 8

Sample Oral Submissions at the Detention Review Hearing of Alfred Blake

Note: The words in brackets and italics are inserted to illustrate the implementation of the road map for the readers and will not be spoken when counsel delivers the oral submissions.

I intend to set out the positive factors that are present in Mr. Blake's immigration history, factors that indicate compliance, explain the reasons for his breach of IRPA and outline the proposed tight conditions of release, as well as some observations about Mr. Blake's evidence at the hearing. Finally, I will briefly comment on the law on detentions under IRPA. I hope my submissions will persuade you to release my client with appropriate conditions. [*road map*]

Mr. Blake has in the past demonstrated the capacity to obey our immigration laws. On two previous occasions, in 2015 and 2016, he was issued a work permit to work at the Farm Workers Program in Canada, and he went back to Jamaica prior to the expiry of the work permits on both occasions. [*history*]

Mr. Blake also demonstrated a degree of responsibility and compliance when he informed the CBSA by letter of his change of address to that of his girlfriend in Orangeville when he moved in with her at the beginning of February 2018. This was a month before the CBSA issued a removal order and a Canada-wide arrest warrant against him. Unfortunately, the change of address did not register within the GCMS—the global case management system—and these documents were sent to his old address at FFP, so that Mr. Blake was not aware of the serious immigration jeopardy he was in. [*compliance*]

Finally, I ask you to consider the reasons he fled from FFP. The abuse at work, which the employer failed to address, and the blossoming romantic relationship that had developed with Ms. St. John, incited him to disregard his obligations under IRPA. I agree with Minister's counsel that these reasons in themselves cannot excuse his breach of our immigration rules, but it does provide a context and reason for his disobedience on this one isolated occasion. [*reasons for breach of IRPA*]

I ask that you weigh the strong factors of Mr. Blake's past compliance with our immigration laws and the responsibility he showed in informing the CBSA of his change of address, as well as the motivation that led to this isolated, one-off breach, in considering alternatives to detention and the release plan that is offered.

At the previous detention review hearing, Mr. Blake was unrepresented and traumatized because of his incarceration. He was not aware of the essential qualities that the bondspersons he proposed must have to make them suitable to supervise him. Both the member of the ID and Minister's counsel were bound to have concerns about that release plan given the complete unsuitability of the bondspersons he proposed, and it was inevitable that his detention would continue.

However, today, the release plan being offered is tight. Both the bondsperson posting the performance bond, Ms. St. John, and the person providing the cash bond, Mr. St. John, are suitable. They have an ongoing relationship with Mr. Blake, and that relationship is strong, as prior to his detention he had lived with them for over three months. It is important to note that they both observed in their affidavits that he complied with the rules and discipline of their household and respected them when he lived with them. They are both solvent with good jobs and can easily provide both the performance bond of $3,000 and the cash bond of $2,000. Furthermore, they have indicated that should you decide to increase the amount of the bonds, they will comply. They are not providing these guarantees blindly. They are aware of Mr. Blake's immigration history and the fact that he is currently illegal in Canada. They know there is a risk that they will lose their bonds if Mr. Blake breaches the conditions of release. However, they are confident he will not, and they will ensure he reports to the CBSA regularly, driving him there if need be. They will be monitoring his mail and will ensure that he attends any immigration proceedings and removal from Canada. The degree of supervision that they will provide is high. It will involve Mr. Blake residing with them and the supervision that naturally results from his residence with them. Ms. St. John works day shifts, but Mr. St. John works at home during the day. When Mr. St. John goes to his shop in town, he will bring Alfred with him. There is, therefore, 24-hour, 7-day supervision. [*conditions of release and 24-hour supervision*]

Mr. Blake's evidence at this detention review is credible. He is deeply grateful for the assistance that the St. Johns will provide through their bonds and their supervision. He has unhesitatingly declared that he will obey them. It will be no different from when he lived with them and obeyed their rules of the household. It is, therefore, unlikely that he will violate any of the conditions of release I propose. I believe the last nine days of detention have been an eye opener for Mr. Blake, and you can be confident that Mr. Blake understands the jeopardy he is in and will not breach any conditions of release that you impose. As he said at the hearing, "I now understand what I did was wrong, and I have no intention of breaking either the rules of Gill and Tony or the immigration laws." [*observation on Blake's evidence at the hearing*]

Regulation 245 of the IRPR lists several factors that are favourable to Mr. Blake's case, namely his previous compliance with IRPA and the fact that he has strong community ties with the St. Johns. It is accepted that an analysis of the length of detention under regulation 248 indicates that Alfred should not face lengthy detention, as he has his current Jamaican passport. The CBSA can remove him without any impediment. However, paragraph (e) of regulation 248 mandates the ID to consider alternatives to detention. The case law is clear that detention is a matter of last resort, especially when there are suitable and compelling alternatives to detention. The landmark case of *Sahin v. Canada*, decided in 1994 in the Federal Court and reported at volume 1 of the 1995 Federal Court Reports, at page 214, must be considered. The principles of law in that case were codified in the IRPR and set out the law that you must follow in deciding whether to release Mr. Blake. I will not go through this with you, sir, as I know you are very familiar with the law on detentions. In my submission, the case for alternatives to detention is compelling and powerful and would justify Mr. Blake's release on the strict conditions I have proposed. [*brief comments on the law*]

I ask that he be released subject to the strict conditions I have outlined and any other conditions you deem appropriate. Thank you for patiently listening to my submissions. [*closing sentence*]

Commentary

Depending on the speed of your speech, these submissions will take less than 15 minutes to deliver! The road map at the start of the submissions provided a logical path for the submissions that followed. The submissions complied with the road map and delivered all the important points in a concise and focused manner. The observations about Blake's evidence at the hearing highlighted the fact that Blake will comply with the rules that the St. Johns will impose on him. The brief commentary on the law is appropriate. It reminds the member that they must comply with the law and that they know *you* know the law. However, it also recognizes that the member is familiar with the law, so the advocate avoids wasting time by tediously going over the law in detail.

I am not suggesting that this is a perfect oral submission. It is not, but it illustrates the methodology involved and the important points that must be made. Each advocate will have their own style and "turn" of language. I encourage you to engage your own personality when making oral submissions at both the ID and in all aspects of your advocacy at the IRB.

CHAPTER 9

It All Comes Together: The 7-Day Detention Review Transcript

The meticulous and thorough preparation for the detention review hearing has been done. How will the detainee's counsel and the detainee fare during this 7-day review? Will Alfred be released or not? We shall see as we examine the transcript and reasons for decision reproduced below.

```
                    1-0007-F1-5-5-DR-09-May-18-BOSWMA-58(1)(b)
```

IMMIGRATION AND REFUGEE BOARD

-IMMIGRATION DIVISION-

Record of a Detention Review held under the
<u>Immigration and Refugee Protection Act</u> concerning

ALFRED BLAKE

HEARING: PUBLIC

HELD AT:	Immigration Holding Centre
DATE:	May 9, 2018
BEFORE:	George Hope -Member

APPEARANCES:

    Alfred Blake   –Person Concerned

    Mr. Thompson   –Minister's Counsel

    Mr. Fink   –Counsel for the Person Concerned

    N/A   –Interpreter

MEMBER: ced Good morning.

This is the detention review of Alfred Blake.

Is that you, sir?

PERSON CONCERNED: Yes.

MEMBER: Today is Wednesday, May 9, 2018.

These proceedings are now being tape recorded. My name is George Hope, and I am a member of the Immigration Division. I will be presiding over your hearing today, Mr. Blake.

Representing the Minister today is Mr. Thompson, and I understand that the person concerned is represented by counsel.

COUNSEL: Yes, sir. I represent Mr. Blake and my name is John Fink.

MEMBER: I understand that there are 2 persons outside, one of whom would like to post a performance bond and the other intends to provide a cash bond. Is that correct, Mr. Fink?

COUNSEL: Yes, sir.

MEMBER: Would these bondspersons like to give evidence at this hearing, Mr. Fink?

COUNSEL: They would, but as you see I have provided comprehensive affidavits from both Gill St. John and Tony St. John. This would be the evidence they would give in chief. I do not want to waste the time of this tribunal by asking them questions about the contents of their affidavits. However, if either you or Minister's counsel wish to question them, they are happy to attend this hearing.

MEMBER: The affidavits you presented from them deal with all the issues that I am concerned about, so I have no questions for them. But perhaps Mr. Thompson may have some question of your bondspersons.

MINISTER'S COUNSEL: The affidavits are detailed and deal with all the issues, so I do not need to question them. However, I reserve the right to comment on the affidavits and draw some inferences. But that's all.

MEMBER: Very well. We will proceed with this hearing without the bondspersons, but I note for the record the detailed affidavit evidence they presented. This will form part of the substantive evidence in this case.

COUNSEL: Thank you, sir.

MEMBER: I am conducting this 7-day review on May 9, 2018. Present is Minister's counsel, Mr. Thompson, and counsel for the person concerned, Mr. Fink. It is agreed by the parties that an interpreter is not required by Mr. Blake as English is his first and native language. Before we commence the hearing, counsel will help me organize and mark the relevant exhibits that will be produced and relied upon at this hearing.

MINISTER'S COUNSEL: I am relying on our GCMS notes on Mr. Blake, which I would like to exhibit as A1.

COUNSEL: On behalf of Mr. Blake, I have here a bundle of documents properly tabbed, paginated with a table of contents, that contains the affidavits of our bondsperson, Gill St. John, and her brother, Tony St. John. Included in the bundle are all the documentary exhibits properly tabbed that are attached to their affidavits. There are also other documents—the issued removal order and arrest warrant. I would like to mark this package of documents as R1.

MEMBER: Very good, so marked—A1, the documents from Minister's counsel, and R1, the documents from Mr. Blake's counsel.

The information I have is that you have been detained by the immigration authorities since April 30, 2018, and that this is your 7-day detention review, having been detained at the 48-hour review by Member Gregory Boswell. Mr. Boswell commented in his reasons for detention that Mr. Blake continued to be a flight risk as the release plan that Mr. Blake presented was weak. I trust that counsel has had an opportunity to read the 48-hour detention review transcript, which I can see he requested from the registrar of the Immigration Division.

COUNSEL: I have reviewed the transcript, sir.

MEMBER: Very well. This is a public hearing. The procedure we shall follow is that, firstly, Minister's counsel will outline your immigration history and the grounds they rely on for your continued detention. Secondly, you will be given an opportunity through your own counsel's questions to say whatever you consider necessary in the case and in response to Minister's counsel. During the process, Minister's counsel and I may ask you some questions to clarify your evidence. Do you understand?

PERSON CONCERNED: Yes, sir.

MEMBER: After this, Minister's counsel will make any submissions he deems appropriate. Finally, your counsel will be given the opportunity to make submissions on your behalf. Yes, Mr. Thompson.

MINISTER'S COUNSEL: Mr. Blake had been accepted in the Farm Workers Program, where he was employed looking after livestock at a farm in Hamilton. His employer was Fresh Farm Produce Inc. (FFP). He received a work permit to work at FFP. I am reading from the GCMS notes. It seems he first came to Hamilton from Jamaica, his country of citizenship and ordinary residence, on May 1, 2014. In accordance with his work permit, he left Canada on February 10, 2015. He received another work permit to work for FFP on May 1, 2015 and left on February 10, 2016 before his work permit expired. However, after he received a work permit to continue work at FFP on June 12, 2017, he did not leave Canada before his work permit expired on February 10, 2018. In fact, the CBSA received a call from FFP that Mr. Blake had abandoned his employment at the farm on February 7, 2018 and then disappeared. Eventually, on March 1, 2018, the CBSA issued a Canada-wide warrant for Mr. Blake's arrest, and shortly thereafter a CBSA officer issued a removal order against Mr. Blake. This removal order was sent to his last known address in Hamilton. As you will recall from reviewing the last detention review transcript, there were some pages missing toward the end of the GCMS notes, which may have dealt with events after the removal order was issued. I have been able to find these missing notes and they seem to suggest that Mr. Blake provided the CBSA with an address in Orangeville. But what is confusing is that the note after that entry says, "unknown address—disregard."

In any event, Mr. Blake has breached IRPA in failing to leave Canada before the expiry of his work permit on

February 10, 2018. Furthermore, he breached his conditions of employment as outlined in the work permit conditions in ceasing work at the farm and effectively fleeing from the program. On April 19, 2018, Hamilton police stopped Mr. Blake for speeding. Upon checking the CPIC system, police became aware of the Canada-wide arrest warrant on Mr. Blake. Police alerted the CBSA, giving them Mr. Blake's address in Orangeville, which was apparently on Mr. Blake's driver's licence. The CBSA arrested Mr. Blake on Monday, April 30, 2018 and detained him at the Rexdale Holding Centre until his 48-hour review, which took place on Wednesday, May 2, 2018. At that hearing, Member Boswell detained Mr. Blake because he provided bondspersons, a Tim O'Connor and James Philpot, who were totally unsuitable for the reasons Member Boswell gave.

At this detention review, the Minister takes the position that Mr. Blake is a flight risk in that he has demonstrated through his actions that he is contemptuous of our immigration laws by breaching IRPA in both leaving FFP in breach of his work permit conditions and failing to leave Canada before the expiry of his work permit. At the last review hearing, the member found that Mr. O'Connor, the proposed bondsperson, and Mr. Philpot, who would provide the cash bond, were unacceptable and inappropriate. Today, we take the position that the bondspersons that Mr. Fink is presenting, namely, Gill St. John and Tony St. John, are also inappropriate. However, that is a matter for you to determine, sir. We therefore seek the continued detention of Mr. Blake.

MEMBER: Thank you, Mr. Thompson. Mr. Fink, you can now proceed with your examination of Mr. Blake.

COUNSEL: Mr. Blake, do you accept that you breached IRPA by not continuing to work for FFP until the expiry of your work permit and that you also breached IRPA by failing to leave Canada after your work permit expired?

PERSON CONCERNED: I did break the law, but I didn't do that the last two times I came to Canada. I did it this time because I fell in love with Gill and I needed peace, as a fellow worker at FFP, Luke Brown, kept harassing me and making racist taunts.

COUNSEL: What did he do? Did you complain to your boss about this man's behaviour toward you?

PERSON CONCERNED: This guy kept wanting to fight me. Every day was hell with this guy, shovelling manure at me and trying to kick me. I complained to the boss, Dick, but Dick did nothing. I had just had enough of all this.

COUNSEL: What about your relationship with Gill? How did that start?

PERSON CONCERNED: I met Gill in the fall of 2017 at a church gathering in Hamilton. It seems that my twin brother, James Blake, knew Tony St. John back in Jamaica. Tony started to talk to me and introduced me to his sister, Gill. Gill and I had a lot in common, and soon after meeting, we dated regularly. She is a super girl, and we fell in love. With this mental case at work I needed peace, and I was desperate to be with Gill, so I left FFP.

COUNSEL: When you left FFP, what did you do?

PERSON CONCERNED: I went to live with Gill and Tony at their house in Orangeville. But I was worried about immigration, so I wrote a letter to immigration and gave them my new address in Orangeville. Gill and I wanted to be engaged. Eventually, our plan was to marry. Gill is a Canadian citizen, you know. She got her citizenship in 2015. She would have sponsored me. She said she would. I'm sorry for what I did, but I don't know what else I could have done with the abuse at work and my deep love for Gill. This is the first time I did this. Before, I always left Canada before my work permit ran out.

MEMBER: Did you tell Gill and Tony that you fled from FFP, and that you stayed in Canada illegally after your work permit expired?

PERSON CONCERNED: No, sir. I told them that I had a job arranged at a dairy farm in Grand Valley, a nearby town. I said I had a good work permit. We just left it at that, sir. However, I did not tell the member at the last hearing that I eventually told Gill and Tony about my illegal status in Canada after I was detained.

MEMBER: So, you lied to Member Boswell? And why didn't you write a letter to an immigration officer, telling the officer of the abuse at work, seeing that FFP was not doing anything about your situation there?

PERSON CONCERNED: I accept I did lie, and I didn't write to immigration because I didn't think they could help me.

COUNSEL: Is Gill employed, and what about Tony?

PERSON CONCERNED: Gill has a good job at the CIBC bank in Orangeville, and Tony is a self-employed carpenter.

COUNSEL: You told Minister's counsel before the hearing started that you had a couple of people who could post a bond and cash as part of your release plan. Can you tell me about them?

PERSON CONCERNED: My girlfriend, soon to be fiancé, Gill St. John, will post bond for $3,000, and her brother, Tony, will provide a $2,000 cash bond.

COUNSEL: How well do you know them?

PERSON CONCERNED: Very well. I lived with them for three months before I got detained by immigration. I respect them, and I obey the rules of their household. I believe they know I would not do anything to risk them losing their bond or cash. I know they are giving me a chance and I certainly will not mess up as I did before. I know I'll be back here if that happens, and this is the last place I ever want to see in my life.

COUNSEL: Do Gill and Tony know your immigration history and about your illegality in Canada?

PERSON CONCERNED: Yes, they do, and I am so glad they still want to help me.

COUNSEL: It seems from the GCMS notes that the CBSA had a record of your change of address to Orangeville. Did you ever receive any mail from the CBSA or Immigration at your address in Orangeville after you went to live there with Gill and Tony?

PERSON CONCERNED: No, sir. I don't understand it, and when I got the removal order after I was arrested by the CBSA, I saw the FFP old address. I was surprised, as that order was issued well after I informed Immigration of my change of address to Orangeville.

COUNSEL: Just to assist you and Minister's counsel, I refer you to page 22 of Exhibit R1, where you will see a copy of the removal order that was issued by the CBSA on March 1, 2018. It clearly shows the old FFP address.

MEMBER: I am most grateful, counsel.

COUNSEL: Have you spoken to Gill and Tony prior to the hearing this morning?

PERSON CONCERNED: Yes, I have. They told me that I must obey their house rules and that I must report for all future immigration proceedings and removal. I told them I would not abuse their kindness by jeopardizing their bond and cash. I told them that I would obey all their rules and will attend all meetings and appointments with immigration even if it's to report for removal from this country. By God I will do all that.

COUNSEL: These are my questions, sir. As you are aware, I will also be relying on the evidence of the affiants, Gill and Tony, their documents and other documents in Exhibit R1 at this review hearing.

MEMBER: I understand, Mr. Fink. Now, Mr. Thompson, are there any questions you have for Mr. Blake?

Cross-Examination by Minister's Counsel of the Person Concerned

MINISTER'S COUNSEL: When you decided to abandon your work at FFP and not leave Canada at the end of your work permit, you knew that what you did was against our immigration laws?

PERSON CONCERNED: Yes, I did.

MINISTER'S COUNSEL: And you went ahead and broke the law?

PERSON CONCERNED: Yes. I needed peace from this maniac at work, as Dick did nothing. I love Gill and needed to be with her in a peaceful place.

MINISTER'S COUNSEL: Is it not obvious to you that Gill is blindly helping you because she loves you and not because she thinks you will comply with conditions of release?

PERSON CONCERNED: Gill knows I will obey her orders as I did when I lived with her. She had a good talk with me over the phone last night. She made it crystal clear that if I didn't obey the rules of her household and comply with all the conditions of release, she would pull her bond. She is a strong woman and says she will not stand any nonsense from me.

MINISTER'S COUNSEL: At the last review hearing you agree you lied when you told the member that Gill and Tony did not know you were illegal here in Canada?

PERSON CONCERNED: I did lie.

MINISTER'S COUNSEL: So, we cannot be sure that you are not lying about abiding with any conditions of release that the member may impose?

PERSON CONCERNED: I'm not lying about that or anything else.

MINISTER'S COUNSEL: I gather that you and Gill have decided to marry, and she will sponsor you for permanent residence. Is that correct?

PERSON CONCERNED: Our plans are uncertain because of my present situation, but that is certainly our intention.

MINISTER'S COUNSEL: So, would it not be fair for me to suggest to you that you have no intention to return to Jamaica as you intend to establish a life here in Canada with your future wife and brother-in-law?

PERSON CONCERNED: No. Whatever plans Gill and I have cannot in any way be such as to cause me to break the immigration laws. If I am ordered to be removed from Canada, I will leave. My counsel did advise me that any spousal sponsorship that may have started in Canada can continue being processed while I am in Jamaica. I am okay with that.

MINISTER'S COUNSEL: Those are my questions, sir.

MEMBER: Do you have any questions in re-examination, Mr. Fink?

COUNSEL: Yes, just a few questions, sir.

MEMBER: Go ahead.

COUNSEL: When did you tell Gill and Tony about what you had done and your illegality here in Canada?

PERSON CONCERNED: After I was arrested by the CBSA and detained.

COUNSEL: Did Gill and Tony know you were illegal when you lived with them?

PERSON CONCERNED: No.

COUNSEL: So, was it necessary to lie when they were innocent of any involvement in your illegal status here in Canada?

PERSON CONCERNED: No. I was just confused and foolish.

COUNSEL: These are my questions, sir.

MEMBER: Very good. We will now move to any submissions that Mr. Thompson would like to make. Is that agreed?

COUNSEL: I would like to summarize the evidence in the affidavits of Gill and Tony as part of my client's case.

MEMBER: It is not necessary. I have read your materials very carefully. If there are matters in R1 you would like to highlight, you can do so in your submissions.

MINISTER'S COUNSEL: I would like to add the following to the submissions I made at the beginning of the hearing to support our contention that Mr. Blake is not likely to appear for removal. Firstly, both Tony and Gill are akin to Mr. Blake's family members. The intensity of this familial relationship has deepened during the last three months when Mr. Blake lived with them. Gill loves the detainee and Tony seems to be a good friend. As is apparent from Gill's affidavit, Tony will eventually become Mr. Blake's brother-in-law. These people are keen, indeed very anxious, to secure Mr. Blake's release. In my submission, their motivation for offering a performance and cash bond is driven by their overwhelming desire to see him back home with them and not through any earnest compulsion to ensure he complies with the conditions of release. I suggest that they are not appropriate and suitable to provide these bonds. I submit that their assurances that their supervision of Mr. Blake will ensure he complies with conditions of release are hollow and cannot persuade you that he will comply with conditions of release. Furthermore, I submit that there is no air of reality to Mr. Blake's insistence that he will return to Jamaica if he is ordered to do so during a spousal sponsorship application brought by Gill. Mr. Blake and Gill are desperate to be together. In my submission, that makes Mr. Blake's assertion that he will return to Jamaica if he is forced to somewhat suspicious and unbelievable.

MEMBER: I just want to understand that submission, Mr. Thompson. Are you saying that if family members or people who are akin to family members put up a performance and cash bond, I should reject them outright because of that kind of relationship? Secondly, in the Chairperson's Guidelines, there is express reference to the fact that members must look to see whether there is a relationship between the detainee and his bondspersons, so it can be determined whether the detainee will obey the bondspersons and their rules. Am I to ignore those guidelines?

MINISTER'S COUNSEL: I agree that can be a dilemma. In some cases, the intensity of the relationship is a positive factor. In others, it may be a negative factor. I take the position that in this case, the relationship of Gill and Tony with Mr. Blake is too intense for you to accept that they will be able to properly supervise Mr. Blake. Unless there are any further questions, sir, these are my submissions.

MEMBER: Thank you, Mr. Thompson. Mr. Fink, please make your submissions.

Fink delivers his oral submissions in accordance with the draft in chapter 8. During the submissions, the following exchange takes place between the member and Fink:

MEMBER: Are you saying that I should accept Mr. Blake's reasons for fleeing from FFP and not leaving Canada, and that they justify his behaviour? Are they even relevant? He clearly breached IRPA.

COUNSEL: No. He accepts that he breached IRPA, as you recall from his evidence. I am not in any way suggesting that the abuse at work and his love for Gill can excuse his behaviour, but it does provide a context for this isolated breach, especially in view of his compliance with IRPA on at least two previous occasions. I submit that if you look at the reasons for non-compliance as background or context for his actions, it does have some relevance.

MEMBER: Do Gill and Tony really appreciate the risk of losing their bond and cash if Blake breaks the conditions of release?

COUNSEL: This issue is dealt with in both of their affidavits when they say that they not only know Mr. Blake's immigration history and illegality, but they know they risk losing their bond and cash if he fails to comply with conditions of release. Sir, they are not going into this pledge blindly. They know Mr. Blake's history and can, therefore, intelligently assess the risks. They also know Mr. Blake well, as he lived with them for three months, and can also assess his ability and willingness to comply with conditions of release and their rules.

MEMBER: What do you say about the fact that your client admitted lying to an ID member at the last review hearing about Gill and Tony not knowing about his illegality in Canada?

COUNSEL: This was the subject of my re-examination of Mr. Blake. It was a foolish lie and perhaps not even a lie, as Gill and Tony did not know about Mr. Blake's illegal status while he lived with them. They only became aware of it after his arrest and detention. It was a harmless utterance by Mr. Blake. He has also demonstrated his honesty and candour with his admission of the lie today. I ask that it is not something that should affect his credibility in any way, as it was innocuous.

MEMBER: I see that you are relying on section 245 of the Immigration and Refugee Protection Regulations and the factor of community ties as favouring release?

COUNSEL: Yes.

MEMBER: But does this not cut two ways, in that it could be argued that the fact that Mr. Blake will eventually marry Gill may motivate him not to report for removal?

COUNSEL: Technically, yes. But here the supervening factor is the strength of the bond and the respect Mr. Blake has for both Gill and Tony. This would make his failure to report for removal very unlikely, as he would know Gill and Tony would lose their bond and cash. Mr. Blake would not do it, because of his loyalty to them and the sense of shame he would feel if he did that.

MEMBER: Alright. Just one last matter. I understand from reading the decision of Member Boswell that Mr. Blake has a current Jamaican passport. Mr. Thompson, is the CBSA in possession of Mr. Blake's passport?

MINISTER'S COUNSEL: No, sir. We would certainly want the passport surrendered to the CBSA as part of any conditions of release, if you do release him.

COUNSEL: I took instructions on this point from Mr. Blake. Gill gave me his passport this morning. Here it is, Mr. Thompson.

MEMBER: Thanks. Let's have a brief 15-minute recess while I consider this matter carefully and then I will deliver my oral decision.

Short Recess

REASONS FOR DECISION

Mr. Blake failed to complete the Farm Workers Program and failed to return to his homeland, Jamaica.

Without any permission from the CBSA, he left the program and went to cohabit with his girlfriend, Gill St. John, in Orangeville. Ms. St. John is originally from Jamaica, but she became a Canadian citizen in 2015.

There was a Canada-wide warrant for Mr. Blake's arrest after the CBSA became aware from his employer that he had fled from the farm in Hamilton where he worked. It seems that Mr. Blake fled from FFP on February 7, 2018. The CBSA also issued a removal order against him, which was sent to his last known residential address. The CBSA made a mistake in failing to properly record the new address in Orangeville that Mr. Blake provided them soon after going to Orangeville. This is a positive factor in this review hearing, as it showed that Mr. Blake was not trying to hide from the Immigration authorities and was responsible in providing them his new address. In any event, the CBSA became aware of his whereabouts when Mr. Blake was stopped by police for speeding in Orangeville on April 19, 2018. The police checked CPIC, and as soon as they knew he was wanted by Immigration, they informed the CBSA. The CBSA now knew his residential address. However, they should have known this new address well before the Canada-wide warrant was issued on March 1, 2018. Several weeks after the police stop, on April 30, 2018, CBSA officers went to his address in Orangeville, and Mr. Blake was arrested on the warrant. The detention review hearing today is the 7-day second detention review hearing. I am aware of the rules and case law establishing that I must conduct this review hearing de novo and not be influenced by the evidence at the previous hearing when Mr. Blake was detained. It is important to note that Mr. Blake was not represented at that hearing and that he misconstrued the function, responsibilities, attributes and duties of the bondspersons he presented. Minister's counsel, Mr. Thompson, has, with his usual thoroughness, explained the facts and the grounds for detaining Mr. Blake.

Essentially, Mr. Blake is a flight risk because he left the Farm Workers Program without permission and did not leave Canada when he was required to do so on February 10, 2018. Instead, he went to cohabit with Ms. St. John in a different town. Through his actions, Mr. Blake demonstrated a complete contempt for our immigration laws by breaking IRPA in two ways. Firstly, he left the Farm Workers Program before he completed the work that he had to do there during the period of his work permit. Secondly, he breached his limited authorization to remain in Canada only until February 10, 2018 by illegally staying in Canada after that date. At the hearing, Mr. Blake told me that he had provided his new residential address in Orangeville to the CBSA. As I said earlier, I accept that he did that, but the CBSA messed up by not properly recording and acknowledging that new address.

Mr. Blake said that he met Ms. St John when he attended a Pentecostal church in Hamilton in the fall of 2017. Ms. St. John attended the church so she could meet various members of her family who live in Hamilton. Apparently, Ms. St John's brother, Tony St. John, knew Mr. Blake's twin brother in Jamaica. Mr. Blake and Tony conversed with each other and that is how Mr. Blake became acquainted with Ms. St. John.

In any event, a relationship blossomed between Mr. Blake and Ms. St. John. The two dated for several months so that by the beginning of February 2018, Mr. Blake and Ms. St John agreed that he would move into her townhouse in Orangeville. Mr. Blake could not hold back his tears when he expressed the intense love he had for Ms. St. John, which led him to leave the program and not return to Jamaica, although it seems that a contributing factor to him leaving FFP was the harassment and abuse he received from a fellow employee.

I note Mr. Blake's love for Ms. St. John and their commitment to each other through their proposed engagement, but that cannot be an excuse for his clear breach of our immigration laws. In my opinion, there are strong and cogent grounds for Mr. Blake's continued detention, as he is clearly a flight risk. However, there are factors here that fall within section 245 of the Immigration and Refugee Regulations that I must consider. Paragraphs (d) and (g) are relevant. Firstly, he complied with two previous work permits that were issued in 2014 and 2015, working at FFP for the full duration of the work permit and leaving Canada before it expired. That is a strong positive factor that points to his ability to comply with our immigration laws. Secondly, he has strong ties to the community in that he is a member of a responsible and law-abiding Canadian family here, through his ties to Gill and Tony, the proposed bondspersons. Finally, one cannot ignore the responsibility he showed in informing the CBSA of his new address when he moved to Orangeville.

I must look at section 248 of the regulations on the issue of the anticipated length of his detention, which will be short as the CBSA is in possession of his current Jamaican passport, so there is no impediment to him being removed to Jamaica. However, despite this, I must consider viable alternatives to detention under section 248. I have looked at the release plan presented by counsel and I believe Mr. Blake is capable of being released through the imposition of appropriate conditions. However, the final analysis of whether there are sufficient and compelling alternatives to detention turns on the issue of the appropriateness and suitability of the bondspersons that are part of the release plan submitted by Mr. Fink. It is a well thought out plan. The affidavits of Gill and Tony demonstrate their knowledge of Mr. Blake and their strong relationship with him. His capacity to obey their rules, including conditions of release, is reflected both through the evidence he gave at the hearing and through the contents of the affidavits. As Mr. Fink stressed, Gill and Tony are familiar with his immigration history and illegality but are nevertheless prepared to offer their bond/

cash, knowing fully the risks they face in the event of the detainee not complying with conditions of release. They know they will lose their bond if Mr. Blake breaks any release conditions. They have produced evidence of their solvency and ability to post the bond/cash. They are responsible Canadian citizens and have no previous criminal convictions. I do not accept the submissions of Minister's counsel that being family members, their motivation to post bond/cash is to have him released to be at home with them, without any concern that he obeys conditions of release. There is no evidence to support these submissions. In fact, everything I have heard during this hearing, especially the heart to heart talk that Mr. Blake had with Gill the night before this hearing, makes it obvious that Gill and Tony are very concerned that he obeys the rules of their household and complies with conditions of release. I have no doubt that Gill and Tony will pull their bond if they see any signs that Mr. Blake may breach any release conditions.

However, I do not believe that the amount of bond and cash offered is sufficient to reduce my concerns as to whether Mr. Blake will likely appear for removal. I therefore increase the amount of the performance bond that Ms. St. John intends to post to $5,000 and the amount of the cash deposit by Tony St. John to $3,000.

As the case law makes clear, as I am departing from the previous detention order by releasing Mr. Blake today, I must provide compelling reasons for doing so. At this review, the release plan offered by Mr. Blake's counsel was tight, with bondspersons who satisfy all the relevant criteria that I have outlined, whereas at the previous hearing the bondspersons who were offered by Mr. Blake when he represented himself were completely inadequate. New evidence was also adduced at this hearing that confirms that Mr. Blake demonstrated a certain level of responsibility by providing the CBSA with his residential address when he moved to Orangeville. At the last review there was an absence of evidence on this issue. These factors, therefore, provide compelling reasons for me to depart from the 48-hour detention decision.

I am releasing Mr. Blake on conditions as set out below:

    a. Residence with Gill St. John and Tony St. John at their residential address at 20 Becca Drive, Orangeville, Ontario.
    b. Gill St. John to provide a performance bond in the sum of $5,000, and Mr. Blake is not to be released until such bond has been provided to the CBSA.

    c. Tony St. John to provide a cash deposit of $3,000, and Mr. Blake is not to be released until such cash deposit has been provided to the CBSA.
    d. Mr. Blake is to notify the CBSA within 48 hours of any change of his residential address.
    e. Monthly reporting by Mr. Blake in person to the CBSA at 6900 Airport Road on the 15th of each month.
    f. To attend for his removal from Canada when that occurs and any immigration proceedings where his attendance is required.
    g. To abide by the rules and discipline of the household of Gill St. John and Tony St. John.
    h. Not to work in Canada unless permitted to do so under IRPA and the Regulations. If Mr. Blake can legally work, he must inform the CBSA within 48 hours of the name and address of his employer.

Those are the conditions of release. If Minister's counsel or Mr. Fink believe I have omitted relevant further conditions, or that any conditions I have outlined ought to be deleted or amended, please advise.

MINISTER'S COUNSEL: No, sir.

COUNSEL: No, sir.

MEMBER: Give me a few moments whilst I draft the release order and sign it. I will provide original release orders to the bondspersons, Mr. Blake and his counsel.

------------REVIEW CONCLUDED-------------

I HEREBY DECLARE THAT THIS IS A TRUE
TRANSCRIPT OF THE RECORDING AND THAT I HAVE
SWORN THE OATH OF SECRECY

_____

Amy Ho—Transcriptionist for Transcribe Inc. / Security # 76638451-0000978011

May 9, 2018

Review Questions

1. Why was this release plan better than the plan submitted by Mr. Blake at the 48-hour review?

2. Name the four factors (not involving a discussion of the bondspersons) at this review hearing that caused the member to find that Mr. Blake was capable of being released and not a substantial flight risk.
3. Would the four factors that you identified persuade the member to release Mr. Blake even if the bondspersons were inadequate?
4. Refer to the Immigration Division Rules at appendix C and outline the rules that Mr. Fink adhered to when he presented his materials at the hearing.
5. In terms of the rules you identified, why is it important that you comply with these rules?
6. Do you believe Mr. Fink's re-examination of Mr. Blake neutralized the potential for adverse credibility findings concerning Mr. Blake's lie at the previous review hearing? Provide reasons.
7. Review the questioning of Mr. Fink by the member and Mr. Fink's answers. Do you believe Mr. Fink prepared his responses to these questions and identified some of the apparent weaknesses in his case prior to the review hearing? Is that something that you think is necessary for you to do when you do a detention review case?
8. Were there occasions when Mr. Fink used his answers to the member's questions to strengthen his arguments for release? Can you identify the counsel's answers that demonstrated this?
9. What was the reason the member decided to increase the amount of the bond and cash?
10. Would the member have done so if Gill and Tony had not said they were flexible on the issue of the amount of their bond and cash in their affidavits? Could it have led to a detention order because the member could not increase the amount of the bond?
11. Review the draft submissions of Mr. Fink in chapter 8 as you read the above transcript. Identify three points in these oral submissions that you believe were highly effective in persuading the member to release Mr. Blake.

CHAPTER 10

Danger Ground for Detention

When the Minister seeks detention of the immigrant on the ground of danger to the public and that ground has been proven by the Minister, devising an effective release plan becomes more difficult because it must now focus on preventing the immigrant from committing offences when released. However, before we embark on an analysis of effective release plans, we must understand the meaning of "danger to the public."

The definition of "danger to the public" has been addressed by the Federal Court of Appeal in the context of ministerial danger opinions in *Canada (Minister of Citizenship and Immigration) v. Williams*, [1997] 2 FC 646 at 668–69 (CA):

> . . . In my view the formulation in subsection 70(5) [under the former Immigration Act-author's note] is sufficiently clear for that purpose. In the context the meaning of "public danger" is not a mystery: it must refer to the possibility that a person who has committed a serious crime in the past may seriously be thought to be a potential re-offender. It need not be proven—indeed it cannot be proven—that the person will re-offend. What I believe the subsection adequately focuses the Minister's mind on is consideration of whether, given what she knows about the individual and what that individual has had to say in his own behalf, she can form an opinion in good faith that he is a possible re-offender whose presence in Canada creates an unacceptable risk to the public. I lay some stress on the word "unacceptable" because, with the impossibility of proof of future conduct, there is always a risk and the extent to

which society should be prepared to accept that risk can involve political considerations not inappropriate for a Minister. She may well conclude, for example, that people convicted of narcotics offences have a greater likelihood of recidivism and that trafficking represents a particular menace to Canadian society. I agree with Gibson J. in the *Thompson* case [footnote omitted] that "danger" must be taken to refer to a "present or future danger to the public." But I am reluctant to assert that some particular kind of material must be available to the Minister to draw a conclusion of present or future danger. I find it hard to understand why it is not open to a Minister to forecast future misconduct on the basis of past misconduct, particularly having regard to the circumstances of the offences and, as in this case, comments made by one of the sentencing judges. A reviewing court may disagree with the Minister's forecast or consider that more weight should have been given to certain material, but that does not mean that the statutory criterion is impermissibly vague just because it allows the Minister to reach a conclusion different from that of the Court.

In *Thompson v. Canada (Minister of Citizenship and Immigration)*, IMM-207-96, 16 August 1996, Justice Gibson indicated that the fact of a conviction alone is not a sufficient basis for a danger to the public finding. Circumstances of the case must, over and above the conviction, indicate that the person poses a "present or future danger" to the public.

Clearly, an immigrant who has been convicted of many criminal offences that involve violence against members of the public is likely to be considered a danger to the public by the member of the ID. Difficulties arise when the Minister relies on allegations of criminal behaviour, as opposed to convictions, as the basis for the danger ground. In that situation, the ID must determine whether the allegations have been proven on a balance of probabilities.

Youth Convictions and Charges that Are Withdrawn

Sometimes, the CBSA will rely on youth convictions that are sealed and expunged to demonstrate that the detainee, now an adult, is a danger to the public. Under sections 118 and 119 of the *Youth Criminal Justice Act*, SC 2002, c 1, there is no access by anyone to a youth record that has been sealed and expunged. This makes good sense, as Parliament's intention is to rehabilitate offenders who have made mistakes in their youth so they can have a fresh start as adults without being forever tainted with their youth record. The Federal Court has pronounced that the CBSA cannot use their knowledge of these sealed youth offences, perhaps through admissions made by the detainee as to the nature of the offences, to support the danger ground. Similarly, charges that are withdrawn should not be used against a detainee to bolster the danger ground.

There is a prohibition on access to the immigrant's youth record if he has not been convicted of any offences since his youth record was expunged.

In that same case, Justice Southcott found "charges that were dismissed or withdrawn, and which did not, therefore, lead to a conviction could not be taken into account by the Minister in supporting a danger opinion."

By implication, this principle would also be applicable if such charges are the basis for the danger ground for detention.

Plans for Release

Unlike flight risk, which does not endanger the public, a finding that the immigrant is a danger to the public does raise the *substantial need to develop a release plan that will minimize the risk of harm to the public.*

The facts of each case are different, and the degree of risk to the public that the particular immigrant poses is immensely variable, necessitating a case by case assessment by the Immigration Division. However, below is a list of conditions that may remove or at least minimize the risk of danger to the public:

- A curfew, if the immigrant's offence was committed at night or in the early hours of the day.
- House arrest conditions so that the immigrant must reside with the bondsperson(s) and not be out of the residence except in the company of the bondsperson(s).
- Compulsory attendance at an addictions program for rehabilitative treatment and counselling where the immigrant committed offences through alcohol and/or drug addiction. If there is no house arrest, an inpatient facility that can closely monitor the immigrant 24/7 to reduce the risk of the immigrant escaping and going out in the public arena without any supervision is preferable to an outpatient facility. The degree and extent of supervision at an addiction rehabilitation facility would involve an assessment of the risk to the public that the immigrant may pose.
- The installation of an electronic monitoring device and GPS on the immigrant's person, although this can be problematic in that the immigrant may be able to find a way to remove the device to either escape or commit offences while under the release order.
- Monthly progress reports from a psychologist or psychiatrist based on weekly counselling and treatment of an immigrant with mental health issues. Can the immigrant obtain this service through the government

health service or can it only be funded privately? The issue of cost may be a factor that would make such a condition impracticable.

Two Federal Court cases, namely *Minister of Public Safety and Emergency Preparedness v. Lunyamila*, 2018 FC 211, a judgment of Justice Blanchard with reference to earlier judgments in that case of the Chief Justice, Justice Crampton, and Justice Harrington; and *Minister of Public Safety and Emergency Preparedness v. Hassan*, 2012 FC 1357, a judgment of Justice Russell, set out some important principles when looking at release plans where the grounds for detention is danger to the public even where the detention is lengthy.

In *Lunyamila*, Justice Blanchard said: *[my emphasis]*

> *Where a person is a danger to the public, the weight given to this factor should vary directly with the extent to which alternatives to detention can mitigate such danger. Stated conversely, the greater the risk that the public would be required to assume under a particular alternative, the more this factor should weigh in favour of continued detention.* Where the conditions of release are such that the public would be required to bear significant risk of danger at the hands of the detainee . . ., this should weigh strongly in favour of continued detention. If it were otherwise, Parliament's public safety and security objectives, which have been prioritized in the IRPA and the Regulations, would be significantly undermined.

Later in the judgment, Justice Blanchard was dismissive of release plans when members of the ID ordered the detainee to a rehabilitative program, as the judge knew the program offered little supervision and had led to the respondent struggling with his substance abuse issues with frequent interaction with the police and the criminal justice system when he had previously been released into this facility. Justice Blanchard said: *[my emphasis]*

> *[A]ny conditions of release would have had to virtually eliminate, on a day-to-day basis, any risk that Mr. Lunyamila would pose to people* living or working at any residence where he may be required to reside, and to the public at large. They would also have to have virtually eliminated any risk that he might disappear into the general public, to avoid future removal. A reasonable alternative to detention for the Respondent is a facility that has the ability to prevent the Respondent from harming another patient or someone who works there and that has a way of ensuring that the Respondent remains on the premises.

In the *Hassan* case, Justice Russell reached a similar conclusion concerning the release plan that the member of the ID had ordered because the residential facility for the respondent's drug addiction where the respondent would reside did not offer the degree of supervision and restrictions that would be necessary to control the extreme violence that the respondent had shown in the past.

The lesson to be learned from these cases and other cases in the Federal Court is that when representing detainees who are dangerous and violent criminals, counsel must present release plans that will severely restrict the liberty of the immigrant in the community. This is necessary so that the risk of harm to the public is substantially reduced or "virtually eliminated," as Justice Blanchard said in *Lunyamila*.

CHAPTER 11

Identity Ground for Detention

The identity ground for detention involves a different approach than the flight risk or danger to the public grounds for detention. The jurisprudence makes it clear that there is an onus on the detainee to cooperate with the CBSA to facilitate the detainee's removal to his or her country of nationality.

The facts that can lead to detention of the foreign national on identity grounds vary case by case. Below, I set out an example where identity can become an issue that can lead to detention.

A Typical Example: The Case of Tariq Mustafa

Tariq arrived in Canada from Pakistan and intends to make a refugee claim. He purchased a false passport in Karachi, Pakistan, in order to flee the city where he lives because of persecution by Muslims there by reason of his Christianity. The false name on this fake passport was "Mohammed Ashraf." At the point of entry at Pearson International Airport in Toronto, he is questioned by a CBSA officer about his identity and whether he can provide his original passport and identity card to prove this. He tells the officer he destroyed his original identity documents but not his birth certificate, which is in his mother's possession. He says the name on the fake passport is wrong and that his true name is Tariq Mustafa. He is held in detention while the CBSA investigates the matter.

He instructs an RCIC to represent him at the forthcoming detention review to secure his release. The CBSA insists that he cannot be released until they are satisfied as to his identity. This is a difficult case, and the whole focus of the representative must be on establishing Tariq's identity. The representative cannot expect or rely on the CBSA to conduct a vigorous and diligent investigation about Tariq's identity. The RCIC must initiate and take the necessary proactive steps to establish Tariq's identity by sending correspondence to and engaging in telephone conferences with Tariq's mother in Karachi and inquiring into Tariq's birth certificate, school records, photos and other documents that can establish his identity. It may be that Tariq has relatives in Toronto. Letters from the relatives confirming Tariq's identity after visiting him in the holding centre would be useful. The representative should advise Tariq to cooperate fully with the CBSA and answer truthfully all questions they ask in assisting them in their investigations about his identity. This is the minimum. Before the detention review, the RCIC ought to provide both the CBSA and the ID with copies of his correspondence with Tariq's mother. The RCIC's notes of the telephone conversations with Tariq's mother may be helpful, and if Tariq has relatives in Toronto, letters from them confirming his identify would also assist. These documents will demonstrate that Tariq has been diligent in attempting to prove his identity and may persuade the member to release him pending the investigation by the CBSA.

The Laird Report (see chapter 16) comments on the fact that a significant number of lengthy detentions occur because the CBSA has been less than diligent in investigating the identity of the foreign national. The issue is that there is a risk the member of the ID may not accept that the CBSA has not been diligent or ignore the facts that establish the CBSA's lack of diligence—hence the urgent need for the detainee and his representative to take proactive steps to establish his identity. Below is an extract from the Laird Report that highlights this problem: *[my emphasis]*

> ### Failure to Question the CBSA on Delay
>
> In long term detentions, there were many examples of CBSA-caused delays that were seldom the focus of questioning in review hearings or remarked upon in ID decisions. *For example, in one case, the detained person agreed in writing in 2012 (and earlier gave oral permission) for the CBSA to publish his photograph in a media release with the goal of finding relatives. Due to delays within the CBSA itself and perhaps at the Ministry of Public Safety and Emergency Preparedness, the media release did not come out until **two years** later. In fact, the media release did not go to the countries where he had possible citizenship until 2016.* Members were not persistent in asking questions about this delay. Decisions repeatedly found that the CBSA was diligent or even "extremely diligent." Notwithstanding this incredible delay, successive decisions rely

on CBSA submissions that the reason for delay in obtaining travel documents is the detainee's "complete lack of cooperation."

In *Minister of Public Safety and Emergency Preparedness v. Lunyamila*, 2018 FC 211, Justice Blanchard, quoting from an earlier judgment in that case of the Chief Justice of the Federal Court, Justice Crampton, said: *[my emphasis]*

> The Chief Justice framed the fundamental issue raised by the applications before him as "how to resolve the tension between, on the one hand, an immigration detainee's refusal to cooperate with a validly issued order for removal from Canada, and on the other hand, the length of detention and uncertainty regarding the duration of future detention that result, in whole or in part, from that refusal" (Lunyamila II at para 1). He held that this tension had to be resolved in favour of continued detention where such refusal to cooperate "has the result of impeding any steps that may realistically contribute in a meaningful way to effecting the removal of a detainee who has been designated to be a danger to the public" or who is "unlikely to appear for removal from Canada" (Lunyamila II at para 2). *To hold otherwise, warned the Chief Justice, would enable such a detainee "to simply produce, or contribute to producing, a 'stalemate,' for the purposes of ultimately obtaining his release from detention" and, therefore, "manipulate our legal system in order to avoid the execution of a validly issued removal order," something, the Chief Justice stated, that runs contrary to the scheme of the Immigration and Refugee Protection Act, SC 2001, c 27 [Act] and which the Respondent appears to be attempting to do* (Lunyamila II at para 3)."

Although this case was decided in the context of a situation where the detainee was under a removal order, having been found to be a flight risk and a danger to the public, the principle of law involved is applicable.

The section in chapter 1 on the identification ground for detention should be stressed, and I repeat it here:

Regulation 247 of the IRPR stipulates that the assessment of whether the immigrant will be detained on identity grounds will depend on several factors:

- Has the foreign national cooperated with the CBSA and the IRCC by providing all the necessary documents that will prove the foreign national's identity? Or has the foreign national deliberately obstructed the government in the process of investigating and establishing the immigrant's identity?

- Has the foreign national destroyed genuine identity documents and used fraudulent identity documents to deliberately conceal his or her identity?
- Has the foreign national provided contradictory evidence to the IRCC and the CBSA that is inconsistent with other identity documents in the government's files?

I would add that in *all* cases where the identity of the foreign national is in issue, the detainee's representative *must* take all the steps that are necessary to demonstrate the detainee has attempted to prove his or her identity.

CHAPTER 12

Detention of Children

Detention of children can raise some difficult questions, especially where the detention of parents can lead to the child being separated from them. It is important for the representative to be aware of the case law and rules when detention of children is at stake.

The CBSA National Directive for the Detention or Housing of Minors (the National Directive) defines Alternatives to Detention (ATDs) as follows:

> A policy or practice that ensures people are not detained at an Immigration Holding Centre (IHC), provincial or any other facility for reasons relating to their immigration status. ATDs allows individuals to live in non-custodial, community-based settings while their immigration status is being resolved. ATDs includes Community Programming (in-person reporting, cash or performance bond and community case management and supervision) and Electronic Supervision tools, such as voice reporting.

The directive says there is a need to consider the humanitarian and compassionate concerns involving the BIOC (best interests of a child) when their decisions adversely affect children. The National Directive deals with this issue in its preamble as follows:

> Canada's international obligations and domestic legislative and policy frameworks are the broad underpinnings of this Directive. Section 60 of the IRPA affirms the principle that the detention of a minor must be a measure of last resort, taking into account other

applicable grounds and criteria, including the best interests of the child (BIOC). A Federal Court decision in 2016 [B.B. and Justice for Children and Youth v MCI, (August 24, 2016), Toronto IMM 5754-15 (FC) [Justice for Children and Youth] by Mr. Justice Hughes] ruled that the interests of a housed minor is a factor that can be taken into the decision to detain or maintain detention of a parent and are to be weighed along with other mandatory factors under R. 248. The United Nations Convention on the Rights of the Child (CRC), to which Canada is a party, states that the BIOC shall be a primary consideration in all state actions concerning children. In recognizing the vulnerability of children and research on the detrimental effects of detention and family separation on children, the CBSA developed the National Directive for the Detention or Housing of Minors for operational use, which takes a balanced approach to achieve better and consistent outcomes for minors affected by Canada's national immigration detention system.

The National Directive defines the BIOC:

> An international principle to ensure children enjoy the full and effective benefit of all their rights recognized in Canadian law and the CRC. It is also a rule of procedure that includes an assessment of the possible impact (positive or negative) of a decision on the child or children concerned.

The National Directive defines one of its objectives to be "to ensure that the detention or housing of a minor or the separation of a minor from his/her detained [parent or legal guardian], where unavoidable, is for the shortest time possible."

Furthermore, the National Directive recognizes that "the BIOC are best achieved where children are united with their families in community-based, non-custodial settings where possible."

Calin v. MPSEP, 2018 FC 731, is an excellent recent judgment by Justice Annis on the detention of a child. After reviewing the National Directive as I have set out above, the justice (at paragraphs 30–33) points to the harshness and inequity of children being separated from their parents because of the latter's detention:

> The Court recognizes that the IRPA distinguishes between the situations of children being in detention and of those being housed with their parents who are in detention. Nevertheless, while the children may not formally have been detained, effectively they were. The BIOC inescapably required them to remain with their mother, rather than being separated in some form of housing that

would prevent the Applicant from providing them with her care and guidance, and likely raise significant anxiety in the children as a result of being separated from their most important caregiver.

In essence, in situations where no real choice exists other than the children being housed with the Applicant, the Board should consider the situation as reflecting the requirement to adhere to section 60 of the IRPA, i.e. that they be detained by extension of their parents' situation "only as a last resort."

Moreover, as the National Directive indicates, this Court has already ruled that the interests of a housed minor is a factor that can be taken into consideration for the decision to detain or maintain detention of a parent to be weighed along with other mandatory factors under section 248 of Immigration and Refugee Protection Regulations, SOR/2002-227 [Regulations].

The Court concludes, on the basis of its foregoing comments, that the Board likely committed a reviewable error by not appropriately considering the BIOC in this matter as a factor that could support their mother's conditional release.

Justice Annis goes on (at paragraphs 57–58) to examine the harm that can be caused to children through being separated from one or both of their parents through their detention:

> There is considerable evidence that the detention of the children can be highly detrimental to them. For instance, the authors Hanna Gros and Yolanda Song in their publication "Mental Health Consequences of Family Separation and Child Detention" in Samer Muscat, ed., *"No Life for a Child" – A Roadmap to End Immigration Detention of Children and Family Separation* (Toronto: International Human Rights Program, University of Toronto Faculty of Law, 2016) state somewhat as a summary as follows at page 23 of their monograph:
>
>> The detrimental effects of immigration detention on children's mental health have been extensively documented worldwide. Unfortunately, Canadian researchers have severely limited opportunities to conduct studies on the subject because they have had little access to immigration detainees held in IHCs or correctional facilities. Only a few Canadian studies on the mental health of immigration detainees are available. Nevertheless, those studies have confirmed that

> detained children experience "high rates of psychiatric symptoms including self-harm, suicidality, severe depression, regression of milestones, physical health problems, and post-traumatic presentations." Younger children in detention also experience developmental delays and regression, separation anxiety and attachment issues, and behavioural changes, such as increased aggressiveness. One of the few Canadian studies to date confirmed that *"immigration detention is an acutely stressful and potentially traumatic experience for children." The same research shows that family separation also has severe detrimental psychological effects on children. As such, neither detention nor family separation account for the best interests of the child.* [my emphasis]

Because these risks occur over the longer time period and do not manifest themselves until after release from detention, it is not possible to present personal evidence of the harm to children who have been detained or housed with parents in detention. Likewise, it is not possible to demonstrate a serious likelihood of jeopardy to the children's health or safety from confinement in immigration detention centres.

Justice Annis concluded that the BIOC was decisive so that the applicant parent ought to be released from detention on suitable conditions so there would be no separation between the parent and her children.

CHAPTER 13

Release

After the member signs the release order, your job is not done, because you need to take all the necessary steps to help the bondspersons post their bond and cash. They must attend the CBSA/Immigration Division Registry with the required documents and explanations, if necessary, to satisfy the CBSA officer that they meet all the qualifications and eligibility requirements to post the performance bond and the cash deposit. The most difficult issue will be the assessment of the solvency of the bondspersons. This is such an important issue that I have reproduced below an extract from ENF 8 that sets out in detail the solvency assessment. *You must become very familiar with it because you have to keep this assessment in mind when you discuss the performance bond and the cash deposit with your bondspersons when you are preparing the case.*

Extract from ENF 8 Current to May 15, 2017

This is an extract from the IRCC enforcement manual that all bondspersons should be aware of and *that you should know thoroughly before you assess the appropriate amount of bond and cash for the bondspersons.* Failure to do this could result in the bondspersons not being able to meet the financial criteria set out below, leading to the continued detention of your client.

8.14 Determining solvency for guarantors

The requirement that a guarantor be solvent, i.e. have sufficient liquid funds to pay the guarantee if it is enforced, is intended to ensure that the Government is able to collect on the debt should the guarantor go into default upon non-compliance by the person concerned with conditions.

The following principles should guide the determination of solvency:

- the guarantor's annual income should be assessed first. The annual income minus liabilities on income should be **three (3) times** the total of the guarantee. For example, a requirement of a guarantee in the amount of $5,000 would require net income of at least $15,000 (3 x $5,000). A person with annual income of $50,000 and annual liabilities totalling $20,000 leaving $30,000 net income would qualify to post the guarantee. If the guarantor's annual net income is insufficient, then the guarantor's assets shall be assessed.
- when assessing income alone, the liabilities to take into account are the total of the annual liabilities, not the total liability. For example, a loan of $15,000 payable monthly in the amount of $200 would constitute a $2,400 annual liability for the guarantor. A rent or mortgage payment of $1000 per month would constitute a $12,000 annual liability.
- assets alone without any income are a strong indication that the individual is likely not solvent, however, officers may consider individual circumstances of the case before making a decision.
- when the amount of the guarantee is too high for the guarantor to qualify on annual income alone, both income and assets are assessed; the guarantor's solvency is calculated by totalling the guarantor's annual income and current assets minus existing total liabilities.
- officers should ask for income and assets in an amount approximately three times the total amount of the guarantee to be posted.
- existing liabilities should be subtracted from the total of the guarantor's combined income and assets for the calculation of solvency. For example, if the guarantor's annual income is $65,000 and they own a house valued at $300,000, and they have no other qualifying assets, their total income and assets would be $365,000. If the guarantor's mortgage on the house is $280,000, their car loan balance is $20,000, their student loan balance is $25,000 and they have a line of credit balance in the amount of $15,000, then their total liabilities are $340,000. They have the net amount of $25,000 ($365,000 − $340,000) available for a guarantee, however, if the guarantee required was $10,000, they would be deemed insolvent as a $10,000 guarantee requires $30,000 in available income and assets.
- liabilities or debts include mortgage balances; outstanding loan balances; student loan balances; credit card balances; line of credit balances;

annual rent obligations; and the average yearly cost of monthly utility payments (e.g. phone, internet, cable, hydro, water, gas/oil).
- original documentation of source of funds must be provided, and if accepted towards the determination of solvency, copies shall be taken and placed on file.
- where reasonable in the circumstances, to assist in the determination of solvency, officers may request proposed guarantors to provide a recent credit report.

Assessing income

Income which is not eligible for solvency determination:

- welfare, social assistance, family allowances, child tax benefits, child support payments, medical disability, and worker's compensation should not be considered in the solvency determination given that these payments are made in the public interest and it is unlikely that the Crown would seek to recover the amount of the guarantee from these payments to pay the debt on default.

Income which is eligible for solvency determination includes:

- employment income, proven by the three most recent Canada Revenue Agency (CRA) Notices of Assessment, pay stubs;
- Employment Insurance benefits, including maternity leave benefits and parental leave benefits, proven by EI statements, or the T4E;
- Canada Pension Plan payments / Quebec Pension Plan payments, proven by pension statements or financial institution statements showing these deposits;
- Old Age Security payments, proven by OAS statements or financial institution statements showing these deposits;
- other pension payments, proven by pension statements or financial institution statements showing these deposits;
- investment income such as dividends or interest, proven by the T5 Statement of Investment Income;
- trust income, proven by T3 Statement of Trust Income;
- rental income, proven by recent income tax forms submitted to the CRA, or financial institution statements showing these payments as deposits combined with proof of title to the rental property and rental agreements;

- earnings on a life insurance policy, proven by statements from the life insurance company;
- spousal support (alimony) payments, proven by most recent income tax form filed, or by financial institution statements showing the deposits combined with the agreement/court order showing the amount to be paid;
- business income, proven by the most recent tax filings, or by financial institution professional business account statements.

Regularly documented cash deposits into a guarantor's accounts may be proof of income; however, officers should require credible evidence of the origin of these deposits and their continuing nature, as well as reasonably satisfying themselves that they are not illegally obtained.

In cases where officers deem it reasonably appropriate in the circumstances, they may accept alternative documentary proof of income or require additional corroborating proof.

Assessing assets

- assets acceptable for a guarantee should be capable for easy liquidation by the Crown.
- equity in property is acceptable as long as the property is in Canada.
- where the guarantor owns an asset with another person or persons, only the percentage of equity owned by the guarantor will be considered for proof of solvency.
- letters of credit, credit limits on credit cards, and unused or available lines of credit are not considered assets.

Assets which should not be accepted for solvency determination:

- assets held in foreign locations (e.g. offshore accounts) due to the difficulty of seizing these assets upon forfeiture;
- assets held in forms of ownership so complicated that enforcing the debt would be overly time consuming and difficult, for example, a commercial building held by a number of owners;
- Registered Retirement Savings Plans (RRSP);
- Registered Educational Savings Plans (RESP);
- value of pension plans, including personal locked-in or prescribed plans such as Locked in Retirement Accounts (LIRA), Life Income

Funds (LIF), Life Registered Income Funds (LRIF), etc. *(Note: all provinces provide unconditional protection against creditors for money held in a pension plan or when transferred out to a personal locked or prescribed plan such as a LIRA, LIF, LRIF)*

- Canada savings bonds and bonds issued by entities other than the Government of Canada;
- vehicles of any type;
- tools;
- machinery;
- personal property such as furniture, antiques, collectibles, jewelry, artwork, clothing, and other personal effects.

Eligible assets for solvency determinations include:

- savings, proven by the previous 12 month period of financial institution statements;
- Guaranteed Investment Certificates (GICs), proven by financial institution statements;
- Treasury bills, proven by financial institution statements;
- bonds issued by the Government of Canada which are transferable (Canada Savings Bonds are not acceptable because they are not transferable), proven by bond certificates;
- stocks, proven by stock certificates, where the principal investment is at least 12 months old;
- equity in real estate, proven by the registered title or deed to the property, the mortgage balance statement or mortgage discharge, where applicable, and the most recent municipal property tax assessment or property evaluation done by the bank or other reputable institution.

Officers may accept other documentary proof of assets or require additional corroborating proof in cases where they deem it appropriate in the circumstances.

CHAPTER 14

Appeals

There will be occasions when your client is detained after a full detention review hearing. However, after the review hearing, you conclude that the member's decision to detain your client was unreasonable. You are concerned that this wrongful detention will lead to continued detention at future reviews. In these circumstances, you have no alternative but to advise the client that the detention order ought to be challenged in judicial review proceedings in the Federal Court. But, irrespective of the merits of a judicial review, the central question will be whether your client and the client's family or friends will have the funds to retain a lawyer to proceed with the appeal. If they are willing to fund an appeal, you need to be aware of some of the rules in connection with leave and judicial review applications (Leave and JR) to the Federal Court to challenge the detention order. This knowledge will also enable you to have a first glance at the merits of the judicial review, although a final opinion must be obtained from an experienced immigration judicial review lawyer to determine whether the challenge will have a reasonable chance of success.

1. The time limit for commencing the Leave and JR is only 15 days from the date of the decision detaining the client.
2. The challenge of the detention decision in the Federal Court involves an analysis by the Federal Court judge at the leave stage of the record before the member decision maker. A Leave and JR application is not a new hearing on the merits. The Federal Court judge is only entitled to look at the record before the ID decision maker. The judge cannot consider any new evidence or additional facts that were not before the ID decision maker.

3. The application for Leave and JR is initially a two-stage process. The first stage is the commencement of the leave application, with any Notice of Appearance that the Department of Justice will serve on the applicant and file. (This Notice consists of the representative of the Minister of Public Safety and Emergency Preparedness (MPSEP) saying that they will respond to the Leave and JR.) At the time of commencement of the Leave and JR, there may be a full written decision, or it may not have been delivered to the applicant yet. If the applicant has received the written decision at the time of the issuance of the Leave and JR application, the applicant (your client) has 30 days from that date of issuance of the leave application to perfect the Leave and JR by preparing an Application Record (AR). If there are no written reasons yet, then the 30-day time limit to perfect the Leave and JR runs from the date the applicant receives the written reasons. The AR will contain the full record that was before the member of the ID, including the Reasons for Decision, any transcript of the hearing, an affidavit from the applicant and memorandum of law and argument from counsel representing the applicant. The memorandum will contain an overview of the case, the facts, the issues and arguments on the law. The Department of Justice, who represents the MPSEP and their counsel, within 60 days of receipt of the applicant's AR must deliver their memorandum of law and argument. A single judge of the Federal Court will then consider all the filed materials and decide whether to give the applicant permission to have his or her challenge heard orally at a judicial review hearing in the Federal Court. If the Federal Court judge decides not to grant leave or permission to allow the matter to go for a full judicial review hearing, there is no appeal of that decision. This ends the Leave and JR application. In my experience and from some statistical data, only about 20 per cent of Leave and JR applications will result in leave being granted. This is not surprising, as the Federal Court judge can only consider the record before the member of the ID, and the test or standard of review, which we will discuss below, is a difficult one.

4. A grasp of the test to obtain leave in detention review cases in the ID is important so that the legal professional can at first glance recognize whether there is merit in the JR challenge. In *Minister of Public Safety and Emergency Preparedness v. Ismail*, 2014 FC 390, at paragraphs 31–33 of the decision of Madam Justice Mactavish, the test is well stated by her in the following passage: *[my emphasis]*

> [31] This Court has recognized that the Immigration Division has particular expertise in interpreting and applying the detention and release provisions of IRPA:

see *Canada (Minister of Citizenship and Immigration) v. Thanabalasingham*, 2003 FC 1225 (CanLII), at para. 42, [2003] F.C.J. No. 1548; aff'd 2004 FCA 4 (CanLII), [2004] 3 F.C.R. 572. *As such, considerable deference must be paid to the Immigration Division's assessment of its enabling legislation.*

[32]   Indeed, the parties agree that in coming to its decision, the Immigration Division was interpreting its home statute in relation to a question that goes to the core of its expertise, namely the review of reasons for detention under IRPA: see section 54. *As such, the Immigration Division's decision is subject to review on the standard of reasonableness.*

[33]   In reviewing a decision against the reasonableness standard, the Court must consider the justification, transparency and intelligibility of the decision-making process, and whether the decision falls within a range of possible acceptable outcomes which are defensible in light of the facts and the law: see *Dunsmuir v. New Brunswick*, 2008 SCC 9 (CanLII) at para. 47, [2008] 1 S.C.R. 190, and *Canada (Citizenship and Immigration) v. Khosa*, 2009 SCC 12 (CanLII) at para. 59, [2009] 1 S.C.R. 339.

It is clear from this passage that a proper analysis must be conducted as to whether the decision of the ID member is reasonable in detaining the applicant. The following questions must be asked in that analysis:

- Was there evidence that justified and made the decision intelligible?
- Were proper reasons given that made the decision-making process transparent?
- Does the decision fall within a range of possible acceptable outcomes that are defensible considering the facts and the law?
- In all the circumstances, was the decision reasonable?

As you can see from the test, for the applicant to have a chance of success in the challenge, there must be irrationality in the decision, a failure to consider relevant and compelling evidence, a substantial absence of reasonableness in the decision and an outcome that was not defensible considering the facts and the law. Therefore, you must take a hard look at the decision, bearing these factors in mind, before you can go to the next step in obtaining an opinion from an experienced Federal Court judicial review lawyer.

If the lawyer who did the detention review is not familiar with JR applications in the Federal Court or the representative at the detention review hearing is a consultant or paralegal (who do not have rights of audience in the Federal Court), an experienced lawyer in this area of law must be found. It is important for the representative who conducted the detention review to have the cell phone number of a few lawyers (so they can be contacted outside normal business hours) who are experienced in judicial review work in the Federal Court so that a quick call can be made to the lawyer soon after the detention decision. This is important because of the short time limit to issue and serve the Leave and JR application.

A detailed examination of the Leave and JR process in the Federal Court is outside the scope of this handbook. However, it is important to note that the lawyer will want to obtain an order from the Federal Court to stay all further reviews scheduled by the ID after the lawyer issues and serves the Leave and JR application. This must be done to prevent further detention reviews taking place that will effectively override and make moot the challenge of the original detention order.

One word of caution: The financial cost of these applications for Leave and JR are significant. The last thing you want to do is to encourage your client to bring such an application after your client is detained unless the challenge is meritorious and has a reasonable chance of success. The opinion of an honest and experienced lawyer on the merits of the challenge is essential. If that opinion is negative, accept it and advise your client accordingly. Always follow the ethical rule that prevails in my practice: *do not accept retainers unless your client has a reasonable chance of success.* To mislead clients by falsely representing that they have a chance of success in these JR cases, and thereby induce them to provide a retainer, is dishonest and unethical. Never do it if you want to maintain your credibility and reputation in the legal profession.

In the next chapter, we will discuss the resources that you need to be aware of to assist detainees who do not have the financial means, even with the help of friends/family, to pay for legal representation at their detention review hearing. We will also look at various government-funded supervision programs that do not require the detainee to provide a bondsperson.

CHAPTER 15

The Impecunious Detainee without a Bondsperson or Residence

This handbook would be deficient if we failed to deal with the common situation where the detainee and her family or friends have no money to retain either an immigration lawyer or a consultant to represent her at a forthcoming detention review hearing. There is also the situation where the detainee has no family or friends in Canada who can be bondspersons. In both situations, it is necessary for you to be aware of the resources that can help the unfortunate detainee.

The lack of access to justice by detainees is reflected in the excerpt reproduced below from an article on the website of Canadian Lawyers for International Human Rights (CLAIHR):

Access to Justice in Immigration Detention

In our recent research, we also identify a series of systematic everyday obstacles that impede access to procedural justice for immigration detainees in Canada. Such obstacles include the arbitrariness of decision-making in detention reviews; the difficulty with gathering new evidence, the standard of proof for detainees, and prohibitive release conditions that collectively diminish the efficacy of monthly reviews of detention sentences; and the overlapping barriers to retaining high-quality legal counsel that include insufficient funding, geographical distancing, and informational hurdles.

A key building block to procedural justice is access to high-quality, affordable legal counsel. Although detainees have a right to be represented in their detention reviews, the government is not obligated to provide counsel. While a recent Canadian Bar Association report and a 2013 Action Committee on Access to Justice in Civil and Family Matters report both detail the difficulties facing marginalized groups of Canadians in obtaining counsel, neither report addresses the plights of non-citizens, let alone those in detention. Yet, legal counsel is found to be the chief determining factor in successful detention bail hearings across national contexts. Advocates in the United States, for example, have been keen to document the deleterious consequences of appearing in immigration court without counsel. The authors of the study determined that "immigrants who are represented by counsel do fare better at every stage of the court process—that is, their cases are more likely to be terminated, they are more likely to seek relief, and they are more likely to obtain the relief they seek." Similarly, in Canada, effective representation of migrants is key to protecting their rights while in detention.

The structure of detention in Canada systematically impedes access to quality legal counsel for detained migrants. These hurdles include: difficulties with gathering case-relevant evidence from detention; one-way telephone communication out from the IHCs [Immigration Holding Centres] and prisons; unjustified and discretionary transfers between detention sites; and the increasing use of video- and teleconferencing over in-person hearings. Counsel-client meetings also vary arbitrarily across detention facilities: in the Toronto IHC, a glass partition separates visitors and detainees who must rely on a patchy two-way telephone system, but at the Laval (Montreal) IHC they are allowed to mingle in the visiting room. In both provincial prisons and IHCs, access to reliable information on available legal counsel is extremely limited, and not always in a language comprehensible to the detainee. IHC detainees are particularly isolated because there is no Internet and interpreters are made available **only** at IRB and CBSA proceedings. [Excerpted from Petra Molnar and Stephanie J. Silverman, "Excluded from Justice? Immigration Detainees in Canada," http://claihr.ca/2016/04/04/excluded-from-justice-immigration-detainees-in-canada/ (footnotes omitted).]

Fortunately, there are government resources that can assist the detainee. However, whether the counsel who is eventually funded by Legal Aid to represent these detainees will have the high level of competence and experience that is demanded in immigration detention cases is doubtful. Firstly, the hourly rate for counsel's work in legal aid cases is low and will naturally attract newly called lawyers who may not have the degree of experience, expertise and skill required in a typical detention review case. Secondly, the number of hours that Legal Aid Ontario will provide to the lawyer is low and insufficient to reflect the amount of work required to properly prepare for the detention review hearing. This may result in a less than thorough preparation of the case. There are competent lawyers who will do this kind of publicly funded work, but the quality of the lawyer who will represent the detainee can sometimes be a matter of luck.

The 2017 Laird Report (see chapter 16) is highly critical of the lack of legal aid and access to counsel in Ontario as opposed to most other provinces. I have reproduced an extract from the report below:

Uneven Access to Legal Services

As reported above, rates of representation by counsel at ID hearings vary significantly across the country, averaging 76% in Eastern Region; 70% in Western Region; and 38% in Central Region, in 2017.[30] Access to counsel also varies within regions as a result of differences in provincial legal aid programs. In our sample, the detained person was represented by counsel in less than 10% of the hearings reviewed in Ontario but at almost all hearings in Quebec and British Columbia. Many unrepresented detainees, in the face of extensive submissions by CBSA Hearings Officers, barely participated in their hearings.

In Quebec, the provincial legal aid plan sends two duty counsel to the Montreal hearing location daily. Duty counsel try to attend all 48-hour and 7-day hearings and attend 30-day hearings based on an assessment of need, if the detained person is unrepresented. Legal aid certificates are available for longer term detentions and continue throughout the period of detention, unlike in Ontario.

Western Region covers British Columbia, Alberta, Manitoba, Saskatchewan, Yukon, the Territories and Nunavut. About 50% of detention hearings in this region take place in person in Vancouver, with the rest being conducted by telephone or video hearing with the detained person usually located in Calgary, Edmonton, Regina, Saskatoon or Winnipeg.[31] At the Vancouver hearing center, the B.C. Legal Services Society has one or two duty counsel on site daily. The duty counsel determines which individuals most require their assistance. They attend most 48-hour hearings and select 7-day and 30-day hearings, based on need.

For detainees in Saskatchewan, no legal aid support is available. Legal Aid Alberta has two staff lawyers responsible for all immigration issues, including detention review hearings, one in Calgary and one in Edmonton. Depending on other responsibilities, they may or may not be available for ID hearings. In Manitoba, the legal aid plan will provide representation to every person in immigration detention.

In Ontario, Legal Aid Ontario's Refugee Law Office (RLO) currently only represents at a limited number of ID hearings, based on capacity. There is no duty counsel program. In our sample from Central Region, the detained person was represented at less than 10% of hearings. This is much lower than the reported rate of representation in Central Region, which was 38% in 2017. The discrepancy is probably explained by the predominance of very long-term detention in our sample of Central Region files.

Apparently Legal Aid Ontario (LAO) will provide a certificate for one or two hearing days to present a release plan but will not continue to fund litigation at the ID. Typically, in our sample, the RLO or private counsel appeared once or twice over many months to present release plans. Although not apparent in the audit, apparently LAO has agreed to start providing RLO support at an expanded number of hearings where the individual has mental health issues or where a Designated Representative has been assigned.

While the question of legal aid funding for legal services is outside the scope of the audit, it is clear that the uneven level of representation across the country not only puts detainees in some provinces at a comparative disadvantage in securing release, but also has an adverse impact on the ID's work. The availability of legal aid-funded counsel in all regions would reduce the power imbalance in the hearing room as between detainees and the CBSA and would greatly assist the ID in the proper execution of its mandate.

Footnotes referred to in the above extract from the Laird Report:

> **30** This section focuses on representation by lawyers, as opposed to immigration consultants or paralegals. In our sample, there were no hearings where a non-lawyer represented a detainee. The audit was told that

"under-representation", by lawyers or paralegals without immigration law expertise, was an issue.

31 Individuals are sometimes detained in smaller communities. In those cases, the 48-hour hearing is generally conducted by telephone from the local RCMP detachment.

Provincial Legal Aid

Legal aid is available to detainees who can demonstrate that they have no or little income or savings to retain counsel privately. There is a strict financial test that must be met, and the argument must be made that if the detainee is not represented by competent counsel at the review hearing, there will be further detention. You are advised to search online for the relevant contact information for legal aid in your province.

Voluntary Organizations and Legal Clinics

Counsel who are assisting detainees in Ontario who do not have friends/family in Canada and, therefore, no bondspersons or a residential address, ought to check out the resources below. The following organizations can help detainees obtain information and assistance in connection with their detention.

Parkdale Community Legal Services – PCLS

www.parkdalelegal.org/

Parkdale Community Legal Services (PCLS) is a teaching clinic with law students from Osgoode Hall Law School who work under the supervision of the staff lawyers. PCLS offers assistance in immigration and refugee cases.

Refugees Lawyers' Association – RLA

www.rlaontario.com/

The Refugee Lawyers' Association (RLA) of Ontario is an association of approximately 200 lawyers in the province of Ontario in Canada advocating on behalf of refugees. The RLA hopes to use its website to present members and others with news in the world of refugee determination in Canada, links to sources of country research, as well as comments on important Federal Court decisions in refugee law. Its newest page, Research Links, features links to general sources of information, including Amnesty International.

Toronto Bail Program

www.torontocentralhealthline.ca/displayService.aspx?id=132824
The detainee who has no bondsperson or a place to reside in as an alternative to detention can apply for supervision and shelter under the Toronto Bail Program.

Counsel in other provinces should contact either or both the immigration section of their local provincial bar association or the Canadian Association of Professional Immigration Consultants (CAPIC) at https://www.capic.ca/ for the necessary resources.

CHAPTER 16

Recent Developments

In this chapter, we will examine some recent developments in 2017 and 2018 that have improved the detention review system by focusing on procedures that enable detainees to be released whose incarceration would have otherwise continued. The Laird Report, with its comprehensive investigation of detention reviews, especially those that involved long periods of detention, led to some much-needed recommendations. However, much more work needs to be done in improving the detention review system, as the Laird Report makes clear.

Chapter ENF 34 of the CBSA manual has established a process whereby detainees can in certain circumstances be released into the community through a community case management and supervision procedure (CCMS). In addition, various electronic monitoring devices have been added to the toolkit of the CBSA to gauge, monitor and supervise the immigrant.

I have set out below an executive summary from the CBSA describing how the system operates.[i] In the last chapter, we examined detainees who may not have either a place to reside or a bondsperson. CCMS may assist them through the imposition of various monitoring systems and also the use of community-based service providers, such as the Salvation Army, the John Howard Society and the Toronto Bail Program, to support the necessary conditions that the ID may impose concerning residence and supervision.

CBSA Executive Summary: Alternatives to Detention (ATD) Program

As a key pillar to the National Immigration Detention Framework, the Alternatives to Detention (ATD) Program provides officers with an expanded set of tools and programs that will enable them to more effectively manage their client-base while achieving balanced enforcement outcomes. The wider availability of ATDs supports recommendations from the United Nations High Commission for Refugees (UNHCR) for a robust ATD program within Canada. This Privacy Impact Assessment (PIA) has been authored to address new program activities that seek to lessen the CBSA's reliance on its Immigration Holding Centres and Provincial Correctional Facilities (PCFs) that currently detain foreign nationals (FNs) and permanent residents (PRs). The ATD Program expands the scope of current CBSA conditions and release mechanisms and develops new tools to close gaps in programming availability and access on a national scale, with priority placed on areas with the highest volume of detainees or potential ATD participants.

Specifically, this PIA examines the ATD Program's expansion of two ATDs to a national level – Voice Reporting (VR) and Community Case Management and Supervision (CCMS); and the introduction of Electronic Monitoring (EM) as a pilot in the Greater Toronto Area Region (GTAR).

Voice Reporting (VR)

For those who agree to VR programming, the individual provides voice samples which are stored in a new information system (the Voice Reporting System – VRS) and compared/matched against future voice reporting events. Once enrolled in VR, the individual is required to call at regular intervals, at which time their voice is compared to the recordings obtained at the time of VR enrollment. The types of personal information collected for VR includes name, address, contact details, and other related information which is most often collected by Immigration Refugees and Citizenship Canada (IRCC) or CBSA during the immigration or refugee application stage. However, the new VR solution also collects a participant's voice recording and, for those ordered to have VR with location-based services (LBS), Global Positioning System (GPS) coordinates will be collected in specific situations.

To collect the GPS coordinates, the CBSA has entered into a contract with a service provider (SP) who will collect the GPS coordinates from cellular providers. The voice recording and GPS coordinates are collected and stored in the new VRS, as well as in the existing immigration enforcement case management system called the National Case Management System (NCMS), which is a CBSA system managed by the CBSA.

Community Case Management and Supervision (CCMS)

CCMS is a risk-based community release program, whereby subsequent to a risk assessment, a CBSA officer or the Immigration Refugee Board (IRB) determines that an individual's risk can be managed in community, resulting in a release from detention. *CCMS is intended to promote detention avoidance or detention release for persons who remain compliant with the CBSA but who may lack a bondsperson, or who require social service support in addition to a bondsperson to mitigate risk upon release into the community.* [my emphasis] Services and programming are provided by three contracted Service Providers (SPs) that are established and experienced in the delivery of community case management to individuals that pose some level of security risk to the public or risk to the integrity of CBSA's immigration enforcement program. Those three SPs are: the Salvation Army, the John Howard Society and the Toronto Bail Program.

The CBSA will continue to utilize existing information (in the NCMS and GCMS systems, as well as information arising from detention reviews) to determine if CCMS is appropriate. The types of personal information collected for CCMS includes name, address, contact details, and other related information which is most often collected by IRCC or CBSA during the immigration or refugee application stage. However, once an individual is supervised by a CCMS SPs, the types of information that could be collected by the CBSA is expected to be detailed but only include information related to the individual's release from detention on CCMS programming. CCMS SPs and their sub-contractors (doctors, mental health counselors, therapists, addiction counselors, etc.) will likely collect medical information, mental health information, diagnoses/prognoses, substance abuse history, and other related information. The CBSA has instructed CCMS SPs to follow Provincial and Federal privacy legislation regulating the transfer and storage of personal medical information.

Electronic Monitoring

In July 2018, along with the other elements of the ATD Program, the CBSA deployed an EM Pilot Project in the Greater Toronto Area Region (GTAR), which is intended to facilitate the release of selected high-risk individuals. The EM system is built upon real-time location data collected and analysed in a central facility and reported to regional staff to investigate for enforcement purposes as appropriate. The CBSA is utilizing the services of Correctional Service of Canada (CSC), who currently maintains a successful, national EM program. A Memorandum of Understanding (MOU) with CSC has been signed to address the details related to policies, procedures, privacy, information sharing and financial arrangements.

By initiating a pilot in one region, CBSA will acquire quantitative and qualitative data about the effectiveness of EM monitoring in an immigration context and align itself with international partners who utilize the technology for immigration purposes. The Pilot has a concrete framework with strict program parameters which will improve on the previous EM option that is being used by the IRB as an acceptable release mechanism. If the GTAR pilot is successful, it will be expanded to a nationally available electronic supervision tool with the ATD Program.

Regarding the collection of information, EM enrollment requires the collection of names, address, telephone numbers, and other biographical information which has already been collected. To enroll a participant in EM, the CBSA provides the telephone number and address information to CSC, but not the name of the individual. Within the CSC EM software application, the CBSA participants will be uniquely identified so as to differentiate them from the CSC EM participants.

Once enrolled, the GPS coordinates of the individual are collected and stored in a software application maintained by CSC, as well as on the server of CSC's vendor. When various alerts occur on an individual, CSC will contact the individual and attempt to resolve the alert. All alert information and CSC's attempts to resolve them are provided to the CBSA. For urgent notification, a CBSA Stand by Officer and/or Duty Manager is available after regular business hours. A PIA was conducted on the CSC EM program and is available as required.

Right of Access

Individuals may formally request access to their personal information, or access to corporate records related to the Alternatives to Detention Program by filing a request with the Access to Information and Privacy Division. More information about this can be found on the Access to Information and Privacy page.

Accountability

Individuals with concerns about the collection, use, disclosure or retention of their personal information may issue a complaint to the CBSA Access to Information and Privacy Division. Complaints should be made in writing, and include the individual's name, contact information, and a brief description of their concerns. Contact the Access to Information and Privacy Division at the CBSA.

The External Audit 2017/2018 on Detention Reviews: The Laird Report

The full audit must be read by all those who represent detainees at detention reviews, as it highlights some of the difficulties and obstacles to release that can be present at these reviews.[ii] Below, I have reproduced important extracts from the report. I have italicized parts of the extracts to emphasize some of the deficiencies in the process.

> This is the report of an external audit commissioned in September 2017 by the then-Chair of the Immigration and Refugee Board (IRB), Mario Dion. *The mandate of the audit is to assess hearings and decisions in randomly selected cases where immigration detention exceeded a minimum of 100 days in order to determine the prevalence of issues relating to the fairness of the process, and its compliance with the* Charter of Rights and Freedoms, *as identified in a series of decisions of the Federal Court, the Federal Court of Appeal, the Alberta and Ontario Courts of Appeal and the Ontario Superior Court of Justice.*[1]
>
> The audit was conducted over a seven-month period by a single auditor, working independently and with the assistance of a second individual who reviewed French-language hearings. The audit completed a detailed review of more than 300 detention

review hearings and decisions conducted under the *Immigration and Refugee Protection Act (IRPA) and Regulations (IRPR)* by the Immigration Division (ID) of the IRB. The hearings and decisions were pulled from 20 files[2] that were randomly selected. The focus was on the conduct of hearings, on whether the hearings met standards of fairness as articulated by the courts, and the related question of whether the decisions fairly reflected the evidence and submissions of the parties.

The audit was not intended to be a legal review of whether the decisions correctly applied immigration law and jurisprudence, outside the particular fairness issues identified for consideration. The auditor and the reviewer brought extensive adjudicative and litigation experience to their work, but not expertise in immigration law.

This was, therefore, a comprehensive examination of many detention review cases, and the observations in the report are shocking, as can be gleaned from the extracts below:

Inaccuracies and Inconsistencies in Factual Findings

ID Members are generally rotated through a detention file, with the result that, every 30 days, a different Member from the same office will chair a hearing to review an individual's continuing detention. This practice is consistent with the requirement to "decide afresh"[37] at every hearing and serves to reassure the detained person that a set of fresh eyes will be examining their case every month. However, a disadvantage is that, in some cases, it was apparent, from month to month, that *the Member conducting the hearing was not sufficiently familiar with factual circumstances which, if considered, might have supported release.*

For example, in one file, a 2016 decision ordering continued detention finds that the detained person caused delay by failing to call her Consulate for scheduled interviews, relying on this in part for a negative flight risk assessment. However, a 2015 decision in the same case had directed CBSA to facilitate the telephone interview with the Consulate; during that hearing, the Member had pointed out to CBSA that the detained person had been prevented from having the interview due to jail lockdowns and other institutional problems preventing telephone access. *In fact, the record showed that it took CBSA four months to arrange a telephone interview that the detained person was at all times willing to participate in. This fact would have been apparent to the second decision-maker if he or she had the opportunity to review transcripts of prior hearings and/or decisions.*

Indeed, one factor affecting the consistency and accuracy of findings is the fact that decisions are not uniformly transcribed, so that successive adjudicators are not necessarily familiar with the evidence or findings at previous hearings.[38]

In some files, one can see an inconsistent or false narrative developing over time. Negative assumptions, not rigorously supported by the evidence, would sometimes gradually become part of the accepted history for the detained person. The problem of factual inaccuracies and even "rank speculation" in detention decisions has been identified by the Federal Court in *Wang*[39] and by the Ontario Superior Court in *Ogiamien*,[40] *Scotland*[41] and *Ali*. In *Ali,* the Court, in referring to the government's position that Mr. Ali was actively thwarting the investigation, stated:

> The authorities cannot discharge the onus that rests on them to demonstrate that the continued detention of Mr. Ali is justified, for immigration purposes, based on skepticism and speculation.[42]

There were several examples of what could be considered "speculation" in our sample. In one file, a 2016 decision declining to order release, relies in part on the fact that the detained person caused the forfeiture of "thousands of dollars" in posted bonds. On the other hand, a 2017 decision in the same case states, correctly, that it appears from the record that there was never any actual forfeiture of bonds in the case. Through months of hearings, decisions go both ways on this factual point, with some later decisions relying on the supposed forfeiture cited in the 2016 decision as a reason for maintaining detention.

In several files, factual findings changed over time, to the detriment of the detained person. In one case, after 24 months of detention, two decisions in 2014 cite, apparently for the first time, a past conviction for possession of a firearm. Earlier decisions, as well as a comprehensive case review in the paper file,[43] do not include any mention of this conviction. In fact, at a 2012 hearing, a Member notes that his "serious convictions are all dated", pointing only to a robbery conviction in 2005 and an attempted robbery in 2007.

Our review of all the available hearing recordings did not find any instance in which CBSA cited a firearms conviction, including the very hearing where the conviction was first cited. Firearms are never mentioned again after the two 2014 decisions, but one decision in 2015 and one in 2016[44] cite "weapons" convictions as a reason for detention. Was there a conviction for possession of a weapon? Perhaps or perhaps not. But if someone is being held for 59 months as a danger to the public, it is important to do so on the basis of an accurate and consistent record of past convictions.

In reviewing successive hearings, it becomes apparent that, in the face of inaccuracies or vague misstatements, individuals in detention become discouraged or desperate, sometimes no longer attending, or attending without speaking, or becoming upset and angry at a hearing.

Perhaps the most glaring example is a hearing at which danger to the public is added as reason for detention, for the first time, after a person has already been held for more than a year. There is no new event; CBSA does not argue for the additional ground. The decision cites an extensive history of convictions occurring "not that long ago," without seeming to seriously take into account that almost all convictions took place more than 10 years earlier. The Member states: "Of course I will maintain the ground of danger ..." without apparently realizing that he is adding a new ground. He gives no basis for deciding differently.[45]

In this case, the ground of public danger is then maintained in subsequent hearings, based on consistency with this decision. In more than one hearing, the detained person tries to challenge the public danger finding. She is unrepresented. At one hearing, her submissions to the effect that she is not a public danger and has never hurt anyone are abruptly cut off. This hearing is presided over by the very presiding Member who first added public danger as a ground; he chides her for not understanding the basis on which she was considered to be a public danger, saying: "You've been through this process of detention review many times now ... I believe you should know that you don't need to have killed someone to be considered to be a danger to the public. You should know that."[46] And yet it was this presiding Member who added public danger as a ground without giving any basis for coming to a different decision on this than at all previous reviews and without any submissions from either party.

The lesson from this extract is that the representative must be diligent in ordering all the previous detention review transcripts to ensure that there are no inconsistencies or inaccuracies that have tainted subsequent hearings.

Related to the inaccuracy issue is the unquestioning reliance by members of the ID on statements made by Hearings Officers on substantially hearsay evidence of CBSA officers, as the extract below demonstrates:

Uncritical Reliance on Statements by CBSA Hearings Officers

Related to the inaccuracy issue, is the fact that *Members too often relied uncritically on statements made by CBSA Hearings Officers.* The danger of inaccurate findings is compounded by the rotation of Hearings Officers representing the CBSA. In some cases, a Hearings Officer will keep a file over a longer period of time but rotation appears to be common. Because the audit listened to every hearing in most files, we were able to identify instances where the Hearings Officer, perhaps because of a lack of familiarity with the history of the case, misstated facts which were then relied upon in the decision. This was particularly a concern in very long-term detentions.

Sometimes inaccuracies in CBSA submissions seemed to minimize delays in their own investigation. One example is a 2015 hearing where CBSA informs the Member that fingerprints were sent "a few months ago" to Interpol. However, it had been reported at a hearing 18 months earlier that fingerprints had in fact been sent to Interpol in 2013.

Over time, inaccurate statements by CBSA officers can become accepted facts that are repeated in decisions, even where these "facts" are contradicted by earlier decisions that are contemporaneous to the events at issue. For example, in a 2015 decision, a Member rejects CBSA submissions that the detained person had recently refused to sign travel documents or had not been cooperative in that regard.[47] However, a few months later, a second decision relies on renewed submissions from CBSA that the detained person caused delay by refusing to sign a travel document. The detained person's own explanation of the delay with the travel document (which is consistent with the finding in the earlier decision) is not taken into account or even acknowledged in the second decision. A few months later, yet another decision states that the detained person caused delay by refusing to sign the travel documents.

The danger of uncritical reliance on CBSA submissions about non-cooperation has specifically been identified in several court decisions.[48] In Brown, the Ontario Superior Court commented on CBSA evidence before the Court (and previously before the ID) that Mr. Brown had hindered his removal process by not providing information about family members in Jamaica. The Court accepted the evidence of Mr. Brown that he had no known family in Jamaica, noting that it could not have constituted a failure to be cooperative if Mr. Brown was unable to provide information regarding his family because he simply did not have that information.[49]

It is, therefore, important to review the statements of Hearings Officers critically. If there are issues, whether it be unreliability based on hearsay evidence or inaccurate and misleading opinions, the representative must ensure the CBSA officer is summoned to attend the hearing for cross-examination to clarify the misleading evidence. The report highlighted the failure of either the member or the detainee's counsel to initiate the process whereby the CBSA officer is summoned to attend the hearing for the purpose of cross-examination.

One of the most disturbing procedures was bondspersons being interviewed outside the hearing room by the Hearings Officer. The officer would then articulate to the member in the hearing room the officer's interpretation or perception of what the bondsperson had said. In one case, the bondsperson was not allowed into the hearing room, and the member made no attempt to have the bondsperson available for questioning by the detainee or his counsel. This process effectively allowed the Hearings Officer to manipulate or interpret what the bondsperson said to justify arguments that the bondsperson was not suitable. Fortunately, since 2017, the process has been changed, at least in the Central Region, so that bondspersons are interviewed in the hearing room. This makes the process more transparent and fair.

The report highlights the failure of the member of the ID to comply with the basic rules of natural justice by not allowing counsel for the detainee to adduce evidence from witnesses to support a release plan. In one case, counsel for the detainee was not allowed to lead evidence by conference call from the director of an institution of the details of supervision and programming for the detainee. The release plan proposed by counsel relied on that evidence. The member, in rejecting the proposed plan, said there were unanswered questions about the level of supervision and the ability of the institution to take the detainee to ID and IAD hearings. But these unanswered questions were caused by the failure of the member to allow counsel to adduce evidence. The report comments on this serious issue:

> The failure to allow a party to present evidence and to hear and question witnesses, is a fundamental breach of natural justice. The Federal Court in *Brown* has recently emphasized this. Citing *Charkaoui*,[54] the Court stated:
>
>> Before the state can detain people for significant periods of time, it must accord them a fair process. This basic principle has a number of facets. It comprises the right to a hearing. It requires that the hearing be before an independent and impartial decision-maker. It demands a decision based on the facts and the law. It entails the right to know the case put against one, and *the right to answer that case*.[55] *[my emphasis]*

The report found that in detention reviews where a detainee had been in detention for a substantial period, there was a consistent failure by ID members to question the lack of diligence by the CBSA in pursuing the removal of the detainee. Usually, these cases centred on identity issues, which prevented the detainee being removed to their country of origin. Members of the ID were prepared to accept the excuses made by the Hearings Officer for the delay without any probing examination by the members of the true reasons for the delay, namely, the lack of diligence by the CBSA in pursuing their investigation. This resulted in the unreasonable continued detention of the detainee.

Some members of the ID did not appreciate the need to explain the detention review process clearly to unrepresented detainees and failed to allow them the opportunity to respond to the allegations of the Hearings Officer.

The report found there was a failure by adjudicators to actively consider alternatives to detention, as the following extract from the report demonstrates:

> Many tribunals[62] have adopted active adjudication tools to ensure an efficient and balanced hearing process. Active adjudication is particularly helpful when there is a power imbalance between parties, including when one side is unrepresented, as in many ID hearings. It is beyond the scope of this report to discuss the elements of an active adjudication practice but for a thorough outline with useful examples, see Michelle Flaherty, Best Practices in Active Adjudication.[63] Today, even the courts generally do not

hesitate to ensure that the necessary evidence is brought forward by questioning witnesses and identifying gaps, particularly when a party is unrepresented.

In the cases reviewed by the audit, there was a pronounced need for a more active adjudication approach in the assessment of alternatives to detention. Under section 248(e) of the *IRPR*, the "existence of alternatives to detention" must be considered at every detention review before a decision is made on detention or release. However, proposals were sometimes rejected without full and fair consideration, often on the basis of missing information that could have been provided, if not immediately, then at a subsequent hearing.

The member of the ID must consider the evidence at each detention review afresh. But as the extract from the report below highlights, some of the members did not do this:

> The requirement to bring a fresh mind to each detention review hearing has long been emphasized by the courts: *Sahin*; *Thanabalasingham*; *Panahi-Dargahlloo*.[66] What may be relatively new is a recognition by the courts that some features of the process can mitigate against meeting this requirement.
>
> The comments of the Alberta Court of Appeal bear repeating:
>
>> The statute contemplates that ID reviews occur frequently in a timely manner. It is an administrative process, with a focus on the factors for detention set out in the regulations. *However, the serial nature of the reviews, the role of the reviewing officer, and the deference given to earlier review decisions can lead to ID decisions becoming cumulative, without constituting a fresh review of the legality of the detention....*" [my emphasis]

The report goes on to comment on the members' heavy reliance on past detention review decisions:

> **Over-Reliance on Past Decisions**
>
> The fact that Members have the authority to reverse previous decisions is cited by the Ontario Superior Court in *Brown* as an important factor in ensuring *Charter* compliance.[70] The Court stated: "... where members are not satisfied that grounds for detention continued to exist or that the circumstances otherwise warrant the grant of release, they can depart from previous review

decisions to continue detention as long as they provide their reasons for doing so."[71]

However, in our sample, the tendency to rely routinely on previous decisions was evident in many cases, particularly after the initial three or four hearings.

As the Ontario Court of Appeal noted in *Chaudhary*: "previous decisions become highly persuasive at the very least" and "... as the length of detention increases, it becomes more and more difficult to argue that an additional 30 days spent in detention since the last review constitutes a "clear and compelling reason" to depart from the earlier disposition.[72]

The Ontario Superior Court has similarly commented on the difficulty of "displacing" previous decisions:

> In effect, once a decision to detain is rendered at the first detention review, for all practical purposes, the CBSA has met its burden, and at every subsequent detention review, it is difficult, if not impossible, to displace the initial decision. Each ID decision, even if later proven to have been based on faulty information, gets relied on and replicated the next time around.[73]

Detainees with mental health problems faced enormous difficulties in being released. As the report suggests, these difficulties were sometimes insurmountable:

Fairness Issues for Detained Persons with Mental Health Problems

The audit reviewed three files with very long periods of detention where the detained person had significant mental health issues. There were extra barriers to release for these individuals.

In these files, like the cases with substance abuse issues, a recurring issue for the detainees was the lack of treatment and counselling services in provincial correctional institutions. It is very difficult to demonstrate rehabilitation as a factor supporting release if there are few, if any, rehabilitative programs available to you. This is an issue that has been noted by the courts.[80]

There is a failure by some members of the ID to apply mandated factors under IRPR 245, 246 and 248 when considering whether to release the detainee. This is clear from the extract below:

Many decisions seemed to adopt a formulaic approach to the exercise of discretion under the legislation and regulations, fettering the ability to view the evidence in more nuanced and contextualized ways. Factors were weighted against release without a detailed consideration of the particular facts in an individual situation. At some hearings, the Member seemed to have little interest in gaining more than a superficial understanding of the factual circumstances that led to the detention.[85]

In our sample, people were held for years based on flight risk, even though they had a history of reporting to CBSA and there was no evidence that they had ever tried to go underground when previously released. People were held as a public danger for years even though their convictions were dated and had all been for minor offences that received short-term sentences, with few if any other factors suggesting that they could pose a danger.[86]

In *Scotland, Brown* and *Ali,* the Ontario Superior Court has stipulated that *Charter* compliance requires detention determinations to be based on a careful and contextualized consideration of the factual circumstances, including the detainee's testimony.[87]

Notably, in many decisions reviewed, there was little indication that, in assessing flight risk and/or danger to the public, Members were mindful of the statutory language requiring release unless satisfied that the enumerated factors were present.

Members seemed to rely on old convictions to continue detentions on the danger ground, as we can see from the extract below:

> Also surprising was the willingness to rely on convictions from many years previously. For example, a 2013 decision relies in part on a trafficking conviction from 2004 as a public danger factor supporting continuation of a detention that is already 17 months long, notwithstanding the absence of any similarly serious convictions for several years. A history of drug use–related offences from prior to 2002 is repeatedly relied on as part of the basis for a public danger finding at hearings in 2016. Decisions in 2016 and 2017 relied on a danger opinion from 2009.

The gross deficiencies and unfairness in the detention review process, especially in the Central Region, identified in the Laird Report led to recommendations of some changes, particularly in the hearing room, to the effect that:

- Appropriate weight is given to the affirmed testimony of the detained person.

- CBSA is questioned rigorously where there are delays in its process.
- Hearings Officers are required to provide affirmed evidence when needed.
- Enforcement Officers are required to testify if investigation has become delayed or the next steps are not clear.
- Members demystify the process and the regulatory factors to enable unrepresented persons to give relevant testimony and make meaningful submissions.
- Both parties are directed to address the balance of probabilities test on the evidence.
- Members remain seized or are re-assigned, where appropriate, to facilitate the parties in agreeing on a release proposal or to ensure CBSA compliance with a direction.
- Members actively consider alternatives to detention at every hearing.

Later in the report, recommendations are made for greater oversight when certain factors are present:

> Factors should be identified that will trigger a closer oversight of individual cases. This would include, at minimum, cases where some combination of the following factors is present:
> - Detention has continued beyond a specified threshold
> - The detained person is unrepresented
> - There is evidence that the detained person has special vulnerabilities by virtue of physical or mental health, disability or age
> - The detained person is refusing to attend hearings
> - The detained person attends hearings but is unable or unwilling to participate
> - The detained person has put forward one or more release plans which have been rejected
> - The major cause of continued detention is non-cooperation
> - The detained person has young children[97]
> - Other factors as may be identified through internal or external consultations

There were substantial and meaningful recommendations made in the report, which included the implementation of assessment forms at each review hearing that summarize the evidence that led to detention, the expedited preparation of detention review transcripts and, where a detention has exceeded six months, bringing in an experienced adjudicator to look at the case with fresh eyes with regard to the mandated factors under the regulations. The report also recommends that in some cases, members should be seized of the case to follow through with release plans that were identified as inadequate but were capable of supporting release with adjustments.

The report says that members must develop an approach to their adjudication that demonstrates compassion and empathy with detainees and recognition of their fundamental *Charter* rights.

I reproduce below the key recommendations in the report for better legal aid funding and the employment of duty counsel at the detention holding centres.

> It is recommended that the ID initiate discussions with provincial legal aid plans to canvass the possibility of increased legal services for persons in detention. Uneven access to counsel across the country is an enormous problem. As discussed above, representation rates across the country vary from a high of 76% in Eastern Region to a low of 38% in Central Region.
>
> The most critical need is in Ontario. Approximately 50% of all hearings and over 70% of detentions that exceed one year are in Central Region,[106] yet Legal Aid Ontario (LAO) reportedly provides only short term certificates for one or two hearings. The Refugee Law Office funded by LAO also provides representation at ID hearings on a limited basis due to over-stretched resources.
>
> Talks with LAO have already been initiated by the Assistant Deputy Chairperson in Central Region with a view to expanding legal services for detained persons living with mental illness. Hopefully these discussions can be expanded to address the need for representation at more detention hearings, so that Ontario can meet the level of representation available in Quebec, British Columbia, Manitoba and Alberta. It would be hugely beneficial if LAO were to establish a duty counsel program based at the IHC to provide representation at ID hearings and to refer detainees to certificate counsel as needed. In Saskatchewan and the Maritime provinces, the need for legal services could possibly be managed through an expansion in the number of legal aid certificates for private representation.
>
> Even apart from the critical barriers to justice faced by vulnerable persons in detention, tribunals generally report that the frequent appearance of lawyers at hearings, including duty counsel, serves to improve the overall quality of the hearing and decision-making process by, in effect, keeping adjudicators "on their toes."
>
> I cannot leave this topic without commenting that the best solution would be a federally-funded national legal services program for

ID hearings, staffed by lawyers and trained paralegals, and based in Toronto, Vancouver and Montreal. I am also aware that the issue of Federal funding to provincial legal aid plans for expanded representation in immigration matters is an area of very long-standing negotiation.

Finally, one of the burning issues is the inherent unfairness of the performance bond and cash bond system, which can needlessly cause the continued detention of detainees, as the extract from the report below highlights:

> It is recommended that the ID and CBSA undertake a re-evaluation of the policies surrounding release on a bond and the use of broader alternatives to detention such as house arrest or curfew. The audit was not in a position to examine the interaction between ID authority and CBSA authority in this area. However, the following potential issues were identified:
> - Is the ID and/or CBSA's approach to bonds generally consistent with Federal Court jurisprudence, including the *M.C.I. v. B188*, wherein the Court upheld an ID decision to not impose a cash bond due to the detained person's limited resources?[107]
> - Is the ID and/or CBSA's approach to bonds consistent, or should it be consistent, with the direction of the Supreme Court of Canada in *R. v. Antic*[108], confirming the principle in criminal cases that release is to be ordered at the earliest opportunity and on the least onerous grounds?
> - Why does the ID approach to cash and performance bonds vary in different parts of the country? Is this dictated by CBSA?
> - Is the requirement that a performance bond be secured against real estate only a requirement in Eastern Region? Are performance bonds against income allowed in other regions?
> - Given that the requirement to secure a performance bond against real estate creates a disproportionate disadvantage to indigent individuals, should this requirement be abandoned in appropriate cases?
> - The Government announced in 2016 that it would invest $138 million to create alternatives to detention: have these funds been committed and will programs be developed to support release for indigent individuals without access to sureties?
> - In light of recent initiatives in at least one province to make bail more accessible to indigent and vulnerable persons,[109] are the requirements imposed in ID hearings too onerous for low-income individuals who

are disproportionally identified with prohibited grounds of discrimination, including disability and race?
- Is CBSA moving forward with plans to offer GPS tracking as a less-costly and more humane alternative to detention?
- Could greater use be made of broader alternatives to detention, such as house arrest or curfews? Could halfway houses be accessed for placements, as suggested by the Ontario Superior Court in *Toure* v. *Minister of Public Safety*.[110]

Making release or detention decisions can be difficult for members, as the report underlines:

> To be clear, these determinations can be very difficult. To get at the truth, to assess credibility fairly, what is needed is the ability to see things from all perspectives, including in particular, that of the person whose liberty is at stake, as well as an effort to try to understand what their actions could mean in the context of their lives.[111]

Footnotes from the Laird Report

1 See Appendix A below for a full list of the judicial review and *habeas corpus* decisions that informed the scope of the audit.

Appendix A

Sahin v. Canada (Minister of Citizenship and Immigration), [1995] 1 F.C. 214 (T.D.)

Canada (Minister of Citizenship and Immigration) v. Lai, [2001] 3 F.C. 326 (T.D.); 2001 FCT 118

M.C.I. v. Kamail, Nariman Zangeneh (F.C.T.D., no. IMM-6474-00), O'Keefe, April 8, 2002; 2002 FCT 381

Canada (Minister of Citizenship and Immigration) v. Thanabalasingham, [2004] 3 F.C.R. 572 (F.C.A.); 2004 FCA 4

Charkaoui v. Canada (Citizenship and Immigration), [2007] 1 S.C.R. 350; 2007 SCC 9

Panahi-Dargahlloo, Hamid v. M.C.I. (F.C., no. IMM-4335-08), Mandamin, October 30, 2009; 2009 FC 1114

M.C.I. v. Li, Dong Zhe (F.C.A., no. A-642-08), Desjardins, Létourneau, Trudel, March 17, 2009; 2009 FCA 85

Arshad v. M.P.S.E.P. (F.C., no. IMM-844-13), Martineau, February 27, 2013; 2013 FC 203

Warssama, Abdirahmaan v. M.C.I. (F.C., no. IMM-1505-15), Harrington, November 24, 2015; 2015 FC 1311

Ahmed, Ali Ahmed v. M.C.I. (F.C., no. IMM-2572-15), LeBlanc, June 24, 2015; 2015 FC 792

Ahmed, Ali Ahmed v. M.C.I. (F.C., no. IMM-3022-15), Fothergill, July 17, 2015; 2015 FC 876

Ahmed, Ahmed Ali v. M.C.I. (F.C., no. IMM-3579-15), Boswell, August 26, 2015; 2015 FC 1012

Wang, Zhenhua and Yan, Chunxiang v. M.P.S.E.P. (F.C., no. IMM-8294-14), Phelan, January 21, 2015; 2015 FC 79

Wang, Zhenhua and Yan, Chunxiang v. M.P.S.E.P. (F.C., no. IMM-1655-15), Gagné, June 8, 2015; 2015 FC 720

Yan, Chunxiang and Wang, Zhenhua v. M.P.S.E.P. (F.C., no. IMM-3915-15), Southcott, September 28, 2015; 2015 FC 1125

B.B. and Justice for Children and Youth v. M.C.I. (F.C. no. IMM-5754-15), Hughes, August 24, 2016 (unpublished Order)

M.P.S.E.P. v. Lunyamila, Jacob Damiany (F.C., no. IMM-3428-16), Crampton, October 27, 2016; 2016 FC 1199

Brown, Alvin John and End Immigration Detention Network v. M.C.I. and M.P.S.E.P. (F.C., no. IMM-364-15), Fothergill, July 25, 2017; 2017 FC 710

Chaudhary v. Canada (Public Safety and Emergency Preparedness), 2015 ONCA 700 (October 20, 2015)

R. v. Ogiamien, 2016 ONSC 4126, June 29, 2016.

Ogiamien v. Ontario, 2016 ONSC 3080, May 10, 2016.

Canada v. Dadzie, 2016 ONSC 6045, September 28, 2016.

Ogiamien v. Ontario (Community Safety and Correctional Services), 2017 ONCA 839 (November 2, 2017)

Ali v. Canada (Attorney General), 2017 ONSC 2660, April 28, 2017

Scotland v. Canada (Attorney General), 2017 ONSC 4850, August 14, 2017

Ebrahim Toure v. Minister of Public Safety, 2017 ONSC 5878, (October 5, 2017),

Chhina v. Canada (Public Safety and Emergency Preparedness), 2017 ABCA 248, July 31, 2017

2 There were 20 files with respect to 18 individuals held in immigration detention. Two detainees were held in Central Region first and then Eastern Region.

37 *Canada (Minister of Citizenship and Immigration v. Thanabalasingham,* [2004] 3 FC 572 (FCA) at para. 8.

38 In our Central Region files, few decisions were transcribed, whereas all decisions were transcribed in the Eastern Region files reviewed. In Western Region, there appeared to be some variation in practice as between Members.

39 *Wang,* 2015 FC 79, at para. 28 and 30.

40 *Ogiamien,* 2016 ONSC 4126 at para. 91.

41 *Scotland,* 2017 ONSC 4850 at para. 15 to 19, 26 and 31.

42 *Ali,* 2017 ONSC 2660 at para. 32.

43 The "Case Review" is undated but appears to have been prepared by an ID Member or manager in 2014. It includes a list of convictions – no violence and no firearms.

44 This decision says "weapons of course" without citing any particular conviction or giving a date.

45 One factor that must have contributed to the problem in this file is that the detained person was transferred from one region to another, after a brief period of criminal incarceration to face theft-under charges that were withdrawn. The paper file was not transferred and only a couple of earlier decisions were brought to the attention of presiding members by CBSA.

46 Finally, after over three years of detention, one Member questions whether he would find that she is a public danger in a future hearing, suggesting that she obtain counsel and bring forward a new release plan (5 or 6 previous release plans had been previously rejected). He notes that he is not "tying my colleagues' hands" at the next 30-day hearing. He is not the Member at any of the subsequent reviews, but a release plan is accepted a couple of months later.

47 The detained person had asked to speak to her counsel before signing but that was specifically found not to be appropriately considered a cause of delay in the contemporaneous 2015 decision.

48 For example, see *Ali,* 2017 ONSC 2660 at para. 32, commenting on the same arguments made repeatedly before the ID. Also see: *Ahmed,* [2015] FC 1012 at para. 14 and 15.

49 *Brown,* 2016 ONSC 7760, para. 71-75.

54 *Charkaoui* 2007 SCC 9.

55 *Brown and End Immigration Detention Network,* 2017 FC 710.

62 In Ontario, examples include the Ontario Labour Relations Board and the Human Rights Tribunal.

63 (2015), 28 Canadian Journal of Administrative Justice and Practice 291. Also, Michelle Flaherty, *Self-represented Litigants, Active Adjudication and the Perception of Bias: Issues in Administrative Law* (2015) 38 Dalhousie Law Journal 119.

66 *Sahin,* [1995] 1 FC 214; Canada *(Minister of Citizenship and Immigration v. Thanabalasingham,* [2004] 3 FC 572 (FCA); *Panahi-Dargahlloo,* 2009 FC 114.

70 *Brown,* 2016 ONSC 7760 at para. 94-100.

71 *Brown,* above, para. 98.

72 *Chardhary,* 2015 ONCA 700 at para. 88-89.

73 *Scotland,* 2017 ONSC 4850 at para. 73.

80 *Ali,* 2017 ONSC 2660, at paras. 35-37; *Toure v. Minister of Public Safety,* 2017 ONSC 5878 at para. 75-88.

85 An example demonstrates how an active adjudication approach could have been helpful, particularly for unrepresented persons. In one case, a woman (previously released pending a PRRA application) was re-apprehended when her bondsperson reported that she was not living with her any longer. She was held for almost 3 years as a flight risk, notwithstanding her undisputed evidence that she had been reporting to CBSA regularly. She was unrepresented. No Member ever asked her why she had moved out without reporting this to CBSA. This would seem to be something useful to know if a person is being held as a flight risk for an extended period. After about 16 months of detention reviews, she blurted out in a hearing that her bondsperson has been forcing her to steal food, but she had been afraid to report this because CBSA would have taken her back in detention. This may or may not have been true; it might or might not have made a difference in the length of her detention if, earlier on, a presiding Member had asked, and she had shared this information. At the very least, it was a missing part of her story and it could have been helpful in assessing her level of flight risk. It was also notable that this evidence was not included as part of decision delivered at the end of the hearing.

86 The Ontario Superior Court has commented negatively on reliance on minor offences as a basis for a finding of public danger: *Ali,* 2017 ONSC 2660 at paras. 24 and 34.

87 See *Scotland,* 2017 ONSC 4850, paras. 9-30; *Brown* 2016 ONS 7760, paras. 71-76; *Ali,* 2017 ONSC 2660, paras. 30-34 and 39.

97 There were no cases in the audit where detained persons had minor children.

106 The percentage for Ontario would be higher, given that Central Region does not include the eastern part of the province which falls under Eastern Region for ID purposes.

107 In this decision, the Court also noted that CBSA could readily re-arrest the detained person if she was found to be inadmissible at his admissibility hearing. 2011 FC 94 at para. 50-51.

108 *R. v. Antic,* 2017 SCC 27.

109 Ontario Bail Directive, Judicial Interim Release, October 30, 2017.

110 *Toure,* 2017 ONSC 5878 at para. 90-91.

111 Two examples illustrate how difficult these determinations can be. See footnote 68 on page 33. In the case discussed, the Ontario Superior Court found that the attempt of a detained person to use a false birth certificate to facilitate his deportation was corroborative of his testimony that he had no contact information with family that could have assisted him in obtaining legitimate identity papers. However, successive ID decisions relied on CBSA submissions to make the opposite finding – specifically that his attempts to get false documents were evidence of his failure to cooperate honestly with CBSA. The main basis for detention over many years was that he was lying when he claimed that he could not provide contact information for family members who could assist in obtaining identity papers.

In this case, CBSA also relied on the fact that the detained person had, years before, obtained a driver's license under a false name. The person explained that he had no choice – he had never in his life held valid identity papers and CBSA had kept the false birth certificate in his name that he had used previously to facilitate his deportation. He testified that he needed the driver's license as an identity document to get housing and work. He relied on the fact that he had continued to report to CBSA under his correct name and never used the false documents to elude immigration authorities.

This explanation was never taken seriously or assessed for its credibility by ID Members. Instead, ID decisions found that the false license application "clearly" demonstrated a high flight risk and grounds for continued detention. In contrast, the Ontario Superior Court was able to interpret the behavior of this person in a much more nuanced way.

Recommendations for Amendments

I reproduce below a letter from the CBA, dated January 11, 2019, to the Immigration Enforcement Policy Unit of the CBSA, outlining some recommendations on bonds, release and forfeiture. The reference to the cases in that letter have been omitted.

Dear Manager:

Re: Proposed Amendments, Immigration and Refugee Protection Regulations Sections 45-49 (Deposits or Guarantees)

I am writing on behalf of the Canadian Bar Association Immigration Law Section (CBA Section) to comment on the Canada Border Services Agency consultation on proposed amendments to the Immigration and Refugee Protection Regulations, clarifying the requirements of bondspersons. The CBA is a national association of 36,000 members, including lawyers, notaries, academics and students across Canada, with a mandate to seek improvements in the law and the administration of justice. The CBA Section is comprised of over 1,000 lawyers, practicing all aspects of immigration law and delivering professional advice and representation on the Canadian immigration system to clients in Canada and abroad. The CBA Section supports this initiative to ensure consistent, transparent and uniform application of a minimum baseline of factors by all decision-makers with respect to bondspersons. We offer the following comments and recommendations regarding the proposed Regulations.

Quantum

One of the proposed factors for consideration is "the bondsperson's financial situation." The meaning of this phrase should be clarified. We recommend that there be no maximum or minimum amount required to post bond so long as the decision-maker is satisfied that the bond is significant for the bondsperson, and that the bondsperson has the capacity to pay the amount.

Release should not be reserved for the wealthy. The Regulations and associated guidelines should not include a set formula for the quantum of bond proposed, so long as the amount is meaningful for the bondsperson. A formulaic approach unduly fetters discretion.

"Own Bail"

The Regulations should permit the possibility of a detained person posting their own bond, without the need for a bondsperson. In the criminal context, "own bail" is a well-established practice. If the sum posted is meaningful for the detainee, this option offers a strong incentive for compliance. "Own bail" can also be combined with a separate bondsperson, with the monetary bond posted by the detainee and the bondsperson identified for other purposes such as living arrangements and ensuring compliance.

Community Groups

The Regulations should permit institutions and community groups to act as bondspersons, without the need to post a pecuniary bond. Such organizations – social services or mental health groups for example – may not have the monetary capacity or legal ability to post bonds for individual detainees but may otherwise be able to serve as a reliable source of support. This can be especially important when the detainee has no connection to a specific individual in Canada. Release should not be reserved for those with a network of family or friends in the country.

Relationship to Detainee

The proposed factor "the relationship of the proposed bondsperson to the person concerned", needs to be clarified. The CBA Section assumes and recommends this will be interpreted to mean that the closer the relationship, the better the bondsperson. It is well-established that a bondsperson must have sufficient knowledge of and connection to a detainee to provide the support and supervision required and to ensure compliance.

Conversely, the closeness of the relationship should never be used to impugn the bondsperson for not having previously ensured compliance. A common illustrative is a spouse who lived with the person prior to detention and is sponsoring them for permanent residence. Barring an adverse criminal or immigration history, the spouse should be considered a strong candidate for bondsperson. It should not be held against the spouse that they did not proactively ensure the detainee's compliance prior to detention.

Criminal Record

We recommend that the requirement to consider the bondsperson's "criminal record and potential criminal associations" be amended to mandate consideration of "prior criminal convictions" only, not "potential criminal associations." The factor must be based on verifiable facts and evidence of a conviction, not evidence that an individual was merely present at a certain place and time but never convicted of an offence. The law must eschew vicarious liability and should not impugn a bondsperson based on association or charges that were later stayed, withdrawn or dismissed.

Alternatives to Detention

The CBA Section recommends that the Regulations affirm that release should be ordered at the earliest possible opportunity and on the least onerous grounds. A non-exhaustive list of alternatives to be considered would include but is not limited to halfway houses, house arrest, curfew, electronic reporting, voice reporting, GPS tracking and release to community agencies. Consideration of these alternatives is important for all detainees, especially those who are vulnerable or indigent. This approach is consistent with the Immigration and Refugee Board's findings following an external audit commissioned in September 2017 of cases where immigration detention had exceeded 100 days.

Forfeiture Proceedings

Section 49(4) of the Regulations states: "A sum of money deposited is forfeited, or a guarantee posted becomes enforceable, on the failure of the person or any member of the group of persons in respect of whom the deposit or guarantee was required to comply with a condition imposed." This leaves open the possibility of the entire bond being forfeited for a minor breach of a condition (for example, failure to report an address change before a move as opposed to one day after a move).

We recommend establishing a formal process under the administrative immigration scheme, in line with bail forfeiture proceedings in the criminal context.

Under a formal process, the Immigration Division would determine whether the magnitude of the breach justifies forfeiture of the whole bond or a partial amount, considering the history of compliance and any mitigating factors in connection with the breach.

The CBA Section appreciates the opportunity to comment on these proposed Regulations. Please let us know if you have any questions about our recommendations.

Yours truly,

(*original letter signed by Sarah MacKenzie for Marina Sedai*)

Marina Sedai

Chair, CBA Immigration Law Section

Comments

After reading this chapter, it will be clear that the major event in the field of detention reviews in Canada is the September 2017 Laird Report, which through its thorough investigation of detention review cases all over Canada has disclosed gross deficiencies in the system. These shortfalls and inadequacies in the system have led to the detention of many immigrants who ought to have been released. Furthermore, there must be serious concerns about the lengthy periods of detentions that some of the immigrants have had to endure because of the flaws in the system. At least now, in 2019, as this book is about to be published, all the persons involved in detention review cases—members of the division, hearings officers, the detainee's counsel, and the detainee—will be aware of the disturbing facts of the deficiencies and injustices. Hopefully, this knowledge will help prevent any repetition of the unfairness that the system had previously generated.

Fortunately, during the publishing process of this book, the new Chairperson's Guidelines took effect on April 1, 2019. These guidelines must be applied by the Immigration Division throughout Canada. It is such a critically important document on detentions that I have been compelled to devote the next chapter to the new guidelines. Representatives of detainees must be aware of the directions in the new guidelines in order to be able to represent detainees effectively and competently.

We need to work on building a better system. The Laird Report and the new Chairperson's Guidelines have made us aware of the gross deficiencies in the way some past reviews have been conducted and given us the tools to improve the process. Now we must work together in ensuring the review process is fair, accountable and transparent. We must strive toward achieving an equitable balance. That balance must be that detention is only ordered when there are no viable alternatives. But the aim must always be to ensure that a person's liberty is only taken away as a matter of last resort.

Notes

i Available online at https://www.cbsa-asfc.gc.ca/agency-agence/reports-rapports/pia-efvp/atip-aiprp/atd-srd-eng.html.

ii The text of the full audit is available online at https://irb-cisr.gc.ca/en/transparency/reviews-audit-evaluations/Pages/ID-external-audit-1718.aspx.

CHAPTER 17

The Amended Chairperson's Guidelines (effective April 1, 2019)

The Laird Report, which we examined in chapter 16, led to a revision of the June 2013 guidelines. These amended guidelines came into force on April 1, 2019. You will find them at appendix D.

I have provided a link to the 2013 guidelines at appendix G. The new guidelines provide clear directions that all members of the ID throughout Canada must follow. It is, therefore, critically important that representatives of detainees are aware of the terms of these guidelines when conducting detention reviews. Below, I have highlighted the parts of the new guidelines that representatives must be mindful of when doing these reviews.

A Robust and Meaningful Review

At article 1.1.8:

> The Charter requires that a person subject to the detention review process under IRPA is entitled to a meaningful and robust review that takes into account the context and circumstances of the individual case. Such persons must have a meaningful opportunity to challenge their detention. Members must consider the evidence and arguments afresh at each detention review and come to their own determinations. Particular attention must be paid to Charter considerations where detention is lengthy and/or where the prospect of removal has become remote.

This article encapsulates the spirit of the new guidelines to the effect that detainees must be given full opportunity to challenge their detention and that members must not rely on earlier decisions to justify continued detention at a review hearing. It must be a robust and meaningful review wherein the member must consider all the evidence and arguments afresh.

Procedural Fairness and Natural Justice

At article 1.1.13:

> Members are subject to the standards of conduct set out in the Code of Conduct for Members of the IRB. The Code requires members to conduct hearings in a courteous and respectful manner while ensuring that the proceedings are fair, orderly and efficient. It also requires members to comply with procedural fairness and natural justice. Members are expected to approach each case with an open mind and, at all times, must be, and must be seen to be, impartial and objective.

In the past, some members have appeared to be biased, preferring and relying on the grounds for detention articulated by Minister's counsel based on the untested and hearsay evidence of the CBSA officers. Now, members are reminded that they must approach each case with an *open* mind without any bias. They must abide by all the necessary procedural safeguards to ensure the detainee has a fair hearing and that the rules of natural justice have been complied with. The rules of natural justice demand that the detainee and his or her witnesses have a right to be heard at the review hearing by being allowed to give evidence. It would be a serious breach of these rules if members blocked any attempt by detainees to give evidence and call witnesses. If this happens, I suggest the representative must raise an objection at that time, not only to prevent the member from trampling over the detainee's fundamental rights but also to ensure that the objection is on the record of the proceedings in case of a judicial challenge later on.

2. Grounds for Detention

2.2 Danger to the public

The guidelines warn members to be vigilant in undertaking a proper assessment of previous criminal convictions to gauge whether they are a reliable indicator of the detainee being a danger to the public. Below I have listed some of the factors that members must be aware of:

- Are the convictions old so that they can no longer be of any assistance in judging whether the detainee is likely to be a danger to the public?

- Do the circumstances of the previous conviction involve violence and weapons? Did the detainee commit numerous such offences? If so, a finding of danger to the public may be justified.

Members should consider any mitigating or aggravating features present at the time of the offence, including the sentence of the criminal court. This is reflected at article 2.2.4 below:

> It is often necessary for members to draw inferences from a person's criminal record in determining whether that person poses a danger to the public. The more serious the criminal offences, the use of violence and weapons and the greater number of offences committed the more they weigh in favour of a finding of danger to the public. A member should also consider the circumstances of the offence, how much time has passed since the criminal conduct, the sentence imposed by the criminal court and any mitigating or aggravating factors at the time of the offence or since that time.

Under the old guidelines, the determination of the Parole Board of Canada as to whether the detainee is a danger to the public was not considered significant. Now, members are urged to consider the Parole Board's evaluation of the risk the detainee poses as the Board looks at the detainee's recent conduct.

Similarly, under the old guidelines, a determination concerning the grant of bail by a criminal court was not to be given any deference. Now, members are specifically directed to consider the court's determinations while considering all the facts in the case in the immigration context.

A welcome change in the new guidelines is that members must consider any vulnerability and addiction issues that led to a finding of danger to the public in the original offence. Article 2.2.10 mandates:

> Members should also consider the circumstances that led to the original determination of danger to the public; for example, whether those circumstances involved a heightened level of vulnerability due to addiction or mental health issues, among others, and whether those vulnerabilities have been mitigated, e.g. through treatment or rehabilitation. However, members should be cautious regarding an absence of evidence of rehabilitation, as persons in detention often do not have access to rehabilitation programs.

2.3 Unlikely to appear

If a member is concerned that a detainee is unlikely to appear for any admissibility hearing or for removal, the detainee must be given the opportunity to address these concerns. When considering a detainee's previous non-compliance with release conditions, the member is obligated to consider mental health, addiction and other vulnerability issues that may have affected the detainee's ability to comply with these conditions and how the detainee can address these issues. The severity and frequency of non-compliance should also be reviewed.

2.5 Identity of foreign national not established

Although the onus is on detainees to establish their identity as this is a matter within their personal knowledge, nevertheless the member must look at the Minister's effort to establish the detainee's identity, and more particularly as set out under article 2.5.4:

> In assessing the reasonableness of the Minister's efforts to establish identity, the member must consider not what the Member thinks should have been done. Rather the focus should be on whether what the Minister has done, is doing and intends to do is rationally connected to the purpose of the provision – that the steps have the potential to uncover relevant evidence and whether the Minister is acting in good faith. The member should be satisfied that the Minister has provided sufficient evidence of its efforts, as well as concrete plans and time estimates.

This provision arose directly as a result of situations disclosed in the Laird Report where the Minister was able to satisfy the member on a low threshold that the Minister had gone through the motions of establishing the detainee's identity, without showing concrete plans and time estimates concerning their investigations into the detainee's identity. This led to unjustified and sometimes lengthy detentions. Now, the member must engage proactively with the CBSA in determining *what the Minister has done and intends to do to uncover relevant evidence and whether the Minister is acting in good faith.*

Representatives of detainees must engage in a vigorous examination of whether the Minister has undertaken all the steps necessary to establish the detainee's identity. If the Minister is found lacking in that endeavour, submissions ought to be made that the detainee's continued detention is unreasonable. The new guidelines have raised the threshold that the Minister must overcome concerning their diligence in establishing identity.

3. Release and Alternatives to Detention

The new guidelines compel members of the ID to vigorously consider alternatives to detention (ATDs) through the imposition of conditions that would minimize the risks inherent in the grounds for detention, whether it be danger to the public, flight risk or identity issues. There is also a recognition that members must be especially vigilant to protect certain detainees who are particularly vulnerable. Article 3.1.7 provides:

> A heightened obligation to consider ATDs also applies to cases involving vulnerable persons such as persons with mental illness, minors, the elderly, individuals with diverse sexual orientation and gender identity and expression, survivors of torture, survivors of genocide and crimes against humanity, survivors of gender-related violence, and survivors of violence based on sexual orientation and gender identity. As the onus on the Minister is heightened, a member should also actively question the steps that the Minister has taken to make an ATD available in the circumstances of these cases.

The new ATD program discussed in chapter 16 provides to the CBSA an expanded set of tools and programs that enables them to propose release of detainees into the community. This is especially important in cases where the detainee has no friends or relatives in the community who can provide support (e.g., by standing as a bondsperson and providing a residential address). Representatives of detainees must, therefore, explore and develop plans of release utilizing these ATD tools to effect the detainee's release. It is submitted that a failure by representatives to consider these ATD programs is tantamount to incompetence.

One of the problems that the Laird Report identified was the "open and shut" nature of the decisions of members of the ID, in that once a member rejected a plan of release, that ended the matter, with the detainee losing all hope of release. Now, the new guidelines have instituted a procedure whereby the possibility of an appropriate ATD is kept open and not closed to the detainee. Articles 3.1.11 and 3.1.12 provide: *[my emphasis]*

> 3.1.11 Parties may come to an agreement on proposed conditions of release before or during the detention review and submit the agreement to the member at the hearing. Members would ordinarily endorse release, after having reviewed the file and conducted the hearing. In the exceptional case where a member does not accept the joint submission due to concerns regarding the adequacy of release conditions, prior to issuing reasons for rejecting the joint submission and ordering continued detention, *the member should give the parties notice of the member's concerns and an opportunity to confer to see if a varied joint submission or different conditions can be presented.* A member must provide a rationale for rejecting the release plan and continuing detention.

3.1.12 Where a release plan is not presented, *the member should encourage both parties to work jointly to develop and present acceptable release plans for future consideration. Members should also look for reasonable opportunities to review any previously unsuccessful proposed release plans presented by any party to the proceedings to determine whether such plans remain available and over time have become suitable.* Members should encourage the person concerned to look at possible release plans on their own or with counsel.

It is essential that representatives of detainees are familiar with these provisions because it keeps the door open for continued negotiations with Minister's counsel and the member toward securing the release of the detainee, perhaps with a more creative release plan that will minimize the relevant risk.

3.2 Release considerations

It is important to look at some of the usual release conditions, but conditions such as house arrest and ankle braces, although a severe restriction on the liberty of the immigrant, may be justified where the grounds for detention involve the immigrant being a danger to the public. Article 3.2.2 sets out some of the standard conditions:

i. report to CBSA periodically (in person or by telephone);
ii. appear whenever required by CBSA, including for removal;
iii. a bondsperson to pay a deposit or post a guarantee for compliance with conditions;
iv. provide CBSA with a travel document or cooperate with CBSA in obtaining a travel document, except in the case of an asylum seeker or refugee who has not exhausted their legal remedies;
v. reside with a bondsperson or other person considered capable of exercising control and influence over the person concerned;
vi. remain within (or outside) a particular location or geographic area;
vii. abide by a curfew;
viii. reside at community housing or a rehabilitation centre;
ix. not have contact with certain people (e.g., the victim of domestic abuse);
x. not commit criminal offences;
xi. report criminal charges or convictions to CBSA;
xii. abide by conditions of parole or conditions imposed by a justice of the peace or criminal court;

xiii. not consume alcohol, drugs or other intoxicating substances, except in accordance with a medical prescription or in the context of a rehabilitative program, to be applied only for persons with a history of addiction and non-compliance;

xiv. make all reasonable efforts to obtain treatment for alcohol or drug abuse, mental illness or anger management;

xv. enroll in a community case management and supervision program;

xvi. not possess a firearm or other weapon;

xvii. not knowingly associate with individuals who have a criminal record;

xviii. refrain from using a cell phone or a computer or have no functioning internet connection in the person's residence (as an exceptional measure);

xix. permit entry into the person's residence at all times by CBSA or designated personnel (as an exceptional measure); and/or

xx. obtain and wear an electronic bracelet to track movements (as an exceptional measure).

3.3 Bondspersons

One of the important changes brought about by the new guidelines is the requirement that the bondsperson give evidence at the detention review hearing. Prior to this, the bondsperson could be interviewed by Minister's counsel outside the hearing room to determine their suitability. The Laird Report criticized this practice as it was not transparent and could lead to a biased and inaccurate assessment of a bondsperson's suitability by both Minister's counsel and the member. Articles 3.3.2–3.3.4 provide:

> **3.3.2** When a bondsperson is present and available to testify, members must hear direct evidence from the bondsperson before determining that the person is not suitable to be a bondsperson. Members cannot rely on bondsperson interviews conducted outside of the hearing room and not in the presence of members in this context. However, upon a joint release recommendation or where the Minister does not object, a member can determine that the bondsperson is acceptable without hearing direct testimony.
>
> **3.3.3** If the proposed bondsperson is unavailable to provide testimony, a member should determine whether an adjournment is required or a decision should be rendered with an early detention review scheduled, depending on the duration of the lack of availability.

3.3.4 Members must ensure that relevant considerations relating to the proposed bondsperson are explored at the detention review in order to assess the suitability of the person put forward.

This new procedure ensures transparency through members questioning the bondsperson in the hearing room to determine suitability so that the detainee or counsel can respond.

The procedure outlined in the Alfred Blake case study, where counsel prepares a detailed affidavit setting out all the factors that will satisfy a member of the bondsperson's suitability, should be carried out in every case. This gives both Minister's counsel and the member the opportunity to consider the bondsperson's evidence and formulate any questions that may be necessary to clarify the affidavit evidence. In my experience, providing this detailed affidavit of the bondsperson to the Minister's counsel before the hearing can induce counsel to agree to the release of detainee on appropriate conditions. If there is no consent release then, under this new procedure, questioning of the affiant by Minister's counsel and the member must be done during the hearing.

4. Minors

The general rule under the new guidelines is set out at articles 4.1.2 and 4.1.3: *[my emphasis]*

> **4.1.2** Members must consider the prescribed factors in the IRPR when determining whether to release or continue detention, including the best interests of the child, as well as all other relevant circumstances. *Members must only detain minors in the most exceptional circumstances, and for the shortest time possible.*
>
> **4.1.3** *The Minister must submit its best interest of the child assessment at each detention review when it is detaining a child.* The person concerned may also advance arguments regarding the best interest of a child, supported by evidence.

Article 4.1.4 sets out some of the factors that must be considered in determining the child's best interest with respect to detention and release of the minor and their parent/guardian:

- the child's physical, emotional and psychological well-being;
- the child's healthcare and educational needs;
- the importance of maintaining relationships and the stability of the family environment, and the possible effect on the child of disrupting those relationships or that stability;

- the care, protection and safety needs of the child; and
- the child's views and preferences, provided the child is capable of forming their own views or expressing their preferences, taking into consideration the child's age and maturity.

The level of dependence of the child on the person for whom there are grounds to detain (parent/guardian) should also be a consideration.

In addition, article 4.1.5 provides:

4.1.5 Members must explain in their reasons for decision how the best interests of the child were considered in the decision to detain the child or their parent/guardian.

5. Vulnerable Persons

As with minors, there is a heightened obligation on members to "consider ATDs and to impose attainable conditions that are connected to the circumstances of the vulnerable person concerned." In addition, article 5.1.7 provides that "early detention reviews are strongly encouraged to ensure that the file is progressing rapidly and the vulnerable person concerned is not unduly affected."

As previously stated, vulnerable persons include the mentally ill or persons with serious addiction issues or persons who have been the victims of trauma and other kinds of emotional or physical abuse.

7. Conducting the Detention Review – Robust Hearing

One of the substantial criticisms in the Laird Report involved the failure of some members at subsequent reviews to conduct a robust fresh hearing with an open mind in considering new evidence or new arguments. This failure led detainees to give up all hope of being released at these subsequent reviews. Under the new guidelines, members must make a fresh determination at each review hearing. Articles 7.2.1 and 7.2.2 provide:

7.2.1 Members must ensure that at each hearing the person concerned is aware of the Division's duty to release under section 58(1) of IRPA unless the Minister proves, on a balance of probabilities, that there is a statutory ground for detention and that continued detention is required, with the onus resting on the Minister.

> **7.2.2** The Minister may elect to rely on having previously established the grounds for detention. However, the member is not bound to accept the previous finding of a member at the last detention review if the Minister has failed to provide reasonably available evidence to justify the detention. This is particularly relevant in long-term detention cases, and cases involving persons concerned with vulnerabilities, especially where the Minister leads insufficient evidence to justify the ground for detention, the length of detention or its uncertain duration, or the necessity of detention rather than less restrictive liberty restraints.

The Minister bears an ongoing burden to prove that detention remains justified, and the member must come to a fresh determination on whether the detainee should continue to be detained. Representatives of detainees must ensure that both Minister's counsel and the member follow this directive if it seems the member is routinely rubber-stamping approval of the detention order at a previous hearing.

Members must explain in their reasons why they have rejected an ATD put forward either by detainees or their representative at the hearing.

As with the previous guidelines and the established case law, members must state their reasons for departing from the detention order at a previous review when releasing the detainee.

7.3 Disclosure and evidence

The rules of natural justice are clearly set out in the new guidelines at article 7.3.1:

> **7.3.1** Both parties have the right to present relevant evidence at a detention review, including witnesses, and to question those witnesses. *Members should ensure that the person concerned understands and has an opportunity to testify, present evidence and counter the Minister's evidence, including by presenting their own sworn testimony should they so choose, calling witnesses, and/or cross-examining the Minister's witnesses. [my emphasis]*

The guidelines expressly provide that the Minister must disclose any document they intend to rely upon at any detention reviews. *They cannot rely on a document that they fail or refuse to disclose.* This is a welcome change from the situation in the past where Minister's counsel could rely on any materials at the hearing, often catching the detainee's representative by surprise. There also existed the unjust situation where Minister's counsel could rely on hearsay evidence without the ability of the detainee's representative to probe that evidence through cross-examination. Now, special rules under articles 7.3.2–7.3.6 have been implemented in the new guidelines, which have made the process fairer and more transparent: *[my emphasis]*

> **7.3.2** The Minister must disclose any document they intend to rely on in any detention review, in compliance with the Division's rules. They cannot rely on a document they refuse/fail to disclose. *Furthermore, evidence from the Enforcement/Removals Officer should be in the form of either a statutory declaration to be disclosed before the hearing or oral testimony.* The type of evidence provided affects the weight to be afforded by the member. *It is not appropriate for the Minister to present information when the primary source of the information has not been made available to the parties*, unless the primary source of information is not compellable (i.e. a consular official).
>
> **7.3.3** Members must ensure that the parties have provided each other with *reasonable notice of the evidence or information that will be relied upon at the detention review*. Members must consider any request to summon the Enforcement Officer to provide testimony at the detention review. Members should summon an Enforcement Officer on their own initiative if they believe that this would be likely to address important gaps in the evidentiary record, in particular where the person concerned is self-represented.
>
> **7.3.4** *The Minister is expected to disclose all relevant evidence, whether or not it is exculpatory, or they intend to rely on it.*
>
> **7.3.5** In circumstances where the Minister's counsel cannot answer questions posed by the member at the hearing, *the member is encouraged to adjourn to allow the source of the information, such as a CBSA Enforcement Officer, to attend the hearing to answer questions or, where impractical or impossible for a timely decision, for the Minister's counsel to obtain the information requested.* An early detention review could also be scheduled, as applicable.
>
> **7.3.6** Where the Minister is unable to provide the information requested, the member must carefully consider whether the Minister has discharged its onus to justify continued detention.

It is important that both detainees and their counsel understand and apply these new rules. If, at the hearing, Minister's counsel is making statements that rely on the untested hearsay evidence of a CBSA officer, the detainee's representative is under a duty to object and ask the member to compel Minister's counsel to summon the CBSA officer so he or she can be cross-examined. If the detainee's representative does not take these proactive steps, these new rules will not be effective in preventing injustice to the detainee. I have incorporated the new disclosure requirements in a precedent correspondence to the ID and the CBSA at appendix F, tab 6.

Members now have an onus to assist detainees by taking an active role in ensuring they have a sufficient evidentiary record upon which to base their decision by:

- active questioning to address any factual gaps;
- giving notice of concerns to the person concerned in plain language and providing an opportunity for a response;
- testing the Minister's representations through active and, where necessary, probing questions to assess their evidentiary basis; and/or
- insisting upon testimony from others with more direct knowledge of the case (for example, Enforcement Officers) where important questions remain after questioning of the Minister's counsel and the person concerned.

8. Sufficiency of Reasons for Decision

The new guidelines define what constitutes sufficient reasons for the decision by the member after the detention review hearing. The member must analyze the evidence adduced at the hearing and explain how the evidence relates to the findings made in the reasons, including why any ATDs proposed were accepted or rejected. There must be a complete evidential record. Article 8.1.4 provides:

> Reasons for decision should be sufficiently detailed to allow the reader to know what grounds and factors the member relied on in support of their decision to order continued detention or release, including the reasons for departing from previous decisions. The reasons should also explain possible ATDs and any barriers to release which, in the member's opinion, must be overcome by the person concerned prior to release.

Conclusion

The amended guidelines have introduced new principles that will make the detention review process fairer to detainees so that there is justice, transparency and accountability. However, only time will tell whether these new amendments will remedy the unfair practices that permeated the detention review process as highlighted by the Laird Report. Representatives of detainees will have an important role to play in how effective the new amendments are by ensuring that ID members enforce them and not merely pay passive lip service to them.

Glossary of Terms, Acronyms and Initialisms

admissibility and admissibility hearing: A foreign national or permanent resident can be found to be inadmissible (either barred from entry to Canada or removed from Canada) for criminality, serious criminality, membership in a criminal organization, human rights violations in their country of nationality and being a threat to Canadian security. This list is not exhaustive. The Immigration Division (ID) is charged with the responsibility of determining whether the CBSA has proven that the foreign national or permanent resident is inadmissible on these grounds.

affiant: The person, usually a bondsperson, who swears an affidavit as to the facts and evidence that counsel will rely upon to support arguments for release of the detainee.

affidavit: A document that is sworn on oath before a commissioner of oaths and contains all the facts necessary for counsel to present at the detention review. As it is sworn, it is regarded as being evidence and is similar to the testimony of a witness in the witness box.

ATDs: Alternatives to detention, part of the focus of community-based support programs to avoid detention.

BIOC: Best interests of the child or children. This principle is of substantial importance in all humanitarian and compassionate applications under section 25 of IRPA and in detention review cases. Children should not be adversely affected by decisions that may affect their well-being.

bondsperson (bond): One or more individuals who are prepared to enter into a performance bond to guarantee that the detainee will comply with conditions of release. (There is no deposit of money but only a pledge by the bondsperson to pay the amount of the bond in the event the released detainee breaches any conditions of release.) It also refers to a bondsperson who is prepared to provide a cash deposit to guarantee that the detainee will comply with conditions of release. One bondsperson can be ordered to provide both a performance bond and a cash deposit. But depending on the seriousness of the grounds for detention, two or more persons may be called upon to provide the performance bond and cash deposit separately.

cash deposit: At the end of a detention review hearing, if the member imposes a condition that the bondsperson provide a cash deposit, it is usually paid to the CBSA in the form of a banker's draft or money order or by credit card to the Receiver General of Canada. This is the current practice in Toronto, but in other locations, the CBSA may have the resources to accept cash.

CBA: The Canadian Bar Association is a body that represents all lawyers in Canada. The CBA has various sections. Their immigration section has made recommendations to the government to implement changes in legislation and the regulations to give everyone the right to fundamental justice.

CBSA: The Canada Border Services Agency and its officers, who are responsible for the enforcement of IRPA and the IRPR in connection with breaches of the Act and Regulations. The

CBSA receives its directives from the Minister of Public Safety and Emergency Preparedness (MPSEP).

CCMS: Community Case Management and Supervision. A community-based support program that attempts to house, supervise and monitor detainees who would otherwise be detained for not having appropriate bondspersons.

CGD/CGV: Chairperson's Guidelines on Detention/Chairperson's Guidelines on Vulnerable Persons. The Chairperson of the Immigration and Refugee Board (IRB) issues various guidelines on subjects that range from the treatment of vulnerable persons appearing in the IRB to guidelines on detention reviews. The CGD contains a comprehensive digest of some of the more important cases on detention reviews. These guidelines are reproduced at appendix D. The CGV assists in understanding some of the unique problems faced by vulnerable persons: children, traumatized immigrants, especially women, and mentally ill individuals. These persons may not understand the nature of the detention review proceeding, and a designated representative may have to be appointed to represent their best interests and provide a channel of communication with counsel and the ID. These guidelines are reproduced at appendix E.

conditions of release: This describes the specific conditions that the released detainee must comply with and which if not complied with, will result in the released person being returned to custody. Some conditions, such as the surrender of the detainee's passport and compliance with bondsperson conditions (namely posting a guarantee and a cash deposit), must be complied with prior to the detainee being released. Other conditions of release, such as the obligation to keep the peace and be of good behaviour, adhering to a curfew or house arrest, residence with the bondsperson(s), periodic reporting to the CBSA and abiding by the rules and discipline of the household of the bondsperson(s), are continuing obligations and duties that the released immigrant must comply with to keep their liberty. There is a trend toward the acceptance by the ID of electronic monitoring conditions and use of these devices in appropriate cases.

curfew: A condition of release that stipulates that the released immigrant must not be out of his or her residence between certain hours. These types of prohibitive conditions tend to be a more common condition in criminal bail than immigration release. However, it is increasingly used to protect the public where the ground for detention is danger to the public.

detainee: The immigrant who has been detained by the CBSA and will be the subject of a detention review hearing in the Immigration Division.

detention review: The hearing whereby a member of the Immigration Division will review whether he or she is satisfied that the CBSA has proved that the detainee ought not to be released because of the likelihood of being a danger to the public or a flight risk or because the immigrant's identity has not been established. See chapter 1 for a more comprehensive review of the three-step approach that a member must engage upon at a detention review hearing.

enforcement: The CBSA is responsible for enforcement where there are breaches of IRPA and the Regulations. The CBSA works under the Minister of Public Safety and Emergency Preparedness (MPSEP). This is a different ministry from Immigration, Refugees and Citizenship Canada (IRCC), which is responsible for the decisions of immigration and visa officers and the members of the divisions of the IRB, namely, the Immigration Appeal Division, the Refugee Protection Division and the Refugee Appeal Division. The MPSEP is responsible for the decisions of CBSA officers and the Immigration Division. The primary duties of CBSA officers in enforcement proceedings are set out under section 48 of IRPA. This section stipulates that an immigrant who is subject to a removal order must be removed out of Canada to their country of nationality as soon as possible.

forfeiture: If an immigrant has broken his or her conditions of release, the bondspersons may lose the performance bond or cash they posted. In the case of a performance bond, the amount of that bond must be surrendered to the CBSA. In the case of a cash deposit, the cash will be permanently retained by the CBSA.

habeas corpus: A remedy brought by writ to the Superior Court of Justice to compel the release of an applicant who has been unlawfully detained. There has been a trend during 2017–2018 to bring such an application in cases where a detainee has been incarcerated by decisions of the ID for a lengthy period.

hearings officer: Represents the CBSA at detention review hearings. Sometimes also referred to as Minister's counsel.

house arrest: A restrictive condition of release that prevents the immigrant being outside the residence unless in the presence of his bondspersons. It is a condition that is usually imposed when the ground for detention is danger to the public.

ICCRC: Immigration Consultants of Canada Regulatory Council. This is the professional supervisory and regulatory body for regulated and licensed Canadian immigration consultants (RCICs).

ID: The Immigration Division of the Immigration and Refugee Board, which is the division that adjudicates on detention issues and admissibility.

IRB: The Immigration Refugee Board is the body that contains all the divisions under IRPA, namely the Immigration Division (ID), which determines the issue of the admissibility and detention of foreign nationals/permanent residents, the Immigration Appeal Division (IAD), which adjudicates on appeals involving permanent residents, the Refugee Protection Division (RPD), which adjudicates on refugee claims and the Refugee Appeal Division (RAD), which is an appellate division of the IRB that adjudicates on appeals where the RPD has denied the applicant's refugee claim.

IRPA: The Immigration and Refugee Protection Act is the Federal statute that governs all aspects of Canadian immigration.

IRPR: The Immigration and Refugee Protection Regulations contains detailed regulations that expand on and deal with various detailed aspects of Canadian immigration. Reference to both IRPA and the IRPR is necessary for an in-depth understanding of Canadian immigration law.

JR: Appeals of detention decisions are brought by the challenge of the decision by way of judicial review proceedings (JR) in the Federal Court. See chapter 14 for a detailed analysis of the procedure.

jurisprudence: A body of law comprising mostly legislation, regulations and court decisions that enunciate a principle of law.

PR: Short form for either permanent residence or a permanent resident.

RCIC: A regulated licensed immigration consultant, who is licensed to practice all aspects of Canadian immigration law under IRPA and the *Citizenship Act*. But an RCIC has no rights of audience in the Federal Court, as only lawyers can appear in that court.

removal order: The order issued either by a CBSA officer for more minor breaches of IRPA or by the ID where there are serious breaches of IRPA such as a breach of section 36(1) that leads to a finding of serious criminality. There are three types of removal orders, namely, a deportation order (the most serious kind of order, which prevents the immigrant from coming back to Canada), an exclusion order (which allows the immigrant to come to Canada after the period of the exclusion if they obtain an authorization to do so) or a departure order, which allows the immigrant to voluntarily leave Canada within 30 days, without any adverse consequences. If the immigrant does not leave Canada within 30 days, it becomes a deportation order.

Appendices

A   Immigration and Refugee Protection Act, sections 54–61
B   Immigration and Refugee Protection Regulations, sections 244–250
C   Immigration Division Rules
D   Chairperson's Guidelines on Detention
E   Chairperson's Guidelines on Vulnerable Persons
F   Precedents and Templates
   1. Lawyer Retainer Agreement
   2. Schedule "A": Waiver and Direction to Pay
   3. Schedule "B": Estimate of Fees
   4. RCIC Retainer Agreement
   5. Correspondence to the Immigration Division in the Alfred Blake Case
   6. Correspondence to the Immigration Division under the Amended Chairperson's Guidelines on Detention, Effective April 1, 2019
   7. Affidavit of Gill St. John
   8. Affidavit of Tony St. John
   9. Counsel Contact Information Form
   10. Bondsperson Forms Issued by the IRB
   11. Sample Release Order

G   Important Resources on Detention

Appendix A

IMMIGRATION AND REFUGEE PROTECTION ACT, SECTIONS 54-61

Part 1: Immigration to Canada

Division 6: Detention and Release

IMMIGRATION DIVISION

54 The Immigration Division is the competent Division of the Board with respect to the review of reasons for detention under this Division.

ARREST AND DETENTION WITH WARRANT

55 (1) An officer may issue a warrant for the arrest and detention of a permanent resident or a foreign national who the officer has reasonable grounds to believe is inadmissible and is a danger to the public or is unlikely to appear for examination, for an admissibility hearing, for removal from Canada or at a proceeding that could lead to the making of a removal order by the Minister under subsection 44(2).

ARREST AND DETENTION WITHOUT WARRANT

(2) An officer may, without a warrant, arrest and detain a foreign national, other than a protected person,

   (a) who the officer has reasonable grounds to believe is inadmissible and is a danger to the public or is unlikely to appear for examination, an admissibility hearing, removal from Canada, or at a proceeding that could lead to the making of a removal order by the Minister under subsection 44(2); or

(b) if the officer is not satisfied of the identity of the foreign national in the course of any procedure under this Act.

DETENTION ON ENTRY

(3) A permanent resident or a foreign national may, on entry into Canada, be detained if an officer

(a) considers it necessary to do so in order for the examination to be completed; or

(b) has reasonable grounds to suspect that the permanent resident or the foreign national is inadmissible on grounds of security, violating human or international rights, serious criminality, criminality or organized criminality.

MANDATORY ARREST AND DETENTION — DESIGNATED FOREIGN NATIONAL

(3.1) If a designation is made under subsection 20.1(1), an officer must

(a) detain, on their entry into Canada, a foreign national who, as a result of the designation, is a designated foreign national and who is 16 years of age or older on the day of the arrival that is the subject of the designation; or

(b) arrest and detain without a warrant — or issue a warrant for the arrest and detention of — a foreign national who, after their entry into Canada, becomes a designated foreign national as a result of the designation and who was 16 years of age or older on the day of the arrival that is the subject of the designation.

NOTICE

(4) If a permanent resident or a foreign national is taken into detention, an officer shall without delay give notice to the Immigration Division.

2001, c. 27, s. 55; 2012, c. 17, s. 23.

RELEASE — OFFICER

56 (1) An officer may order the release from detention of a permanent resident or a foreign national before the first detention review by the Immigration Division if the officer is of the opinion that the reasons for the detention no longer exist. The officer may impose any conditions, including the payment of a deposit or the posting of a guarantee for compliance with the conditions, that the officer considers necessary.

PERIOD OF DETENTION — DESIGNATED FOREIGN NATIONAL

(2) Despite subsection (1), a designated foreign national who is detained under this Division and who was 16 years of age or older on the day of the arrival that is the subject of the designation in question must be detained until

(a) a final determination is made to allow their claim for refugee protection or application for protection;

(b) they are released as a result of the Immigration Division ordering their release under section 58; or

(c) they are released as a result of the Minister ordering their release under section 58.1.

CONDITIONS — INADMISSIBILITY ON GROUNDS OF SECURITY

(3) If an officer orders the release of a permanent resident or foreign national who is the subject of either a report on inadmissibility on grounds of security that is referred to the Immigration Division or a removal order for inadmissibility on grounds of security, the officer must also impose the prescribed conditions on the person.

DURATION OF CONDITIONS

(4) The prescribed conditions imposed under subsection (3) cease to apply only when one of the events described in paragraphs 44(5)(a) to (e) occurs.

2001, c. 27, s. 56; 2012, c. 17, s. 24; 2013, c. 16, ss. 22, 36.

REVIEW OF DETENTION

57 (1) Within 48 hours after a permanent resident or a foreign national is taken into detention, or without delay afterward, the Immigration Division must review the reasons for the continued detention.

FURTHER REVIEW

(2) At least once during the seven days following the review under subsection (1), and at least once during each 30-day period following each previous review, the Immigration Division must review the reasons for the continued detention.

PRESENCE

(3) In a review under subsection (1) or (2), an officer shall bring the permanent resident or the foreign national before the Immigration Division or to a place specified by it.

INITIAL REVIEW — DESIGNATED FOREIGN NATIONAL

57.1 (1) Despite subsections 57(1) and (2), in the case of a designated foreign national who was 16 years of age or older on the day of the arrival that is the subject of the designation in question, the Immigration Division must review the reasons for their continued detention within 14 days after the day on which that person is taken into detention, or without delay afterward.

FURTHER REVIEW — DESIGNATED FOREIGN NATIONAL

(2) Despite subsection 57(2), in the case of the designated foreign national referred to in subsection (1), the Immigration Division must review again the reasons for their continued detention on the expiry of six months following the conclusion of the previous review and may not do so before the expiry of that period.

PRESENCE

(3) In a review under subsection (1) or (2), the officer must bring the designated foreign national before the Immigration Division or to a place specified by it.

2012, c. 17, s. 25.

RELEASE — IMMIGRATION DIVISION

58 (1) The Immigration Division shall order the release of a permanent resident or a foreign national unless it is satisfied, taking into account prescribed factors, that

   (a) they are a danger to the public;

   (b) they are unlikely to appear for examination, an admissibility hearing, removal from Canada, or at a proceeding that could lead to the making of a removal order by the Minister under subsection 44(2);

   (c) the Minister is taking necessary steps to inquire into a reasonable suspicion that they are inadmissible on grounds of security, violating human or international rights, serious criminality, criminality or organized criminality;

   (d) the Minister is of the opinion that the identity of the foreign national — other than a designated foreign national who was 16 years of age or older on the day of the arrival that is the subject of the designation in question — has not been, but may be, established and they have not reasonably cooperated with the Minister by providing relevant information for the purpose of establishing their identity or the Minister is making reasonable efforts to establish their identity; or

(e) the Minister is of the opinion that the identity of the foreign national who is a designated foreign national and who was 16 years of age or older on the day of the arrival that is the subject of the designation in question has not been established.

CONTINUED DETENTION — DESIGNATED FOREIGN NATIONAL

(1.1) Despite subsection (1), on the conclusion of a review under subsection 57.1(1), the Immigration Division shall order the continued detention of the designated foreign national if it is satisfied that any of the grounds described in paragraphs (1)(a) to (c) and (e) exist, and it may not consider any other factors.

DETENTION — IMMIGRATION DIVISION

(2) The Immigration Division may order the detention of a permanent resident or a foreign national if it is satisfied that the permanent resident or the foreign national is the subject of an examination or an admissibility hearing or is subject to a removal order and that the permanent resident or the foreign national is a danger to the public or is unlikely to appear for examination, an admissibility hearing or removal from Canada.

CONDITIONS

(3) If the Immigration Division orders the release of a permanent resident or a foreign national, it may impose any conditions that it considers necessary, including the payment of a deposit or the posting of a guarantee for compliance with the conditions.

CONDITIONS — DESIGNATED FOREIGN NATIONAL

(4) If the Immigration Division orders the release of a designated foreign national who 16 years of age was or older on the day of the arrival that is the subject of the designation in question, it shall also impose any condition that is prescribed.

CONDITIONS — INADMISSIBILITY ON GROUNDS OF SECURITY

(5) If the Immigration Division orders the release of a permanent resident or foreign national who is the subject of either a report on inadmissibility on grounds of security that is referred to the Immigration Division or a removal order for inadmissibility on grounds of security, it shall also impose the prescribed conditions on the person.

DURATION OF CONDITIONS

(6) The prescribed conditions imposed under subsection (5) cease to apply only when one of the events described in paragraphs 44(5)(a) to (e) occurs.

2001, c. 27, s. 58; 2012, c. 17, s. 26; 2013, c. 16, ss. 23, 36.

RELEASE — ON REQUEST

58.1 (1) The Minister may, on request of a designated foreign national who 16 years of age was or older on the day of the arrival that is the subject of the designation in question, order their release from detention if, in the Minister's opinion, exceptional circumstances exist that warrant the release.

RELEASE — MINISTER'S OWN INITIATIVE

(2) The Minister may, on the Minister's own initiative, order the release of a designated foreign national who 16 years of age was or older on the day of the arrival that is the subject of the designation in question if, in the Minister's opinion, the reasons for the detention no longer exist.

CONDITIONS

(3) If the Minister orders the release of a designated foreign national, the Minister may impose any conditions, including the payment of a deposit or the posting of a guarantee for compliance with the conditions, that he or she considers necessary.

CONDITIONS — INADMISSIBILITY ON GROUNDS OF SECURITY

(4) If the Minister orders the release of a designated foreign national who is the subject of either a report on inadmissibility on grounds of security that is referred to the Immigration Division or a removal order for inadmissibility on grounds of security, the Minister must also impose the prescribed conditions on the person.

DURATION OF CONDITIONS

(5) The prescribed conditions imposed under subsection (4) cease to apply only when one of the events described in paragraphs 44(5)(a) to (e) occurs.

2012, c. 17, s. 27; 2013, c. 16, s. 36.

INCARCERATED FOREIGN NATIONALS

59 If a warrant for arrest and detention under this Act is issued with respect to a permanent resident or a foreign national who is detained under another Act of Parliament in an institution, the person in charge of the institution shall deliver the inmate to an officer at the end of the inmate's period of detention in the institution.

MINOR CHILDREN

60 For the purposes of this Division, it is affirmed as a principle that a minor child shall be detained only as a measure of last resort, taking into account the other applicable grounds and criteria including the best interests of the child.

REGULATIONS

61 The regulations may provide for the application of this Division, and may include provisions respecting
- **(a)** grounds for and criteria with respect to the release of persons from detention;
  - **(a.1)** the type of conditions that an officer, the Immigration Division or the Minister may impose with respect to the release of a person from detention;
  - **(a.2)** the type of conditions that the Immigration Division must impose with respect to the release of a designated foreign national who was 16 years of age or older on the day of the arrival that is the subject of the designation in question;
  - **(a.3)** the conditions that an officer, the Immigration Division or the Minister must impose with respect to the release of a permanent resident or foreign national who is the subject of either a report on inadmissibility on grounds of security or a removal order for inadmissibility on grounds of security;
- **(b)** factors to be considered by an officer or the Immigration Division; and
- **(c)** special considerations that may apply in relation to the detention of minor children.

2001, c. 27, s. 61; 2012, c. 17, s. 28; 2013, c. 16, s. 36.

Appendix B

IMMIGRATION AND REFUGEE PROTECTION REGULATIONS, SECTIONS 244–250

Part 14: Detention and Release

FACTORS TO BE CONSIDERED

244 For the purposes of Division 6 of Part 1 of the Act, the factors set out in this Part shall be taken into consideration when assessing whether a person

   (a) is unlikely to appear for examination, an admissibility hearing, removal from Canada, or at a proceeding that could lead to the making of a removal order by the Minister under subsection 44(2) of the Act;

   (b) is a danger to the public; or

   (c) is a foreign national whose identity has not been established.

FLIGHT RISK

245 For the purposes of paragraph 244(a), the factors are the following:

   (a) being a fugitive from justice in a foreign jurisdiction in relation to an offence that, if committed in Canada, would constitute an offence under an Act of Parliament;

   (b) voluntary compliance with any previous departure order;

   (c) voluntary compliance with any previously required appearance at an immigration or criminal proceeding;

(d) previous compliance with any conditions imposed in respect of entry, release or a stay of removal;

(e) any previous avoidance of examination or escape from custody, or any previous attempt to do so;

(f) involvement with a people smuggling or trafficking in persons operation that would likely lead the person to not appear for a measure referred to in paragraph 244(a) or to be vulnerable to being influenced or coerced by an organization involved in such an operation to not appear for such a measure; and

(g) the existence of strong ties to a community in Canada.

DANGER TO THE PUBLIC

246 For the purposes of paragraph 244(b), the factors are the following:

(a) the fact that the person constitutes, in the opinion of the Minister, a danger to the public in Canada or a danger to the security of Canada under paragraph 101(2)(b), subparagraph 113(d)(i) or (ii) or paragraph 115(2)(a) or (b) of the Act;

(b) association with a criminal organization within the meaning of subsection 121(2) of the Act;

(c) engagement in people smuggling or trafficking in persons;

(d) conviction in Canada under an Act of Parliament for

  (i) a sexual offence, or

  (ii) an offence involving violence or weapons;

(e) conviction for an offence in Canada under any of the following provisions of the *Controlled Drugs and Substances Act*, namely,

  (i) section 5 (trafficking),

  (ii) section 6 (importing and exporting), and

  (iii) section 7 (production);

(f) conviction outside Canada, or the existence of pending charges outside Canada, for an offence that, if committed in Canada, would constitute an offence under an Act of Parliament for

  (i) a sexual offence, or

  (ii) an offence involving violence or weapons; and

(g) conviction outside Canada, or the existence of pending charges outside Canada, for an offence that, if committed in Canada, would constitute an offence under any of the following provisions of the *Controlled Drugs and Substances Act*, namely,

(i) section 5 (trafficking),

(ii) section 6 (importing and exporting), and

(iii) section 7 (production).

SOR/2016-136, s. 13(F); SOR/2018-170, s. 2.

IDENTITY NOT ESTABLISHED

247 (1) For the purposes of paragraph 244(c), the factors are the following:

(a) the foreign national's cooperation in providing evidence of their identity or assisting the Department or the Canada Border Services Agency in obtaining evidence of their identity, in providing the date and place of their birth as well as the names of their mother and father, in providing detailed information on the itinerary they followed in travelling to Canada or in completing an application for a travel document;

(b) in the case of a foreign national who makes a claim for refugee protection, the possibility of obtaining identity documents or information without divulging personal information to government officials of their country of nationality or, if there is no country of nationality, their country of former habitual residence;

(c) the foreign national's destruction of their identity or travel documents, or the use of fraudulent documents by the foreign national in order to mislead the Department or the Canada Border Services Agency, and the circumstances under which the foreign national acted;

(d) the provision of contradictory information by the foreign national with respect to their identity during the processing of an application by the Department or the Canada Border Services Agency; and

(e) the existence of documents that contradict information provided by the foreign national with respect to their identity.

NON-APPLICATION TO MINORS

(2) Consideration of the factors set out in paragraph (1)(a) shall not have an adverse impact with respect to minor children referred to in section 249.

SOR/2004-167, s. 65(E); SOR/2016-136, s. 14(E); SOR/2017-214, s. 6.

OTHER FACTORS

248 If it is determined that there are grounds for detention, the following factors shall be considered before a decision is made on detention or release:

(a) the reason for detention;

(b) the length of time in detention;

(c) whether there are any elements that can assist in determining the length of time that detention is likely to continue and, if so, that length of time;

(d) any unexplained delays or unexplained lack of diligence caused by the Department, the Canada Border Services Agency or the person concerned; and

(e) the existence of alternatives to detention.

SOR/2017-214, s. 7.

SPECIAL CONSIDERATIONS FOR MINOR CHILDREN

249 For the application of the principle affirmed in section 60 of the Act that a minor child shall be detained only as a measure of last resort, the special considerations that apply in relation to the detention of minor children who are less than 18 years of age are

(a) the availability of alternative arrangements with local child-care agencies or child protection services for the care and protection of the minor children;

(b) the anticipated length of detention;

(c) the risk of continued control by the human smugglers or traffickers who brought the children to Canada;

(d) the type of detention facility envisaged and the conditions of detention;

(e) the availability of accommodation that allows for the segregation of the minor children from adult detainees who are not the parent of or the adult legally responsible for the detained minor children; and

(f) the availability of services in the detention facility, including education, counselling and recreation.

Applications for travel documents

250 If a completed application for a passport or travel document must be provided as a condition of release from detention, any completed application provided by a foreign national who makes a claim for refugee protection shall not be divulged to government officials of their country of nationality or, if there is no country of nationality, their country of previous habitual residence, as long as the removal order to which the foreign national is subject is not enforceable.

Part 15: Prescribed Conditions

INADMISSIBILITY ON GROUNDS OF SECURITY — CONDITIONS

250.1 For the purposes of subsections 44(4), 56(3), 58(5), 58.1(4), 77.1(1) and 82(6) of the Act, the conditions that must be imposed on a foreign national or permanent resident are the following:

    (a) to inform the Canada Border Services Agency in writing of their address and, in advance, of any change in that address;

    (b) to inform the Canada Border Services Agency in writing of their employer's name and the address of their place of employment and, in advance, of any change in that information;

    (c) unless they are otherwise required to report to the Canada Border Services Agency because of a condition imposed under subsection 44(3), 56(1), 58(3) or 58.1(3) or paragraph 82(5)(b) of the Act, to report once each month to the Agency;

    (d) to present themselves at the time and place that an officer, the Immigration Division, the Minister or the Federal Court requires them to appear to comply with any obligation imposed on them under the Act;

    (e) to produce to the Canada Border Services Agency without delay the original of any passport and travel and identity documents that they hold, or that they obtain, in order to permit the Agency to make copies of those documents;

    (f) if a removal order made against them comes into force, to surrender to the Canada Border Services Agency without delay any passport and travel document that they hold;

    (g) if a removal order made against them comes into force and they do not hold a document that is required to remove them from Canada, to take without delay any action that is necessary to ensure that the document is provided to the Canada Border Services Agency, such as by producing an application or producing evidence verifying their identity;

    (h) to not commit an offence under an Act of Parliament or an offence that, if committed in Canada, would constitute an offence under an Act of Parliament;

    (i) if they are charged with an offence under an Act of Parliament or an offence that, if committed in Canada, would constitute an offence under an Act of Parliament, to inform the Canada Border Services Agency of that charge in writing and without delay;

(j) if they are convicted of an offence under an Act of Parliament or an offence that, if committed in Canada, would constitute an offence under an Act of Parliament, to inform the Canada Border Services Agency of that conviction in writing and without delay; and

(k) if they intend to leave Canada, to inform the Canada Border Services Agency in writing of the date on which they intend to leave Canada.

SOR/2017-214, s. 8.

Appendix C

IMMIGRATION DIVISION RULES

SOR/2002-229

IMMIGRATION AND REFUGEE PROTECTION ACT
Registration 2002-06-11
Immigration Division Rules
P.C. 2002-999 2002-06-11

The Chairperson of the Immigration and Refugee Board, pursuant to subsection 161(1) of the *Immigration and Refugee Protection Act*[a] and subject to the approval of the Governor in Council, in consultation with the Deputy Chairpersons and the Director General of the Immigration Division, hereby makes the annexed *Immigration Division Rules*.

Ottawa, May 7, 2002

Her Excellency the Governor General in Council, on the recommendation of the Minister of Citizenship and Immigration, pursuant to subsection 161(1) of the *Immigration and Refugee Protection Act*,[a] hereby approves the annexed *Immigration Division Rules*, made on May 7, 2002 by the Chairperson of the Immigration and Refugee Board, in consultation with the Deputy Chairpersons and the Director General of the Immigration Division.

[a]S.C. 2001, c. 27

Definitions

DEFINITIONS

1 The following definitions apply in these Rules.

Act means the Immigration and Refugee Protection Act. (*Loi*)

admissibility hearing means a hearing held under subsection 44(2) of the Act. (*enquête*)

contact information means a person's name, postal address and telephone number and the person's fax number and electronic mail address, if any. (*coordonnées*)

detention review means a forty-eight-hour review, a seven-day review and a thirty-day review. (*contrôle des motifs de détention*)

Division means the Immigration Division. (*Section*)

forty-eight-hour review means the review of the reasons for continued detention under subsection 57(1) of the Act. (*contrôle des quarante-huit heures*)

party means a permanent resident or foreign national, as the case may be, and the Minister. (*partie*)

proceeding means an admissibility hearing, a detention review, a conference or an application. (*procédure*)

registry office means a business office of the Division. (*greffe*)

seven-day review means the review of the reasons for continued detention required to be held during the seven days following a forty-eight-hour review, under subsection 57(2) of the Act. (*contrôle des sept jours*)

thirty-day review means the review of the reasons for continued detention required to be held during the thirty days following each previous review, under subsection 57(2) of the Act. (*contrôle des trente jours*)

Communicating with the Division

COMMUNICATING WITH THE DIVISION

2   All communication with the Division must be directed to the registry office specified by the Division.

Part 1: Rules Applicable to Admissibility Hearings

Information

INFORMATION PROVIDED BY THE MINISTER

3   When the Minister requests the Division to hold an admissibility hearing, the Minister must provide to the Division and the permanent resident or foreign national, as the case may be, any relevant information or document that the Minister may have, including

(a) the name and other contact information in Canada of the permanent resident or foreign national;
(b) the person's date of birth, sex and citizenship;
(c) whether the person is single, married, separated or divorced or is a common-law partner;
(d) the inadmissibility report and the Minister's referral;
(e) whether the person has made a claim for refugee protection;
(f) the name and address of the place of detention, if the person is detained;
(g) the language — English or French — chosen by the person for communicating with the Division;
(h) if an interpreter is required, the language or dialect to be interpreted;
(i) if the person has counsel, the counsel's contact information;
(j) the client identification number given to the person by the Department of Citizenship and Immigration;
(k) the names, sex, date of birth, citizenship, and other contact information of any family member whose case has been referred to the Division, and the client identification number given to them by the Department of Citizenship and Immigration;
(l) the date on which the Minister makes the request;
(m) the name and title of the Minister's counsel;
(n) whether the Minister has made an application for non-disclosure of information;
(o) whether the Minister believes that the person is less than 18 years of age or is unable to appreciate the nature of the proceedings; and
(p) the evidence to be presented by the Minister.

CHANGE TO CONTACT INFORMATION

4   If the contact information changes, the permanent resident or foreign national, unless detained, must without delay provide the changes in writing to the Division and the Minister.

Withdrawing a Request by the Minister for an Admissibility Hearing

ABUSE OF PROCESS

5 (1)   Withdrawal of a request for an admissibility hearing is an abuse of process if withdrawal would likely have a negative effect on the integrity of

the Division. If no substantive evidence has been accepted in the proceedings, withdrawal of a request is not an abuse of process.

WITHDRAWAL IF NO EVIDENCE HAS BEEN ACCEPTED

(2) If no substantive evidence has been accepted in the proceedings, the Minister may withdraw a request by notifying the Division orally at a proceeding or in writing. If the Minister notifies in writing, the Minister must provide a copy of the notice to the other party.

WITHDRAWAL IF EVIDENCE HAS BEEN ACCEPTED

(3) If substantive evidence has been accepted in the proceedings, the Minister must make a written application to the Division in order to withdraw a request.

Reinstating a Request by the Minister for an Admissibility Hearing

APPLICATION FOR REINSTATEMENT OF WITHDRAWN REQUEST

6 (1) The Minister may make a written application to the Division to reinstate a request for an admissibility hearing that was withdrawn.

FACTORS

(2) The Division must allow the application if it is established that there was a failure to observe a principle of natural justice or if it is otherwise in the interests of justice to allow the application.

FAVOURABLE DECISION

7 (1) If the decision at the conclusion of an admissibility hearing is in favour of the permanent resident or foreign national, the member making the decision must date and sign a notice of decision and provide a copy to the parties.

UNFAVOURABLE DECISION

(2) If the decision is not in favour of the permanent resident or foreign national, the member must date and sign an order indicating the applicable provisions of the Act and provide a copy to the parties. The member must also notify the permanent resident or foreign national of
   (a) their right to appeal to the Immigration Appeal Division; or
   (b) if they do not have the right to appeal, their right to file an application for judicial review in the Federal Court.

WHEN DECISION TAKES EFFECT

(3) A decision made orally at a hearing takes effect when a Division member states the decision. A decision made in writing takes effect when the member signs and dates it.

REQUEST FOR WRITTEN REASONS

(4) A request made by a party for written reasons for a decision may be made orally at the end of an admissibility hearing or in writing. A request in writing must be received by the Division no later than 10 days after the decision takes effect.

Part 2: Rules Applicable to Detention Reviews

Information

INFORMATION PROVIDED BY THE MINISTER

8 (1) If a foreign national or a permanent resident is subject to a detention review, the Minister must provide the Division and the person detained with the following information:

(a) the person's name, sex, date of birth and citizenship;

(b) whether the person is single, married, separated or divorced or is a common-law partner;

(c) whether the person has made a claim for refugee protection;

(d) the language — English or French — chosen by the person for communicating with the Division;

(e) if an interpreter is required, the language or dialect to be interpreted;

(f) if the person has counsel, the counsel's contact information;

(g) the date and time that the person was first placed in detention;

(h) the name and address of the place where the person is being detained;

(i) whether the Minister is seeking a detention review after the first forty-eight-hour detention or after a seven-day or thirty-day review;

(j) the identification number given to the person by the Department of Citizenship and Immigration;

(k) the provision of the Act under which the review of the reasons for continued detention is required;

(l) whether an application for non-disclosure of information has been made; and

(m) whether the Minister believes that the person is less than 18 years of age or is unable to appreciate the nature of the proceedings.

TIME LIMIT

(2) The information must be received by the Division and the person detained

(a) in the case of a forty-eight-hour review, as soon as possible; and

(b) in the case of a seven-day or thirty-day review, at least three days before the date fixed for the review.

APPLICATION FOR EARLY REVIEW

9 (1) A party may make a written application to the Division requesting a detention review before the expiry of the seven-day or thirty-day period, as the case may be.

FACTOR

(2) The Division may allow the application if the party sets out new facts that justify an early review of the detention.

REMOVAL BEFORE DETENTION REVIEW

10 The Minister must notify the Division as soon as a permanent resident or foreign national is removed from Canada prior to a scheduled detention review.

Decisions

NOTICE TO THE PARTIES

11 (1) At the conclusion of a detention review, the member must notify the parties of the member's decision.

ORDER

(2) The member must date and sign an order for detention or release indicating the applicable provisions of the Act and provide a copy to the parties.

WHEN DECISION TAKES EFFECT

(3) A decision made orally at a hearing takes effect when a Division member states the decision. A decision made in writing takes effect when the member signs and dates it.

REQUEST FOR WRITTEN REASONS

(4) A request made by a party for written reasons for a decision may be made orally at the end of a detention review or in writing. A request in writing must be received by the Division no later than 10 days after the decision takes effect.

Part 3: Rules that Apply to Both Admissibility Hearings and Detention Reviews

Information Relating to Counsel

COUNSEL'S CONTACT INFORMATION

12 A permanent resident or foreign national who is represented by counsel must, on obtaining counsel, provide the counsel's contact information in writing to the Division and the Minister. If that information changes, the permanent resident or foreign national must without delay provide the changes in writing to the Division and the Minister.

Counsel of Record

BECOMING COUNSEL OF RECORD

13 As soon as counsel for a permanent resident or foreign national agrees to a date for a proceeding, or becomes counsel after a date has been fixed, the counsel becomes counsel of record.

WITHDRAWAL AS COUNSEL OF RECORD

14 To withdraw as counsel of record, counsel must notify the Division and the Minister in writing as soon as possible. Counsel is no longer counsel of record as soon as the Division receives the notice.

REMOVAL OF COUNSEL OF RECORD

15 To remove counsel as counsel of record, the permanent resident or foreign national must notify the Division and the Minister in writing as soon as possible. Counsel is no longer counsel of record when the Division receives the notice.

Language of Proceedings

CHANGING THE LANGUAGE OF PROCEEDINGS

16 (1) A permanent resident or foreign national may make an application to the Division to change the language of the proceedings to English or French
   (a) orally or in writing in the case of a forty-eight hour or seven-day review or an admissibility hearing held at the same time; and
   (b) in writing in all other cases.

TIME LIMIT

(2) A written application must be received by the Division
   (a) as soon as possible, in the case of a forty-eight hour or seven-day review or an admissibility hearing held at the same time; and
   (b) in all other cases, at least five days before the hearing.

REQUESTING AN INTERPRETER

17 (1) If a party or a party's witness needs an interpreter for a proceeding, the party must notify the Division in writing and specify the language or dialect of the interpreter. The notice must be received by the Division

    (a) as soon as possible, in the case of a forty-eight hour or seven-day review or an admissibility hearing held at the same time; and

    (b) in all other cases, at least five days before the hearing.

INTERPRETER'S OATH

    (2) The interpreter must take an oath or make a solemn affirmation to interpret accurately.

Designated Representatives

DUTY OF COUNSEL TO NOTIFY THE DIVISION

18 If counsel for a party believes that the Division should designate a representative for the permanent resident or foreign national in the proceedings because they are under 18 years of age or unable to appreciate the nature of the proceedings, counsel must without delay notify the Division and the other party in writing. If counsel is aware of a person in Canada who meets the requirements to be designated as a representative, counsel must provide the person's contact information in the notice.

REQUIREMENTS FOR BEING DESIGNATED

19 To be designated as a representative, a person must

    (a) be 18 years of age or older;

    (b) understand the nature of the proceedings;

    (c) be willing and able to act in the best interests of the permanent resident or foreign national; and

    (d) not have interests that conflict with those of the permanent resident or foreign national.

Conference

REQUIREMENT TO PARTICIPATE AT A CONFERENCE

20 (1) The Division may require the parties to participate at a conference to discuss issues, relevant facts and any other matter that would make the proceedings more fair and efficient.

INFORMATION OR DOCUMENTS

(2) The Division may require the parties to give any information or document at or before the conference.

DECISIONS NOTED

(3) The Division must make a written record of any decisions and agreements made at the conference or state them orally at the hearing.

Fixing a Date

FIXING A DATE

21 The Division must fix the date for a hearing and any other proceeding relating to the hearing. The Division may require the parties to participate in the preparation of a schedule of proceedings by appearing at a scheduling conference or otherwise providing information.

Notice to Appear

NOTICE TO APPEAR

22 The Division must notify the parties, orally or in writing, of the date, time and location of a hearing.

Permanent Resident or Foreign National in Custody

ORDER

23 The Division may order the person who holds a permanent resident or foreign national in custody to bring the permanent resident or foreign national to a hearing at a location specified by the Division.

Documents

Form and Language of Documents

DOCUMENTS PREPARED BY PARTY

24 (1) A document prepared for use by a party in a proceeding must be typewritten on one side of 21.5 cm by 28 cm (8½" x 11") paper and the pages must be numbered.

PHOTOCOPIES

(2) Any photocopy provided by a party must be a clear copy of the document photocopied and be on one side of 21.5 cm by 28 cm (8½" x 11") paper and the pages must be numbered.

NUMBERED DOCUMENTS

(3) A party must number consecutively each document provided by the party.

LIST OF DOCUMENTS

(4) If more than one document is provided, the party must provide a list of the documents and their numbers.

LANGUAGE OF DOCUMENTS

25 (1) All documents used at a proceeding must be in English or French or, if in another language, be provided with an English or French translation and a translator's declaration.

LANGUAGE OF MINISTER'S DOCUMENTS

(2) If the Minister provides a document that is not in the language of the proceedings, the Minister must provide a translation and a translator's declaration.

TRANSLATOR'S DECLARATION

(3) A translator's declaration must include the translator's name, the language translated and a statement signed by the translator that the translation is accurate.

Disclosure of Documents

DISCLOSURE OF DOCUMENTS BY A PARTY

26 If a party wants to use a document at a hearing, the party must provide a copy to the other party and the Division. The copies must be received

(a) as soon as possible, in the case of a forty-eight hour or seven-day review or an admissibility hearing held at the same time; and

(b) in all other cases, at least five days before the hearing.

How to Provide a Document

GENERAL PROVISION

27 Rules 28 to 31 apply to any document, including a notice or a written request or application.

PROVIDING DOCUMENTS TO THE DIVISION

28 (1) A document provided to the Division must be provided to a Division member at a proceeding or to the registry office specified by the Division.

PROVIDING DOCUMENTS TO THE MINISTER

(2) A document provided to the Minister must be provided to the Minister's counsel.

PROVIDING DOCUMENTS TO A PERMANENT RESIDENT OR FOREIGN NATIONAL

(3) A document provided to a permanent resident or foreign national must be provided to them or, if they have counsel, to their counsel.

HOW TO PROVIDE A DOCUMENT

29 A document can be provided in the following ways:
   (a) by hand;
   (b) by regular mail or registered mail;
   (c) by courier or priority post;
   (d) by fax if the recipient has a fax number and the document has no more than 20 pages, unless the recipient consents to receiving more than 20 pages; and
   (e) by electronic mail if the Division allows.

IF DOCUMENT CANNOT BE PROVIDED UNDER RULE 29

30 If a party after making reasonable efforts is unable to provide a document in a way required by rule 29, the party may make an application to the Division to be allowed to provide the document in another way or to be excused from providing the document.

WHEN A DOCUMENT IS CONSIDERED RECEIVED BY THE DIVISION

31 (1) A document provided to the Division is considered received by the Division on the day the document is date stamped by the Division.

WHEN A DOCUMENT PROVIDED BY REGULAR MAIL IS CONSIDERED RECEIVED BY A PARTY

(2) A document provided by regular mail to a party is considered to be received seven days after the day it was mailed. If the seventh day is a Saturday, Sunday or other statutory holiday, the document is considered to be received on the next working day.

Witnesses

PROVIDING WITNESS INFORMATION

32 (1) If a party wants to call a witness, the party must provide in writing to the other party and the Division the following witness information:

(a) the purpose and substance of the witness's testimony or, in the case of an expert witness, a summary of the testimony to be given signed by the expert witness;

(b) the time needed for the witness's testimony;

(c) the party's relationship to the witness;

(d) in the case of an expert witness, a description of their qualifications;

(e) whether the party wants the witness to testify by videoconference or telephone; and

(f) the number of witnesses that the party intends to call.

TIME LIMIT

(2) The witness information must be received by the Division and the other party

(a) as soon as possible in the case of a forty-eight hour or seven-day review or an admissibility hearing held at the same time; and

(b) in all other cases, at least five days before the hearing.

APPLICATION FOR A SUMMONS

33 (1) A party who wants the Division to order a person to testify at a hearing must make an application to the Division for a summons, either orally at a proceeding or in writing.

FACTORS

(2) In deciding whether to issue a summons, the Division must consider any relevant factors, including

(a) the necessity of the testimony to a full and proper hearing; and

(b) the ability of the person to give that testimony.

USING THE SUMMONS

(3) If a party wants to use a summons, the party must

(a) provide the summons to the summoned person by hand;

(b) provide a copy of the summons to the Division with a written statement of how and when the summons was provided; and

(c) pay or offer to pay the summoned person the applicable witness fees and travel expenses set out in Tariff A of the *Federal Court Rules, 1998*.

CANCELLING A SUMMONS

34 A person summoned to appear may make a written application to the Division to cancel the summons.

ARREST WARRANT

35 (1) If a person does not obey a summons to appear, the party who requested the summons may make a written application to the Division to issue a warrant for the arrest of the person.

SUPPORTING EVIDENCE

(2) The party must provide supporting evidence for the written application by affidavit or statutory declaration.

REQUIREMENTS FOR ISSUE OF ARREST WARRANT

(3) The Division may issue a warrant if
- **(a)** the person was provided the summons by hand or the person is avoiding being provided the summons;
- **(b)** the person was paid or offered the applicable witness fees and travel expenses set out in Tariff A of the *Federal Court Rules, 1998*;
- **(c)** the person did not appear at the hearing as required by the summons; and
- **(d)** the person's testimony is still needed for a full and proper hearing.

CONTENT OF A WARRANT

(4) A warrant issued by the Division for the arrest of a person must include directions concerning detention and release.

EXCLUDED WITNESS

36 Unless allowed by the Division, no person shall communicate to a witness excluded from a hearing room any testimony given while the witness was excluded until that witness has finished testifying.

Applications

GENERAL PROVISION

37 Unless these Rules provide otherwise, a party
- **(a)** who wants the Division to make a decision on any matter in a proceeding, including the procedure to be followed, must make an application to the Division under rule 38;
- **(b)** who wants to respond to the application must respond under rule 39; and
- **(c)** who wants to reply to a response must reply under rule 40.

How to Make an Application

APPLICATION TO THE DIVISION

38 (1) Unless these Rules provide otherwise, an application must follow this rule.

TIME LIMIT AND FORM OF APPLICATION

(2) The application must be made orally or in writing, and as soon as possible or within the time limit provided in the Act or these Rules.

PROCEDURE IN ORAL APPLICATION

(3) For an application made orally, the Division determines the applicable procedure.

CONTENT OF WRITTEN APPLICATION

(4) A party who makes a written application must

   (a) state the decision that the party wants the Division to make;

   (b) give reasons why the Division should make that decision;

   (c) include any evidence that the party wants the Division to consider in deciding the application; and

   (d) in the case of an application that is not specified in these Rules, include supporting evidence in the form of a statutory declaration or affidavit.

PROVIDING THE APPLICATION

(5) A party who makes a written application must provide

   (a) to the other party, a copy of the application; and

   (b) to the Division, the original application, together with a written statement of how and when the party provided the copy to the other party.

How to Respond to a Written Application

RESPONDING TO A WRITTEN APPLICATION

39 (1) A response to a written application must be in writing. In a response the party must

   (a) state the decision the party wants the Division to make;

   (b) give reasons why the Division should make that decision;

   (c) include any evidence that the party wants the Division to consider when it decides the application; and

   (d) include supporting evidence in the form of a statutory declaration or affidavit, if the response is to an application that is not provided for by these Rules.

PROVIDING THE RESPONSE

(2) A party who responds to a written application must provide

(a) to the other party, a copy of the response; and

(b) to the Division, the original response, together with a written statement of how and when the party provided the copy to the other party.

TIME LIMIT

(3) Documents provided under this rule must be received by their recipients

(a) as soon as possible, in the case of a forty-eight hour or seven-day review or an admissibility hearing held at the same time; and

(b) in all other cases, no later than five days after the party received a copy of the application.

How to Reply to a Written Response

REPLYING TO A WRITTEN RESPONSE

40 (1) A reply to a written response must be in writing.

PROVIDING THE REPLY

(2) A party who replies must provide

(a) to the other party, a copy of the reply; and

(b) to the Division, the original reply, together with a written statement of how and when the party provided the copy to the other party.

TIME LIMIT

(3) Documents provided under this rule must be received by their recipients

(a) as soon as possible, in the case of a forty-eight hour or seven-day review or an admissibility hearing held at the same time; and

(b) in all other cases, no later than three days after the party received a copy of the response.

Non-disclosure of Information

APPLICATION TO PROHIBIT DISCLOSURE

41 (1) An application made by the Minister for non-disclosure of information must be made in writing as soon as possible.

EXCLUSION FROM HEARING ROOM

(2) If an application is made during a hearing, the Division must exclude the permanent resident or foreign national, and their counsel, from the hearing room.

PROVIDING SUMMARY TO THE MINISTER

(3) The summary that the Division proposes to provide to the permanent resident or foreign national under paragraph 78(h) of the Act may be provided to the Minister by any means that ensures its confidentiality.

Changing the Location of a Hearing

APPLICATION TO CHANGE THE LOCATION OF A HEARING

42 (1) A party may make an application to the Division to change the location of a hearing.

FACTORS

(2) In deciding the application, the Division must consider any relevant factors, including

    (a) whether a change of location would allow the hearing to be full and proper;

    (b) whether a change of location would likely delay or slow the hearing;

    (c) how a change of location would affect the operation of the Division;

    (d) how a change of location would affect the parties; and

    (e) whether a change of location would endanger public safety.

DUTY TO APPEAR AT THE HEARING

(3) Unless a party receives a decision from the Division allowing the application, the party must appear for the hearing at the location fixed and be ready to start or continue the hearing.

Changing the Date or Time of a Hearing

APPLICATION TO CHANGE THE DATE OR TIME OF A HEARING

43 (1) A party may make an application to the Division to change the date or time of a hearing.

FACTORS

(2) In deciding the application, the Division must consider any relevant factors, including

    (a) in the case of a date and time that was fixed after the Division consulted or tried to consult the party, the existence of exceptional circumstances for allowing the application;

    (b) when the party made the application;

    (c) the time the party has had to prepare for the hearing;

(d) the efforts made by the party to be ready to start or continue the hearing;

(e) the nature and complexity of the matter to be heard;

(f) whether the party has counsel;

(g) any previous delays and the reasons for them;

(h) whether the time and date fixed for the hearing was peremptory; and

(i) whether allowing the application would unreasonably delay the proceedings or likely cause an injustice.

DUTY TO APPEAR AT THE HEARING

(3) Unless a party receives a decision from the Division allowing the application, the party must appear for the hearing at the date and time fixed and be ready to start or continue the hearing.

Joining or Separating Hearings

APPLICATION TO JOIN HEARINGS

44 (1) A party may make an application to the Division to join hearings.

APPLICATION TO SEPARATE HEARINGS

(2) A party may make an application to the Division to separate hearings that are joined.

FACTORS

(3) Before deciding an application, the Division must consider any information provided by the applicant and any other relevant information, including

(a) whether the hearings involve similar questions of law or fact;

(b) whether allowing the application would promote the efficient administration of the work of the Division; and

(c) whether allowing the application would likely cause an injustice.

Proceedings Conducted in Private

APPLICATION FOR PROCEEDING CONDUCTED IN PRIVATE

45 (1) A person who makes an application to the Division to have a proceeding conducted in private must apply in writing and follow this rule.

CONTENT OF APPLICATION

(2) In the application, the person must state the decision that the person wants the Division to make and may request that the hearing of the application be conducted in private.

PROVIDING THE APPLICATION

(3) The person must provide a copy of the application to the parties and the original application to the Division.

TIME LIMIT

(4) A document provided under this rule must be received by its recipient

 (a) as soon as possible, in the case of a forty-eight hour or seven-day review or an admissibility hearing held at the same time; and

 (b) in all other cases, at least five days before the hearing.

HEARING OF THE APPLICATION

(5) At the hearing, the person must give reasons why the Division should conduct the proceeding in private and present any evidence that the person wants the Division to consider in deciding the application.

Proceeding Conducted in Public

APPLICATION FOR PROCEEDING CONDUCTED IN PUBLIC

46 (1) A person who makes an application to the Division to have a proceeding conducted in public must apply in writing and follow this rule.

CONTENT OF APPLICATION

(2) In the application, the person must

 (a) state the decision that the person wants the Division to make;

 (b) give reasons why the Division should make that decision; and

 (c) include any evidence that the person wants the Division to consider in deciding the application.

PROVIDING THE APPLICATION

(3) The person must provide the original application and two copies to the Division. The Division must provide a copy of the application to the parties.

TIME LIMIT

(4) A document provided under this rule must be received by the Division

 (a) as soon as possible, in the case of a forty-eight hour or seven-day review or an admissibility hearing held at the same time; and

 (b) in all other cases, at least five days before the hearing.

Notice of Constitutional Question

NOTICE OF CONSTITUTIONAL QUESTION

47 (1) A party who wants to challenge the constitutional validity, applicability or operability of a legislative provision must complete a notice of constitutional question.

FORM AND CONTENT OF NOTICE

(2) The party must provide notice using either Form 69, "Notice of Constitutional Question", set out in the *Federal Court Rules, 1998*, or any other form that includes

   (a) the name of the party;

   (b) the Division file number;

   (c) the date, time and place of the hearing;

   (d) the specific legislative provision that is being challenged;

   (e) the relevant facts relied on to support the constitutional challenge; and

   (f) a summary of the legal argument to be made in support of the constitutional challenge.

PROVIDING THE NOTICE

(3) The party must provide

   (a) a copy of the notice of constitutional question to the Attorney General of Canada and to the attorney general of every province and territory of Canada, in accordance with section 57 of the *Federal Courts Act*;

   (b) a copy of the notice to the other party; and

   (c) the original notice to the Division, together with a written statement of how and when a copy of the notice was provided under paragraphs (a) and (b).

TIME LIMIT

(4) Documents provided under this rule must be received by their recipients no later than 10 days before the day the constitutional argument will be made.

2002, c. 8, s. 182.

Oral Representations

ORAL REPRESENTATIONS

48 Representations made by a party must be made orally at the end of a hearing unless the Division orders otherwise.

General Provisions

NO APPLICABLE RULE

49 In the absence of a provision in these Rules dealing with a matter raised during the proceedings, the Division may do whatever is necessary to deal with the matter.

POWERS OF THE DIVISION

50 The Division may

(a) act on its own, without a party having to make an application or request to the Division;

(b) change a requirement of a rule;

(c) excuse a person from a requirement of a rule; and

(d) extend or shorten a time limit, before or after the time limit has passed.

FAILING TO FOLLOW A RULE

51 Unless proceedings are declared invalid by the Division, a failure to follow any requirement of these Rules does not make the proceedings invalid.

Coming into Force

COMING INTO FORCE

52 These Rules come into force on the day on which section 161 of the Act comes into force.

[Note: Rules in force June 28, 2002, *see* SI/2002-97.]

Appendix D

CHAIRPERSON'S GUIDELINES ON DETENTION

Effective Date: April 1, 2019

Guidelines Issued by the Chairperson, Pursuant to paragraph 159(1)(h) of the Immigration and Refugee Protection Act

TABLE OF CONTENTS

1. Objectives and Principles
2. Grounds for Detention
    2.1 General Principles
    2.2 Danger to the Public (Section 58(1)(a))
    2.3 Unlikely to Appear (Section 58(1)(b))
    2.4 Minister Inquiring into Security, Violations of Human or International Rights, Criminality, Serious Criminality or Organized Criminality (Section 58(1)(c))
    2.5 Identity of Foreign National Not Established (Section 58(1)(d))

3. Release and Alternatives to Detention
    3.1 General principles
    3.2 Release considerations
    3.3 Bondspersons
    3.4 Change in Conditions

4. Minors
5. Vulnerable Persons
6. Designated Representatives
7. Conducting the Detention Review – Robust Hearing
   7.1 Accessible Hearings
   7.2 Fresh Determination
   7.3 Disclosure and Evidence
8. Sufficiency of Reasons for Decision
9. Statutory Timeframes
10. Enquiries

Annex A – Immigration and Refugee Protection Act
Annex B – Immigration and Refugee Protection Regulations

1. Objectives and Principles

1.1.1 The objective of this Guideline is to assist members of the Immigration Division of the Immigration and Refugee Board (IRB) in carrying out their duties as decision-makers by promoting consistency, coherence and fairness in the review of detention.

1.1.2 Although Chairperson's guidelines are not binding, members are expected to follow them, unless compelling or exceptional reasons exist to depart from them.[1] Members must explain in their reasons why they are not following a guideline when, based on the facts or circumstances of the case, they would otherwise be expected to follow it.

1.1.3 Canadian law regards detention as an exceptional measure. This general principle emerges from statute and case law, and is enshrined in the *Canadian Charter of Rights and Freedoms*[2] (the Charter). *International law, as reflected in the International Covenant on Civil and Political Rights*, the *Optional Protocol to the International Covenant on Civil and Political Rights* and the *Convention on the Rights of the Child*, respects the same principle.[3]

1.1.4 The members of the IRB's Immigration Division are required to conduct detention reviews regarding permanent residents and foreign nationals who are detained under Division 6 of Part 1 of the *Immigration and Refugee Protection Act* (IRPA).[4] The detention reviews must be conducted in accordance with the IRPA,[5] the *Immigration and Refugee Protection Regulations* (IRPR), the *Immigration Division Rules*, the Charter, international law, and the jurisprudence.

1.1.5 This Guideline provides guidance with respect to the detention review process under the IRPA for the grounds enumerated in section 58(1).[6]

1.1.6 Under IRPA, members of the Immigration Division must order the release of a permanent resident or a foreign national unless one of the grounds for detention is met. At a detention review, the onus is always on the Minister[7] to demonstrate, on a balance of probabilities, that there are reasons which warrant detention in all circumstances of the case. Members must ensure that the onus and evidentiary burden remains on the Minister at every detention review.[8]

1.1.7 Members must take into account the prescribed factors set out in Part 14 of the IRPR that relate to the grounds for detention and release.[9] If a member determines that there are grounds for continued detention, there must be a consideration of "other factors"[10] in section 248 of the IRPR before a decision is made on detention or release to determine whether further detention is justified in light of all the circumstances of the case. These factors are not exhaustive.

1.1.8 The Charter requires that a person subject to the detention review process under IRPA is entitled to a meaningful and robust review that takes into account the context and circumstances of the individual case. Such persons must have a meaningful opportunity to challenge their detention.[11] Members must consider the evidence and arguments afresh at each detention review and come to their own determinations. Particular attention must be paid to Charter considerations where detention is lengthy and/or where the prospect of removal has become remote.[12]

1.1.9 All detention and release decisions must be made with Charter considerations in mind,[13] in particular, Sections 7, 9 and 12. Detention and other liberty constraints (including release on conditions) must be reasonable, necessary and proportionate, in the particular circumstances of the case.

1.1.10 A minor shall be detained only as a measure of last resort.[14] The *Convention on the Rights of the Child* states that "no child shall be deprived of his or her liberty unlawfully or arbitrarily. The arrest, detention or imprisonment of a child shall be in conformity with the law and shall be used only as a measure of last resort and for the shortest appropriate period of time."[15] Members should make all efforts to ensure that an assessment of the best interests of the child is conducted by the Minister in each case, and by the Member at each hearing, and that all options for alternatives to detention are canvassed before deciding to continue detention of a child or their parents/legal guardians.

1.1.11 Vulnerable persons require special consideration, including making procedural accommodations for such persons so that they are not disadvantaged in presenting their cases. Members should take into account vulnerabilities when weighing evidence and determining release conditions, if any.

1.1.12 The availability, effectiveness and appropriateness of alternatives to detention needs to be adequately assessed in each individual case. In cases where release from detention is ordered, conditions of release are not always required, but where they are, they should be tailored to the particular circumstances of the individual, given that they are restrictions on liberty. Conditions of release need to be proportionate with the level of risk determined and the specific risk determined. Members must ensure that the conditions imposed affect the liberty right of the person concerned as little as possible, while ensuring that their purpose is met.

1.1.13 Members are subject to the standards of conduct set out in the Code of Conduct for Members of the IRB.[16] The Code requires members to conduct hearings in a courteous and respectful manner while ensuring that the proceedings are fair, orderly and efficient. It also requires members to comply with procedural fairness and natural justice. Members are expected to approach each case with an open mind and, at all times, must be, and must be seen to be, impartial and objective.

2. Grounds for Detention

2.1 GENERAL PRINCIPLES

2.1.1 The Immigration Division shall order the release of a permanent resident or a foreign national unless it is satisfied, taking into account prescribed factors, that

  a. they are a danger to the public;
  b. they are unlikely to appear for examination, an admissibility hearing, removal from Canada, or at a proceeding that could lead to the making of a removal order by the Minister under subsection 44(2) (hereinafter "unlikely to appear");
  c. the Minister is taking necessary steps to inquire into a reasonable suspicion that they are inadmissible on grounds of security, violating human or international rights, serious criminality, criminality or organized criminality;
  d. the Minister is of the opinion that the identity of the foreign national — other than a designated foreign national who was 16 years of age or older on the day of the arrival that is the subject of the designation in question — has not been, but may be, established and they have not reasonably cooperated with the Minister by providing relevant information for the purpose of establishing their identity or the Minister is making reasonable efforts to establish their identity; or

e. the Minister is of the opinion that the identity of the foreign national who is a designated foreign national and who was 16 years of age or older on the day of the arrival that is the subject of the designation in question has not been established.

2.1.2 Set out below are specific considerations guiding the determination of each ground.

2.1.3 While non-exhaustive, members must consider the prescribed factors listed in the IRPR when determining the grounds below, as well as any other relevant factors including those listed in section 248 of the IRPR.

2.2 DANGER TO THE PUBLIC (SECTION 58(1)(A))

2.2.1 The Immigration Division shall order the release of a permanent resident or a foreign national unless it is satisfied, taking into account prescribed factors, that the grounds set out in section 58(1) of IRPA are met. Section 58(1)(a) sets out the ground of danger to the public.[17] Neither the IRPA nor the case law explicitly defines the phrase "danger to the public." This phrase relates to the objectives of the IRPA, namely, "to protect public health and safety and to maintain the security of Canadian society."[18]

2.2.2 Members must consider the prescribed factors[19] listed in the IRPR when determining whether the person concerned is a danger to the public, as well as any other relevant factors.

2.2.3 Members must assess whether the person represents a "present and future danger to the public." This assessment is being done under IRPA and must be hinged to the immigration objective. In determining future danger, the probability of danger has to be determined from the circumstances of each case.

2.2.4 It is often necessary for members to draw inferences from a person's criminal record in determining whether that person poses a danger to the public. The more serious the criminal offences, the use of violence and weapons and the greater number of offences committed the more they weigh in favour of a finding of danger to the public. A member should also consider the circumstances of the offence, how much time has passed since the criminal conduct, the sentence imposed by the criminal court and any mitigating or aggravating factors at the time of the offence or since that time.

2.2.5 Members must consider evidence that the person has associated with a criminal organization even if that person has no criminal convictions.

2.2.6 While members are not bound to follow a determination of the Parole Board of Canada as to whether the person is a danger to the public, they should take into account the Parole Board's evaluation of the risk posed by the person since their assessment usually takes into account recent conduct of the person.

2.2.7 While members are not bound to follow determinations made in a criminal court with respect to the granting or not of bail, members should consider the court's determinations while taking into account all the facts in the case within the immigration context.

2.2.8 The Minister's opinion that the person constitutes a danger to the public[20] is a factor to take into account at a detention review but is not in itself sufficient for finding that the person is a danger to the public.

2.2.9 Members should consider that danger to the public may dissipate over time given the passage of time since the offense and/or length of time that the person has been in detention or because evidence supporting the ground of detention has turned stale.[21] Therefore members must consider whether there is ongoing danger to the public, especially for persons who have been in detention for a long period of time.

2.2.10 Members should also consider the circumstances that led to the original determination of danger to the public; for example, whether those circumstances involved a heightened level of vulnerability due to addiction or mental health issues, among others, and whether those vulnerabilities have been mitigated, e.g. through treatment or rehabilitation. However, members should be cautious regarding an absence of evidence of rehabilitation, as persons in detention often do not have access to rehabilitation programs.

2.3 UNLIKELY TO APPEAR (SECTION 58(1)(B))

2.3.1 The Immigration Division shall order the release of a permanent resident or a foreign national unless it is satisfied, taking into account prescribed factors, that the grounds set out in section 58(1) of IRPA are met. Section 58(1)(b) sets out the ground "unlikely to appear for examination, an admissibility hearing, removal from Canada, or at a proceeding that could lead to the making of a removal order by the Minister under section 44(2)."[22]

2.3.2 Members must consider the prescribed factors[23] listed in the IRPR when determining whether the person concerned is unlikely to appear, as well as any other relevant factors.

2.3.3 The prescribed factors listed in section 245 of the IRPR are not exhaustive and can include the best interests of a child of the person concerned in Canada as a factor in assessing whether the person will be motivated, because of the needs of the child, to comply with conditions of release, including being present when requested for removal.

2.3.4 Factors to be considered, such as previous compliance or non-compliance, or the lack or existence of strong community/family ties in Canada, should not automatically lead to a conclusion that the person concerned is unlikely to appear. Rather, they should be considered in the specific context of the case. Where a member has concerns that these facts may give rise to risk that the person concerned is unlikely to appear, these concerns should be articulated to the person concerned for a response, as they may be able to address these concerns.

2.3.5 When considering previous compliance and non-compliance, members need to consider the particular circumstances in each case, including mental illness, addiction or other vulnerabilities, the severity of the non-compliance, frequency, the type of compliance and the impact of non-compliance, as well as any evidence as to how the person concerned is addressing these issues.

2.4 MINISTER INQUIRING INTO SECURITY, VIOLATIONS OF HUMAN OR INTERNATIONAL RIGHTS, CRIMINALITY, SERIOUS CRIMINALITY OR ORGANIZED CRIMINALITY (SECTION 58(1)(C))

2.4.1 The Immigration Division shall order the release of a permanent resident or a foreign national unless it is satisfied, taking into account prescribed factors, that the grounds set out in section 58(1) of IRPA are met. Section 58(1)(c) sets out as a ground that the Minister is taking necessary steps to inquire into a reasonable suspicion that they are inadmissible on grounds of security, violating human or international rights, criminality, serious criminality or organized criminality.[24]

2.4.2 It is up to the Minister to satisfy the member that the Minister is taking necessary steps to investigate their suspicion relating to security, violating human or international rights, criminality, serious criminality or organized criminality.

2.4.3 The question that must be answered by the member is not whether the evidence relied upon by the Minister is true or compelling, but whether that evidence is reasonably capable of supporting the Minister's suspicion of potential inadmissibility. It is for the Minister to decide what further investigatory steps are needed. The member's supervisory jurisdiction on this issue is limited to examining whether the proposed steps have the potential to uncover relevant evidence bearing on the Minister's suspicion and to ensuring that the Minister is conducting an ongoing investigation in good faith and within a reasonable time.[25]

2.5 IDENTITY OF FOREIGN NATIONAL NOT ESTABLISHED (SECTION 58(1)(D))

2.5.1 The Immigration Division shall order the release of a foreign national unless it is satisfied, taking into account prescribed factors, that the grounds set out in section 58(1) of IRPA are met. Section 58(1)(d) sets out as a ground that the Minister is of the opinion that the identity of the foreign national – other than a designated foreign national who was 16 years of age or older on the day of the arrival that is subject of the designation in question – has not been, but may be, established and they have not reasonably cooperated with the Minister by providing relevant information for the purpose of establishing their identity or the Minister is making reasonable efforts to establish their identity.[26]

2.5.2 At every detention review where the Minister has indicated an opinion that the identity of the foreign national has not been established but may be, the member must assess whether the Minister is making reasonable efforts to establish identity and whether the person has reasonably cooperated with the Minister by providing relevant information for the purpose of establishing their identity. Even if the foreign national has reasonably cooperated with the Minister, the ground may be established if the Minister shows that the Minister is making reasonable efforts to establish the identity of the foreign national. Members must consider the prescribed factors[27] in the IRPR, except for minors with respect to cooperation, when determining whether the person is a foreign national whose identity has not been established.

2.5.3 The obligation to establish one's identity rests first and always with the foreign national. The Minister's obligation is to make reasonable efforts but the determination of "reasonable efforts" may be conditioned by the efforts of the person who has an obligation to not obstruct and to cooperate and hence there must be an evaluation of the efforts on the part of both parties.[28] Special consideration should be given to claimants of refugee protection, particularly with respect to the availability or possibility of obtaining identity documents or information. The member should consider whether the level of cooperation requested of the person concerned is reasonable, particularly in the context of claimants of refugee protection, minors and other vulnerable persons.

2.5.4 In assessing the reasonableness of the Minister's efforts to establish identity, the member must consider not what the Member thinks should have been done. Rather the focus should be on whether what the Minister has done, is doing and intends to do is rationally connected to the purpose of the provision – that the steps have the potential to uncover relevant evidence and whether the Minister is acting in good faith.[29] The member should be satisfied that the Minister has provided sufficient evidence of its efforts, as well as concrete plans and time estimates.

3. Release and Alternatives to Detention

3.1 GENERAL PRINCIPLES

3.1.1 Where the member is satisfied that one or more of the above grounds exists, the Member must nevertheless assess whether to release the individual or maintain detention, having regard to all of the circumstances and relevant factors, including those listed in section 248, and bearing in mind overall Charter considerations.

3.1.2 Release without conditions should be the first consideration, and members should apply conditions of release as necessary to manage heightened risk. Release conditions imposed must be tailored to the specific circumstances of the case. They should be linked to risk and be effective in adequately mitigating those risk factors. The principles of proportionality and attainability must apply to every interference with/deprivation of liberty. Each condition imposed is a restriction on a person's liberty. There must be a justification for each condition. Therefore, any condition that is imposed must have a rational connection to the circumstances of the case and the specific ground of detention. This connection should be clearly explained in the reasons for decision.

3.1.3 Members must actively consider and reassess alternatives to detention (ATDs) at each review. This may include reassessing ATDs previously considered and refused at previous detention reviews if those ATDs are still available, recognizing that circumstances may change from one review to another.

3.1.4 Where a member determines that an ATD is necessary or may be appropriate, each element of a proposed ATD must be weighed by the member in order to determine its overall adequacy and necessity in managing the applicable risk. A member should always articulate any concerns with a proposed ATD and give an opportunity to both parties to respond, including calling witnesses where appropriate, prior to rendering a decision. A member should ensure that a person concerned be made aware of the availability of early detention reviews if a response to a concern regarding an ATD cannot be provided at the hearing.

3.1.5 In circumstances where detention is lengthy, the member is under a heightened obligation to consider ATDs, specifically release with appropriate conditions.[30] The burden on the Minister to justify continued detention increases over time as the length of detention continues. The Minister must establish that the detention remains hinged to a legitimate immigration outcome. Detention is not justified if it is no longer necessary to further the immigration purpose, or if the immigration outcome is no longer achievable.[31]

3.1.6 Detention, even for valid reasons, cannot be indefinite.[32] Increased diligence is required in assessing viable ATDs when detention becomes lengthy. The actual or anticipated length of detention under the IRPA is one factor to be considered at a detention review and could be determinative depending on the circumstances and other factors at issue.

3.1.7 A heightened obligation to consider ATDs also applies to cases involving vulnerable persons such as persons with mental illness, minors, the elderly, individuals with diverse sexual orientation and gender identity and expression,[33] survivors of torture, survivors of genocide and crimes against humanity, survivors of gender-related violence, and survivors of violence based on sexual orientation and gender identity.[34] As the onus on the Minister is heightened, a member should also actively question the steps that the Minister has taken to make an ATD available in the circumstances of these cases.

3.1.8 The lack of an established identity does not mean that a member may not consider ATDs.

3.1.9 A decision to detain must not be made solely on the basis of a refusal to cooperate with the Minister's removal efforts. The other factors in s. 248 of the IRPR, and any other relevant factors, must always be considered and weighed before reaching a decision.[35]

3.1.10 Canada Border Services Agency (CBSA) has implemented an ATD Program,[36] which provides them with an expanded set of tools and programs that enables them to more effectively propose release of individuals into the community, commensurate with an individual's risk profile, while ensuring that public safety is preserved. Members should encourage CBSA to consider the availability of the ATD Program for persons concerned. However, members should also ensure that the ATDs considered are commensurate with the level of risk. In addition, members should ensure that other ATDs are canvassed, outside of the CBSA Program, that while not as comprehensive as the CBSA program may still offset risk.

3.1.11 Parties may come to an agreement on proposed conditions of release before or during the detention review and submit the agreement to the member at the hearing. Members would ordinarily endorse release, after having reviewed the file and conducted the hearing. In the exceptional case where a member does not accept the joint submission due to concerns regarding the adequacy of release conditions, prior to issuing reasons for rejecting the joint submission and ordering continued detention, the member should give the parties notice of the member's concerns and an opportunity to confer to see if a varied joint submission or different conditions can be presented. A member must provide a rationale for rejecting the release plan and continuing detention.

3.1.12 Where a release plan is not presented, the member should encourage both parties to work jointly to develop and present acceptable release plans for future consideration. Members should also look for reasonable opportunities to review any previously unsuccessful proposed release plans presented by any party to the proceedings to determine whether such plans remain available and over time have become suitable. Members should encourage the person concerned to look at possible release plans on their own or with counsel.

3.1.13 If ordering continued detention, members must indicate in their reasons the ATD options that were considered and why they are being rejected. Members should also highlight any specific elements that may be lacking to satisfy the member that the release plan appropriately addresses the risk associated to release.

3.1.14 When considering release from immigration detention for a person who has been released by the Parole Board of Canada, members must take into consideration the conditions that have been imposed on the person concerned and the additional supervision that will be afforded by Correctional Service of Canada (Parole Officers). Any release conditions imposed by the member must not contradict the release conditions already imposed by the Parole Board.

3.2 RELEASE CONSIDERATIONS

3.2.1 Where conditions of release are imposed, they should include (1) providing an address and reside at that address; and (2) advising CBSA of a change of address prior to moving.

3.2.2 If deemed necessary to offset a higher level of risk, additional conditions may be imposed,[37] taking into account proportionality and attainability, as well as a rational connection to the circumstances of the case and specific ground of detention. Conditions may include the following:
  i. report to CBSA periodically (in person or by telephone);
  ii. appear whenever required by CBSA, including for removal;
  iii. a bondsperson to pay a deposit or post a guarantee for compliance with conditions;

iv. provide CBSA with a travel document or cooperate with CBSA in obtaining a travel document, except in the case of an asylum seeker or refugee who has not exhausted their legal remedies;
v. reside with a bondsperson or other person considered capable of exercising control and influence over the person concerned;
vi. remain within (or outside) a particular location or geographic area;
vii. abide by a curfew;
viii. reside at community housing or a rehabilitation centre;
ix. not have contact with certain people (e.g., the victim of domestic abuse);
x. not commit criminal offences;
xi. report criminal charges or convictions to CBSA;
xii. abide by conditions of parole or conditions imposed by a justice of the peace or criminal court;
xiii. not consume alcohol, drugs or other intoxicating substances, except in accordance with a medical prescription or in the context of a rehabilitative program, to be applied only for persons with a history of addiction and non-compliance;
xiv. make all reasonable efforts to obtain treatment for alcohol or drug abuse, mental illness or anger management;
xv. enroll in a community case management and supervision program;
xvi. not possess a firearm or other weapon;
xvii. not knowingly associate with individuals who have a criminal record;
xviii. refrain from using a cell phone or a computer or have no functioning internet connection in the person's residence (as an exceptional measure);
xix. permit entry into the person's residence at all times by CBSA or designated personnel (as an exceptional measure); and/or
xx. obtain and wear an electronic bracelet to track movements (as an exceptional measure).

3.3 BONDSPERSONS

3.3.1 If a member determines that a bondsperson is necessary to motivate compliance by the person, the bond should be proportionate to the identified risk.

3.3.2 When a bondsperson is present and available to testify, members must hear direct evidence from the bondsperson before determining that the person is not suitable to be a bondsperson. Members cannot rely on bondsperson interviews conducted outside of the hearing room and not in the presence of members in this context. However, upon a joint release recommendation or where the Minister does not object, a member can determine that the bondsperson is acceptable without hearing direct testimony.

3.3.3 If the proposed bondsperson is unavailable to provide testimony, a member should determine whether an adjournment is required or a decision should be rendered with an early detention review scheduled, depending on the duration of the lack of availability.

3.3.4 Members must ensure that relevant considerations relating to the proposed bondsperson are explored at the detention review in order to assess the suitability of the person put forward.

3.3.5 Members should consider how long the proposed bondsperson has known the person concerned and the nature of their relationship.

3.3.6 In instances where a proposed bondsperson was aware of the person's past immigration or criminal history and did not take steps to ensure past compliance, members must consider whether the proposed bondsperson, in their new role as bondsperson, will exercise sufficient influence to motivate the person concerned to comply with conditions of release.

3.3.7 In instances where a proposed bondsperson was unaware of the person's past immigration or criminal history, members must consider whether the proposed bondsperson, now with that knowledge, is still willing to be considered as a bondsperson and whether they will exercise sufficient influence to motivate the person concerned to comply with conditions of release.

3.3.8 Members must assess whether the proposed bondsperson is reliable and whether there has been a previous failure of that bondsperson to ensure compliance with conditions of release by the person concerned, if they were acting as a bondsperson or under a similar obligation in the prior circumstances. Members must assess whether the proposed bondsperson is able to exert influence, provide supervision, and motivate the person concerned to comply with the conditions of release.

3.3.9 In assessing the adequacy of the bondsperson, the factors as set out in the IRPR need to be considered and assessed against the objective of ensuring compliance by the person concerned, including the proportionality of the bond to the financial capacity of the bondsperson and the impact of forfeiture on the bondsperson.

3.3.10 If a bondsperson meets the eligibility requirements under section 47 of the IRPR and has been rejected at a prior detention review, members should re-consider such bondspersons when taking a fresh look at the case, keeping in mind that an increased length of detention does not transform an unsuitable bondsperson into a suitable one.[38] Members must articulate their reasons to depart from past decisions regarding previously considered bondspersons.[39]

3.3.11 If a member determines that a bondsperson is necessary as a condition of release, it is preferable that a named bondsperson be included on the order for release, since it is usually necessary to consider the circumstances of the person putting up the deposit and their relationship to the person concerned.[40]

3.3.12 In some instances the person concerned has no family network or friends in Canada and has been unable to present a proposal for a supervising bondsperson, which could result in a lengthier period of detention. In those circumstances members should encourage counsel for the person concerned, or the person concerned if unrepresented, to seek a suitable alternative to detention within the community,[41] including a group of individuals, such as a religious community, or a community program in lieu of a bondsperson, such as organizations that work to help with housing and other supports, and organizations that help in supporting individuals with mental illness or addictions.

3.4 CHANGE IN CONDITIONS

3.4.1 An application for a change of conditions of release may be made by the Minister, the person concerned or his or her counsel. A response to the application must be received by the Division and the other party within five days. A decision will be made by the Assistant Deputy Chairperson or a member. A decision will be rendered as soon as practicable and can include convocation of a hearing.

3.4.2 A bondsperson may also apply to change conditions, such as a request to be removed.

4. Minors

4.1.1 Pursuant to the requirements of the *Convention on the Rights of the Child*,[42] members must take into account the best interests of any child, whether detained under the IRPA or not, and whether housed with a parent or not, as a key consideration in any detention-related decision of the parent or guardian. Where a child is neither detained nor housed, the parties who intend to rely on the best interest of a child must raise the issue before the Division.

4.1.2 Members must consider the prescribed factors in the IRPR when determining whether to release or continue detention, including the best interests of the child, as well as all other relevant circumstances.[43] Members must only detain minors in the most exceptional circumstances, and for the shortest time possible.

4.1.3 The Minister must submit its best interest of the child assessment at each detention review when it is detaining a child. The person concerned may also advance arguments regarding the best interest of a child, supported by evidence.

4.1.4 The best interests of a directly affected child who is under 18 years of age must be considered before making a decision on detention of the minor or their parent/guardian. The following is a non-exhaustive list of factors that the members must consider when determining a child's best interests with respect to detention and release of the minor and their parent/guardian, regardless of whether the child is detained or housed:

- the child's physical, emotional and psychological well-being;
- the child's healthcare and educational needs;
- the importance of maintaining relationships and the stability of the family environment, and the possible effect on the child of disrupting those relationships or that stability;
- the care, protection and safety needs of the child; and
- the child's views and preferences, provided the child is capable of forming their own views or expressing their preferences, taking into consideration the child's age and maturity.

The level of dependence of the child on the person for whom there are grounds to detain (parent/guardian) should also be a consideration.[44]

4.1.5 Members must explain in their reasons for decision how the best interests of the child were considered in the decision to detain the child or their parent/guardian.

4.1.6 Early detention reviews are strongly encouraged to ensure that the file is progressing rapidly and the impacted minor is not unduly affected.

4.1.7 In the extraordinary event that a minor is detained or housed, ATDs must be actively considered and continually reassessed taking into consideration all past release proposals. Conditions of release must be crafted to protect as far as possible the child's best interests.

5. Vulnerable Persons

5.1.1 Members must consider how certain vulnerabilities,[45] such as mental illness, may affect the person's ability to comply with conditions of release and whether a less restrictive alternative to detention would be viable before continuing detention.

5.1.2 To help enable a vulnerable person concerned to present their case before the Division, the need for procedural accommodations may arise, pursuant to the Chairperson's Guideline 8: *Procedures With Respect to Vulnerable Persons Appearing before the IRB.*[46]

5.1.3 There is no need for a person to have been declared "vulnerable" pursuant to the Vulnerable Persons Guideline in order to take account of a mental health condition or other vulnerability that is either established by the evidence or apparent in the hearing context.

5.1.4 Accommodations under Guideline 8 must be considered by the member, whether requested by a party or on the member's own initiative, wherever it is appropriate to do so.

5.1.5 Such vulnerabilities should also be accounted for when assessing all of the section 248 factors in the IRPR, including when determining a person's ability and capacity to cooperate with removal arrangements and/or identity investigations. Such vulnerabilities may be a separate and relevant factor, in addition to the section 248 factors, for considering whether to release or detain.

5.1.6 Where vulnerabilities are identified, a member is under a heightened obligation to consider ATDs and to impose attainable conditions that are connected to the circumstances of the vulnerable person concerned.

5.1.7 Early detention reviews are strongly encouraged to ensure that the file is progressing rapidly and the vulnerable person concerned is not unduly affected.

6. Designated Representatives

6.1.1 Members must designate a representative where the person concerned is under 18 years of age or the person is unable to appreciate the nature of the proceedings, at the earliest point at which the member becomes aware of those facts. In cases where a designated representative is required, members are encouraged to retain the same designated representative in all proceedings before the Immigration Division. The designated representative should be provided with all relevant documents in the Division file as soon as possible.

6.1.2 Members should question the designated representative on the steps taken to assist the person concerned, for instance in retaining counsel, informing the person concerned about the various stages in the detention review process, finding suitable ATDs, including contacting potential bondspersons and gathering evidence. Members are encouraged to replace a designated representative when it is apparent that relevant and necessary steps to assist the person concerned have not been taken.

7. Conducting the Detention Review – Robust Hearing

7.1 ACCESSIBLE HEARINGS

7.1.1 Detention reviews are public hearings. The open court principle (i.e., hearings being open and accessible to the public and the media.) supports the integrity and transparency of the Division's proceedings. An exception to the open court principle applies for a person who has a pending proceeding before the Refugee Protection Division or the Refugee Appeal Division, or a pending application for protection to the Minister.[47] The Division may hold a detention review in the absence of the public under other exceptional circumstances,[48] such as for minors and other vulnerable persons, as appropriate.

7.1.2 The Immigration Division shall deal with all proceedings before it as informally and quickly as the circumstances and the considerations of fairness and natural justice permit. In practice, hearings may take place at an IRB office, at an Immigration Holding Centre, in provincial or federal correctional facilities, in CBSA offices and in other facilities such as Courts. Hearings may be held in person, by videoconference and by teleconference and parties can participate from multiple locations.

7.1.3 In-person hearings are preferable from a fairness and natural justice perspective, but the Immigration Division's mandate is also to deal with proceedings as informally and quickly as the circumstances permit. Members should balance these interests when determining how best to proceed with the hearing when considering the circumstances of the individual case.

7.2 FRESH DETERMINATION

7.2.1 Members must ensure that at each hearing the person concerned is aware of the Division's duty to release under section 58(1) of IRPA unless the Minister proves, on a balance of probabilities, that there is a statutory ground for detention and that continued detention is required, with the onus resting on the Minister.

7.2.2 The Minister may elect to rely on having previously established the grounds for detention. However, the member is not bound to accept the previous finding of a member at the last detention review if the Minister has failed to provide reasonably available evidence to justify the detention. This is particularly relevant in long-term detention cases, and cases involving persons concerned with vulnerabilities, especially where the Minister leads insufficient evidence to justify the ground for detention, the length of detention or its uncertain duration, or the necessity of detention rather than less restrictive liberty restraints.

7.2.3 Members must explain why they have rejected the ATDs proposed and any barriers to release in their reasons for decisions when deciding to continue detention.

7.2.4 At each detention review the Immigration Division member must come to a fresh determination on whether the detained person should continue to be detained. The Minister bears an ongoing burden to prove that detention remains justified. However, previous decisions by the Immigration Division to detain the person concerned must be considered at subsequent reviews and the subsequent decision-maker must articulate their reasons for departing from previous decisions.

7.2.5 A departure from a prior decision could result from, but does not necessarily require, new evidence or new legal arguments. The admission of relevant new evidence, a reassessment of the prior evidence based on new arguments or on a different assessment, the proposal of an acceptable alternative to detention, vulnerabilities of the person concerned, the passage of time since the last detention review or a prolonged detention could be a valid basis for departing from a prior decision to detain.

7.2.6 The credibility of the person concerned and of witnesses is often an issue at detention reviews. Where a member had the opportunity to observe the demeanor of a witness and assess credibility, the subsequent decision-maker must give a clear explanation of why the prior decision-maker's assessment of the evidence does not justify continued detention. In addition, a reassessment of the prior evidence based on new arguments could also be a sufficient reason to depart from a prior decision to detain. The member must expressly explain in the reasons what the former decision stated and why they are departing from the previous decision.

7.3 DISCLOSURE AND EVIDENCE

7.3.1 Both parties have the right to present relevant evidence at a detention review, including witnesses, and to question those witnesses. Members should ensure that the person concerned understands and has an opportunity to testify, present evidence and counter the Minister's evidence, including by presenting their own sworn testimony should they so choose, calling witnesses, and/or cross-examining the Minister's witnesses.

7.3.2 The Minister must disclose any document they intend to rely on in any detention review, in compliance with the Division's rules. They cannot rely on a document they refuse/fail to disclose. Furthermore, evidence from the Enforcement/Removals Officer should be in the form of either a statutory declaration to be disclosed before the hearing or oral testimony. The type of evidence provided affects the weight to be afforded by the member. It is not appropriate for the Minister to present information when the primary source of the information has not been made available to the parties, unless the primary source of information is not compellable (ie a consular official).

7.3.3 Members must ensure that the parties have provided each other with reasonable notice of the evidence or information that will be relied upon at the detention review. Members must consider any request to summon the Enforcement Officer to provide testimony at the detention review.[49] Members should summon an Enforcement Officer on their own initiative if they believe that this would be likely to address important gaps in the evidentiary record, in particular where the person concerned is self-represented.

7.3.4 The Minister is expected to disclose all relevant evidence, whether or not it is exculpatory, or they intend to rely on it.

7.3.5 In circumstances where the Minister's counsel cannot answer questions posed by the member at the hearing, the member is encouraged to adjourn to allow the source of the information, such as a CBSA Enforcement Officer, to attend the hearing to answer questions or, where impractical or impossible for a timely decision, for the Minister's counsel to obtain the information requested. An early detention review could also be scheduled, as applicable.

7.3.6 Where the Minister is unable to provide the information requested, the member must carefully consider whether the Minister has discharged its onus to justify continued detention.

7.3.7 The member should play an active role in ensuring they have a sufficient evidentiary record upon which to base their decision, in particular where the person concerned is unrepresented. This may include (but is not limited to):

- active questioning to address any factual gaps;
- giving notice of concerns to the person concerned in plain language and providing an opportunity for a response;
- testing the Minister's representations through active and, where necessary, probing questions to assess their evidentiary basis; and/or
- insisting upon testimony from others with more direct knowledge of the case (for example, Enforcement Officers) where important questions remain after questioning of the Minister's counsel and the person concerned.

7.3.8 Members should carefully review all efforts taken by the Minister to effect removal, including an assessment of the likelihood of removal given the actual circumstances that exist in relation to removal to that country. The member must be satisfied that the Minister has acted with reasonable diligence and expeditiousness to effect removal of the person concerned.[50] Members should also explore with the person concerned opportunities to help effect removal.

8. Sufficiency of Reasons for Decision

8.1.1 At the beginning of their reasons for decision, members must briefly set out the person's name, the initial date of detention and its purpose, and the grounds that the Minister is relying on for continued detention. The member should also state whether it is a private or public hearing, if there is a designated representative and if the person concerned is a minor or has been identified as a vulnerable person.

8.1.2 Members must mention in their reasons for decision the most important evidence adduced at the detention review and how that evidence relates to the findings made in the reasons. All decisions must be grounded in the established factual record.

8.1.3 While members are not required in their reasons for decision to deal with every matter or issue raised by the parties at a detention review, the reasons for decision must adequately explain the basis of their decisions, including any ATDs proposed, and why a particular alternative to detention has been accepted or rejected.

8.1.4 Reasons for decision should be sufficiently detailed to allow the reader to know what grounds and factors the member relied on in support of their decision to order continued detention or release, including the reasons for departing from previous decisions. The reasons should also explain possible ATDs and any barriers to release which, in the members opinion, must be overcome by the person concerned prior to release.

9. Statutory Timeframes

9.1.1 The timing of detention reviews must reflect the statutory scheme as set out in the IRPA as closely as possible. While the member has some discretion to postpone or adjourn a detention review or reserve a decision with respect to the issue of detention, that discretion should be exercised very cautiously. There is an obligation on the member to conduct a detention review and deliver a decision within the timeframes stated in the IRPA.

9.1.2 The member may conduct a detention review outside the timeframes set out in the IRPA in limited circumstances to ensure a fair hearing. For example, a member may exercise discretion to vary the timeframes when an interpreter is not available until the day after the scheduled detention review, where counsel asks for an additional day to prepare in cases involving voluminous and complicated evidence, or where a bondsperson or another witness, such as an Enforcement Officer, is not available. Any variation in the timeframes, however, should be strictly limited to the time needed to conduct a fair hearing.

9.1.3 In very limited circumstances it may be difficult for a member to give a decision within the statutory timeframes, such as following the receipt of voluminous evidence or extensive submissions by the parties or where the member is departing from previous decisions on a long-term detention. The member may reserve the decision for a brief period of time, as necessary, to consider the evidence and submissions.

9.1.4 A party may apply for an early detention review, before the expiry of the seven-day or thirty-day period, if there are new facts that would justify an early review of detention.[51] Examples in which an early detention review may be granted are ATDs to be presented, including the existence of a bondsperson or the acceptance into a program, a change in the circumstances surrounding removal efforts and satisfaction of identity.

9.1.5 If the Federal Court has ordered a stay of a previous release order and has not made any order as to whether or not the Immigration Division should continue to conduct detention reviews pending the outcome of the leave application and judicial review, the Immigration Division should conduct detention reviews according to the timeframes in the IRPA, while taking into account the order of the Federal Court.

10. Enquiries

For information, contact:
IRB.Policy-Politiques.CISR@irb-cisr.gc.ca
OR
Senior Director, Policy, Outreach and Engagement Directorate
Policy, Planning and Corporate Affairs Branch
Minto Place – Canada Building
344 Slater Street, 12th floor
Ottawa, Ontario K1A 0K1

Signed by Richard Wex
Chairperson, Immigration and Refugee Board of Canada
March 14, 2019

Annex A – Immigration and Refugee Protection Act

[Annex A consists of sections 58 and 58.1 of the Act, which can be found in appendix A.]

Annex B – Immigration and Refugee Protection Regulations

[Annex B consists of regulations 245–250.1, which can be found in appendix B.]

Notes

1 Policy on the use of Chairperson's Guidelines, Policy no. 2003-07 of the Immigration and Refugee Board of Canada (IRB), October 27, 2003.

2 Canadian Charter of Rights and Freedoms, Part 1 of the Constitution Act, 1982, being Schedule B to the Canada Act, 1982, (UK), 1982, c. 11.

3 International Covenant on Civil and Political Rights, (1976) 999 UNTS 107, in force on March 23, 1976, sections 9, 10 and 11, and Optional Protocol to the International Covenant on Civil and Political Rights, (1976) 999 UNTS 216, in force on March 23, 1976. These two instruments confer status in law on the civil and political rights set out in the Universal Declaration of Human Rights, U.N. Doc. A/810, p. 71 (1948). The United Nations. "Convention on the Rights of the Child," Treaty Series 1577 (1989), in force on September 2, 1990, Article 37(b).

4 S.C. 2001, c. 27. Section 54 of the IRPA states that the "Immigration Division is the competent Division of the Board with respect to the review of reasons for detention under this Division."

5 Section 3(3)(d) of IRPA states that the Act is to be construed and applied in a manner that ensures that decisions taken are consistent with the Charter. In addition, Section 3(3)(f) of IRPA states that the Act is to be construed and applied in a manner that complies with international human rights instruments to which Canada is a signatory.

6 See Annex A of this Guideline.

7 The Minister in these Guidelines refers to the Minister of Public Safety and Emergency Preparedness, through its hearings officers.

8 *Canada (Minister of Citizenship and Immigration) v. Thanabalasingham*, [2004] 3 F.C.R. 572 (F.C.A.); 2004 FCA 4.

9 IRPR, ss. 245, 246, 247 (See Annex B of this Guideline).

10 IRPR, s. 248 (See Annex B of this Guideline). Section 248 codifies the factors developed by the Federal Court to ensure that continued detention is consistent with the rights guaranteed by section 7 of the Charter, and these factors, the so-called "Sahin factors," are relevant in all cases involving detention. See *Sahin v. Canada (Minister of Citizenship and Immigration)*, [1995] 1 F.C. 214 (T.D.), appeal dismissed in *Sahin, Bektas v. M.C.I.* (F.C.A., no. A-575-94), Stone MacGuigan, Robertson, June 8, 1995.

11 *Charkaoui v. Canada (Citizenship and Immigration)*, [2007] 1 S.C.R. 350.

12 *Brown Alvin John and End Immigration Detention Network v. M.C.I. and M.P.S.E.P.* (F.C., no. IMM-364-15), Fothergill, July 25, 2017; 2017 FC 710.While the Courts have found that the provisions in the IRPA and the IRPR comply with the Charter, for a review of detention to be Charter compliant the provisions must be properly interpreted and applied.

13 *Sahin v. Canada (Minister of Citizenship and Immigration)*, [1995] 1 F.C. 214 (T.D.), appeal dismissed.

14 IRPA, s. 60.

15 The United Nations. "*Convention on the Rights of the Child*," Treaty Series 1577 (1989), in force on September 2, 1990, Article 37(b).

16 https://irb-cisr.gc.ca/en/members/Pages/MemComCode.aspx#Toc343154616.

17 IRPA, s. 58(1)(*a*)

18 IRPA, s. 3(1)(*h*).

19 IRPR, ss. 244(b), 246 and 248.

20 IRPR, s. 246(*a*).

21 *M.C.I. v. Sittampalam, Jothiravi* (F.C. nos. IMM-3876-04 and IMM-8256-04), Blais, December 17, 2004; 2004 FC 1756.

22 IRPA, s. 58(1)(*b*).

23 IRPR, ss. 244(*a*), 245 and 248.

24 IRPA, s. 58(1)(*c*).

25 *Canada (Citizenship and Immigration)v. X*, [2011] 1 F.C.R. 493; 2010 FC 112.

26 IRPA, s. 58(1)(*d*).

27 IRPR, s. 247.

28 *M.C.I. v. X* (F.C., no. IMM-5427-10), Phelan, November 5, 2010; 2010 FC 1095.

29 Ibid.

30 *Ahmed v. Canada (Citizenship and Immigration)*, 2015 FC 876 at para 34.

31 See *Ali v. Canada (Attorney General)*, 2017 ONSC 2660, April 28, 2017 referred to in *Brown Alvin John and End Immigration Detention Network v. M.C.I. and M.P.S.E.P.*, supra, foot11.

32 *Charkaoui*, supra, foot9.

33 IRB Chairperson Guideline 9: Proceedings Before the IRB Involving Sexual Orientation and Gender Identity and Expression.

34 IRB Chairperson Guideline 8: Procedures With Respect to Vulnerable Persons Appearing Before the IRB.

35 *M.P.S.E.P v. Lunyamila* (F.C. no. IMM-3428-16 et al), Crampton, October 27, 2016; 2016 FC 1199. Appeal dismissed in *Lunyamila v. Canada (Public Safety and Emergency Preparedness)* (A-444-16), Stratas, Woods, Laskin, January 19, 2018; 2018 FCA 22 without consideration of the certified question. The Chief Justice said that in situations of "extremely lengthy" detention due to the person's failure to fully cooperate with the Minister's removal efforts, it should be resolved in favour of continued detention; however this assumes no material changes in the other factors required to be

considered under s. 248 of the IRPR, including alternatives to detention. In *Ali*, 2017 ONSC 2660 the Court said that to hold a person indefinitely, solely on the basis of non-cooperation, would be fundamentally inconsistent with the principles underlying ss. 7 and 9 of the Charter. In *Ali*, the Court also confirmed that detention under the IRPA cannot be for the purpose of punishment, but must be necessary to further a legitimate immigration purpose.

36 https://www.cbsa-asfc.gc.ca/security-securite/detent/nidf-cndi-eng.html.

37 This list is not exhaustive.

38 *Muhammad, Arshad v. M.P.S.E.P.* (F.C. no. IMM-844-13), Martineau, February 27, 2013; 2013 FC 203. See also *M.C.I. v. B 147* (F.C. no. IMM-2451-12), Rennie, May 29, 2012; 2012 FC 655.

39 Ibid.

40 *Canada (Minister of Citizenship and Immigration) v. Zhang*, 2001 FCT 522, 205 F.T.R. 91, affirmed in *M.P.S.E.P. and M.C.I. v. Iamkhong, Suwalee* (F.C. no. IMM-254-09), Shore, January 21, 2009; 2009 FC 52.

41 *Re Almrei* (F.C. no. DES -3-08), Mosley, January 2, 2009; 2009 FC 3.

42 Section 3(3)(f) of IRPA states that the Act is to be construed and applied in a manner that complies with international human rights instruments to which Canada is a signatory.

43 IRPA, s. 60, and IRPR, s. 249. Please CBSA's National Directive for the Detention or Housing of Minors, section 7, for more on the best interests of the child as a primary consideration.

44 Canada Gazette, Part I, Volume 152, Number 40: Regulations Amending the Immigration and Refugee Protection Regulations, October 6, 2018. While not in force, these proposed amendments codify the jurisprudence.

45 *Guideline on Vulnerable Persons* of the IRB, December 15, 2012. Section 2.1 defines "vulnerable persons" as "individuals whose ability to present their cases before the IRB is severely impaired" and includes "the mentally ill." Some other vulnerabilities are listed in section 3.1.7. of this Detention Guideline.

46 The IRB has a broad discretion to tailor procedures to meet the particular needs of a vulnerable person, and, where appropriate and permitted by law, the IRB may accommodate a person's vulnerability by various means, including: a. allowing the vulnerable person to provide evidence by videoconference or other means; b. allowing a support person to participate in a hearing; c. creating a more informal setting for a hearing; d. varying the order of questioning; e. excluding non-parties from the hearing room; f. providing a panel and interpreter of a particular gender; g. explaining IRB processes to the vulnerable person; and h. allowing any other procedural accommodations that may be reasonable in the circumstances.

47 IRPA, s. 166.

48 IRPA, s. 166(b).

49 *Brown, Alvin John and End Immigration Detention Network*, supra, footnote 11.

50 *Brown, Alvin John and End Immigration Detention Network*, supra, footnote 11.

51 Immigration Division Rules, s. 9.

Appendix E

CHAIRPERSON'S GUIDELINES ON VULNERABLE PERSONS

Effective date: December 15, 2006
Amended: December 15, 2012

Guideline issued by the Chairperson pursuant to paragraph 159(1)(h) of the *Immigration and Refugee Protection Act*

TABLE OF CONTENTS

1. Introduction
2. Definition of vulnerable persons
3. Objectives
4. Procedural accommodations
5. General principles
6. Proceedings with more than one party
7. Early identification
8. Expert evidence
9. Scheduling
10. Questioning the vulnerable person
11. Decisions and reasons
12. Designated representative

13. Self-represented persons
14. Women fearing gender-related persecution
15. Minors
16. LGBTI individuals
17. References
18. Inquiries

1. Introduction

1.1 The intention of this guideline is to provide procedural accommodation(s) for individuals who are identified as vulnerable persons by the Immigration and Refugee Board of Canada (IRB). Chairperson's guidelines are issued to assist members in carrying out their duties as decision-makers under the *Immigration and Refugee Protection Act* (IRPA)[1] and to promote consistency, coherence and fairness in the treatment of cases at the IRB.

1.2 Appearing at an IRB hearing is a process that can be difficult because of language and cultural barriers and because of the fact that the outcome of the hearing is so significant for those involved. The IRB makes decisions on immigration and refugee matters, including admissibility, detention, removal, refugee protection, permanent resident status, and family reunification — all matters that directly and profoundly affect the lives of individuals.

1.3 The IRB's four divisions, the Immigration Division (ID), the Immigration Appeal Division (IAD), the Refugee Protection Division (RPD) and the Refugee Appeal Division (RAD), are committed to providing fair proceedings to all persons appearing before them in a manner that is guided and informed by the objectives set out in section 3 of the IRPA. This guideline is intended to apply to the four divisions of the IRB.

1.4 The IRB occasionally hears cases involving persons for whom a hearing or other case process is a particularly difficult experience because their ability to present their cases is severely impaired given a physical or psychological frailty or for other reasons. The vulnerability of these persons has always required special consideration, and over the years, the IRB has adopted case-by-case procedures to deal with their cases. This guideline articulates the IRB's continuing commitment to making procedural accommodations for such persons so that they are not disadvantaged in presenting their cases.

1.5 A person's vulnerability may be due to having experienced or witnessed torture or genocide or other forms of severe mistreatment; however, it may also be due to innate or acquired personal characteristics such as a physical or mental illness, or age. What vulnerable persons appearing before the IRB have in common is their severe difficulty in going through the hearing process or other IRB processes without special consideration being given to their individual situations. Like all persons appearing before the IRB, vulnerable persons need to be treated with sensitivity and respect, but they also need to have their cases processed taking into account their specific vulnerabilities.

2. Definition of vulnerable persons

2.1 For the purposes of this guideline, vulnerable persons are individuals whose ability to present their cases before the IRB is severely impaired. Such persons may include, but would not be limited to, the mentally ill, minors, the elderly, victims of torture, survivors of genocide and crimes against humanity, women who have suffered gender-related persecution, and individuals who have been victims of persecution based on sexual orientation and gender identity.

2.2 The definition of vulnerable persons may apply to persons presenting a case before the IRB, namely, to refugee protection claimants (in the RPD), appellants (in the IAD and in the RAD), and persons concerned (in the ID). In certain circumstances, close family members of the vulnerable person who are also presenting their cases before the IRB may qualify as vulnerable persons because of the way in which they have been affected by their loved one's condition.

2.3 Persons who appear before the IRB frequently find the process difficult for various reasons, including language and cultural barriers and because they may have suffered traumatic experiences that resulted in some degree of vulnerability.[2] IRB proceedings have been designed to recognize the very nature of the IRB's mandate, which inherently involves persons who may have some vulnerabilities. In all cases, the IRB takes steps to ensure the fairness of the proceedings. This guideline addresses difficulties that go beyond those that are common to most persons appearing before the IRB. It is intended to apply to individuals who face particular difficulty and who require special consideration in the procedural handling of their cases. It applies to the more severe cases of vulnerability.

2.4 Wherever it is reasonably possible, the vulnerability must be supported by independent credible evidence[3] filed with the IRB Registry.

3. Objectives

The objectives of this guideline are as follows:

3.1 To recognize that certain individuals face particular difficulties when they appear for their hearings or other IRB processes because their ability to present their cases is severely impaired.

3.2 To ensure that such vulnerable persons are identified and appropriate procedural accommodations are made.

3.3 To the extent possible, to prevent vulnerable persons from becoming traumatized or re-traumatized by the hearing process or another IRB process.

3.4 To ensure the ongoing sensitization of members and other hearing room participants to the impact of severe vulnerability.

4. Procedural accommodations

4.1 Depending on the nature of a person's vulnerability, they may face particular difficulties in presenting or addressing evidence that should be taken into account in determining the procedural accommodations to be made. Such difficulties may include the following:

a. a person's vulnerability may affect memory, behaviour and their ability to recount relevant events;

b. the vulnerable person may be suffering from symptoms that have an impact on the consistency and coherence of their testimony;

c. vulnerable persons who fear persons in a position of authority may associate those involved in the hearing process with the authorities they fear; and

d. a vulnerable person may be reluctant or unable to talk about their experiences.

4.2 The IRB has a broad discretion to tailor procedures to meet the particular needs of a vulnerable person, and, where appropriate and permitted by law, the IRB may accommodate a person's vulnerability by various means, including:

a. allowing the vulnerable person to provide evidence by videoconference or other means;

b. allowing a support person to participate in a hearing;

c. creating a more informal setting for a hearing;

d. varying the order of questioning;[4]

e. excluding non-parties from the hearing room;

f. providing a panel and interpreter of a particular gender;

g. explaining IRB processes to the vulnerable person; and

h. allowing any other procedural accommodations that may be reasonable in the circumstances.

5. General principles

5.1   A person may be identified as vulnerable, and procedural accommodations made, so that the person is not disadvantaged in the presentation of their case. The identification of vulnerability will usually be made at an early stage, before the IRB has considered all the evidence in the case and before an assessment of the person's credibility has been made.

5.2   A person may be identified as vulnerable based, in part, on alleged underlying facts that are also central to the ultimate determination of their case before the IRB. An identification of vulnerability does not indicate the IRB's acceptance of the alleged underlying facts. It is made for the purpose of procedural accommodation only. Thus, the identification of a person as vulnerable does not predispose a member to make a particular determination of the case on its merits. Rather, a determination of the merits of the case will be made on the basis of an assessment of all the evidence.

5.3   Similarly, evidence initially used to identify a vulnerable person and to make procedural accommodations may not have been tested through credibility assessments or other means. If such evidence is then used to adjudicate the merits of the case, the member should ensure that the parties are given an opportunity to address this evidence as it relates to the merits of the case. This means that submissions may be made about the relevance of the evidence, and the evidence may be tested through such means as questioning by the parties and the member, and other methods. The credibility and probative value of the evidence may then be assessed by the member, even though the IRB previously accepted the evidence, for the purpose of identifying vulnerability and making procedural accommodations.

6. Proceedings with more than one party

6.1   Some IRB hearings are adversarial in nature, and the rules of natural justice apply equally to both parties. Identification of vulnerable persons and procedural accommodations for vulnerable persons cannot have the effect of denying any party a fair opportunity to present their case. Where the Minister[5] is a party, the Minister's views will be sought on whether a person should be identified as a vulnerable person and, if so, on the nature of any procedural accommodations to be made, except for accommodations of an administrative or minor nature.

7. Early identification

7.1   A person can be identified as vulnerable at any stage of the proceedings. It is preferable to identify vulnerable persons at the earliest opportunity.

7.2   In the course of early review of the file, the IRB may find information disclosing that the ability of the person to present their case may be severely impaired. The IRB may initiate early contact with the person, the designated representative, counsel or any other person to gather evidence that is relevant to whether the individual should be identified as a vulnerable person and that is relevant to the types of procedural accommodations that might be made.

7.3   Counsel for a person who may be considered vulnerable is best placed to bring the vulnerability to the attention of the IRB and is expected to do so as soon as possible. Others who are associated with the person or who have knowledge of facts indicating that the person may be vulnerable (counsel for the Minister or any other person) are encouraged to do the same. Wherever it is reasonably possible, independent credible evidence documenting the vulnerability must be filed with the IRB Registry.

7.4   Counsel for a person who wishes to be identified as a vulnerable person must make an application under the Rules of the Division.[6] The application must specify the nature of the vulnerability, the type of procedural accommodations sought and the rationale for the particular accommodations. The IRB will be sensitive to the barriers that may be created by the formal requirements related to making applications in the case of self-represented persons and other situations and will waive or modify the requirements or time limits set out in the Rules, as appropriate. The IRB may also act on its own initiative.

7.5   A member manager may identify an individual as a vulnerable person and may take appropriate measures to accommodate the person at an early stage and before a member has been assigned to conduct a proceeding. The assigned member is not bound by the IRB's early identification. The assigned member will consider this guideline and whether the identification and any procedural accommodations made will be maintained, amended or discontinued.

7.6 To the extent practicable, once a person has been declared a vulnerable person under this guideline, a member will be assigned at an early stage in the file and will be responsible for that file until the proceeding is concluded.

7.7 The IRB may hold conferences prior to and during hearings to assist in identifying vulnerable persons and to establish the nature of the procedural accommodations required.

8. Expert evidence

8.1 A medical, psychiatric, psychological, or other expert report regarding the vulnerable person is an important piece of evidence that must be considered. Expert evidence can be of great assistance to the IRB in applying this guideline if it addresses the person's particular difficulty in coping with the hearing process, including the person's ability to give coherent testimony.

8.2 The IRB may suggest that an expert report be submitted but will not order or pay for it.

8.3 Generally, experts' reports should contain the following information:

   a. the particular qualifications and experience of the professional that demonstrate an expertise that pertains to the person's particular condition;

   b. the questions that were posed to the expert by the person who requested the expert report;

   c. the factual foundation underlying the expert's opinion;

   d. the methodology used by the expert in assessing the person, including whether an interview was conducted, the number and length of interviews, whether tests were administered, and, if so, what those tests were and the significance of the results;

   e. whether the person is receiving treatment and, if so, the nature of the treatment and whether the treatment is controlling the condition;

   f. whether the assessing expert was also treating the person at the time of producing the report; and

   g. the expert's opinion about the person's condition and ability to participate in the hearing process, including any suggested procedural accommodations and why particular procedural accommodations are recommended.

8.4 Experts should not offer opinions on issues within the exclusive jurisdiction of the decision-maker, such as the merits of the person's case.

8.5 An expert's opinion is not in itself proof of the truthfulness of the information upon which it is based. The weight given to the report will depend, among other things, on the credibility of the underlying facts in support of the allegation of vulnerability.

8.6 The absence of expert evidence does not necessarily lead to a negative inference about whether the person is in fact vulnerable. The IRB will consider whether it was reasonably possible to obtain such evidence.

9. Scheduling

9.1 The IRB has a duty to determine all proceedings before it as informally and quickly as the circumstances and the considerations of fairness and natural justice permit.[7] Moreover, the uncertainty and anxiety caused by delay can be particularly detrimental to some vulnerable persons. In such cases, those persons may be given scheduling priority. Where giving scheduling priority would not facilitate the objectives of this guideline, other procedural accommodations may be provided as appropriate.

10. Questioning the vulnerable person

10.1 The IRB ensures that all those who appear at its hearings or other proceedings are questioned with sensitivity and respect. This obligation is all the more important in the case of vulnerable persons. In probing the information provided by the person, the IRB will attempt to avoid traumatizing or re-traumatizing the vulnerable person.[8]

11. Decisions and reasons

11.1 The uncertainty and anxiety generated by waiting for a decision and reasons for decision may be particularly stressful for vulnerable persons. Generally, decisions and reasons for decisions involving vulnerable persons will be delivered as soon as possible, and orally wherever appropriate. In individual cases, members may determine that written reasons are preferable.

12. Designated representative

12.1 In some cases, vulnerable persons may be under 18 years of age or unable, in the opinion of the IRB, to appreciate the nature of the proceedings. In such cases, the IRB shall designate a person to represent the person, as required by subsection 167(2) of IRPA.[9]

13. Self-represented persons

13.1 Self-represented persons are entitled to the same procedural safeguards as those who are represented, and the IRB will endeavour to ensure that the process outlined in this guideline is both accessible and understandable to these persons. The IRB will take extra care to ensure that self-represented vulnerable persons can participate as meaningfully as possible in their own hearings.

14. Women fearing gender-related persecution

14.1 The RPD and the RAD will consider the IRB guideline entitled *Women Refugee Claimants Fearing Gender-Related Persecution* in all cases involving women refugee cases based on gender.[10] This guideline comprehensively sets out the relevant considerations and explicitly recognizes the special problems faced by women who fear gender-related persecution.

15. Minors

15.1 In all cases involving minors, the RPD will continue to consider and apply the IRB guideline entitled *Child Refugee Claimants - Procedural and Evidentiary Issues*.[11]

15.2 In all cases involving minors appearing before the ID, the IAD or the RAD, these respective divisions will consider and apply the IRB guideline entitled *Child Refugee Claimants - Procedural and Evidentiary Issues*, making necessary modifications in respect of any provisions in this guideline that are not relevant to the ID, the IAD or the RAD.

16. LGBTI individuals

16.1 Lesbian, gay, bisexual, transgender and intersex (LGBTI) individuals may have suffered negative experiences due to homophobia in their respective countries of origin, most specifically discrimination, bullying, ostracism, violence, sexual assault, and so on. The IRB has been sensitive and will continue to be sensitive and alert to the impact that these particular circumstances may have on some LGBTI individuals; it will also ensure that when identified as vulnerable, those individuals, like other persons identified as vulnerable, are not disadvantaged in presenting their cases to the IRB.

17. References

- Immigration and Refugee Protection Act, S.C. 2001, c. 27.
- Refugee Protection Division Rules, SOR/ 2012-0256.
- Refugee Appeal Division Rules, SOR/2012-0257.
- Immigration Appeal Division Rules, SOR/2002-230.
- Immigration Division Rules, SOR/2002-229.

- Immigration and Refugee Board of Canada. Guideline 3 - Child Refugee Claimants: Procedural and Evidentiary Issues. 1996.
- Immigration and Refugee Board of Canada. Guideline 4 - Women Refugee Claimants Fearing Gender-Related Persecution. 1996. Update.
- Immigration and Refugee Board of Canada. Guideline 7 - Concerning Preparation and Conduct of a Hearing in the Refugee Protection Division. 2003. Amended 15 December 2012.

18. Inquiries

For more information, please contact:
Director, Policy and Procedures Directorate
Immigration and Refugee Board of Canada
Minto Place - Canada Building
344 Slater Street, 14th Floor
Ottawa, Ontario K1A 0K1
Fax: 613-952-9083

Notes

1 S.C. 2001, c. 27.

2 For example, paragraph 209 of the *UNHCR Handbook on Procedures and Criteria for Determining Refugee Status under the 1951 Convention and the 1967 Protocol Relating to the Status of Refugees* (Geneva, December 2011) states that "some degree of mental disturbance is frequently found in persons who have been exposed to severe persecution." Such persons regularly appear before the IRB, and the processes of the IRB have been designed to ensure that all persons are treated with sensitivity and respect. This Guideline will not necessarily apply to all such persons since it is intended to apply to those individuals whose ability to present their cases before the IRB is severely impaired.

3 Such as a detailed report by an expert following an in-depth assessment of the person.

4 See section 3.2 of IRB, *Guideline 7 – Concerning Preparation and Conduct of a Hearing in the Refugee Protection Division.* December 1, 2003. Amended December 15, 2012.

5 The Minister of Citizenship and Immigration and the Minister of Public Safety and Emergency Preparedness.

6 RPD rule 50 (SOR/2012-0256), ID rule 38 (SOR/2002-229), IAD rule 43 (SOR/2002-230) and RAD rule 35 (SOR/2012-0257).

7 IRPA, subsection 162(2).

8 For a useful guide on questioning, see the *Training Manual on Victims of Torture* developed by the Learning and Professional Development Directorate (LPDD) of the IRB. The principles suggested in the manual with respect to torture victims can be adopted, with necessary modifications, to the questioning of other vulnerable persons.

9 See also RPD rule 20 (SOR/2012-0256), ID rules 18 and 19 (SOR/2002-229), IAD rule 19 (SOR/2002-230) and RAD rule 21 (SOR/2012-0257).

10 Guideline 4 – *Women Refugee Claimants Fearing Gender-Related Persecution.* Update, November 25, 1996.

11 Guideline 3 – *Child Refugee Claimants: Procedural and Evidentiary Issues.* September 30, 1996.

Appendix F

PRECEDENTS AND TEMPLATES

1. Lawyer Retainer Agreement

TO: John Fink (LSUC # 32161V)
      Barrister and Solicitor
      c/o Fink Law
      10 Denver Street, New Town
      Ontario N2V 70D
      Tel: 232-765-8976
      Fax: 232-766-8790

I HEREBY RETAIN and instruct you to act on my behalf in connection with the detention review scheduled for _____ and to use your best efforts to secure my release.

I UNDERSTAND that this retainer does not include work in connection with any judicial review proceedings or any other appeal.

I UNDERSTAND that at the conclusion of the detention review hearing, whether I am released or not, you will no longer be responsible to do any further work on this matter, unless I further retain you to do so.

I ACKNOWLEDGE that you will charge a fixed fee of $3,000.00 plus HST and that for the purpose of your dockets for work done on my file, your hourly rate is $250.00 per hour.

I ACKNOWLEDGE that pursuant to the Law Society of Ontario rules, you must submit interim and final fee and disbursement billings in accordance with the hourly rate set out above.

I UNDERSTAND you may assign other clerks to work on my detention review file and I acknowledge that they will be billed out to an hourly rate of $75.00 per hour.

I HAVE READ the waiver at Schedule "A," and through my signature, I waive any client-consultant privilege/confidentiality as I am aware that Gill St. John and Tony St. John and other persons I may name need to be familiar with the facts of my file in order to assist me in securing my release.

I ACCEPT that although you have charged a fixed fee, there may be circumstances where further work may have to be done on my file as set out below:

The case becomes more complex requiring further preparation and legal research time than would usually be the case.

The detention review scheduled for _____ is adjourned and that adjournment is outside your control.

You request an adjournment, which is necessary in my best interests.

There may be other circumstances that necessitate a fee higher than the aforesaid fixed fee and you will inform me in writing of the reasons that required the fees to be higher than the fixed fee.

I HAVE READ, UNDERSTOOD AND AGREE through my initials the estimate of how the fixed fees are calculated and your billing periods as stated at Schedule "B" attached to this retainer agreement.

I UNDERSTAND AND ACCEPT that you can only advance my best interests in securing my release if you have my full cooperation and that of the bondsperson(s). I accept that in the event there is lack of cooperation, you will be entitled to terminate the within retainer upon the provision of three days' written notice to me. Furthermore, I accept that I must inform you immediately of my change of address, telephone numbers and email address and that of my bondsperson(s) as well within 48 hours. I further agree that I and my bondsperson(s) will communicate with you immediately upon request by you. I understand my failure to abide with the aforesaid can also result in you terminating the within retainer.

Finally, if I fail to pay your periodic/interim fee billing within three days of it being rendered, that will also be a ground for you to terminate the retainer. The provision of the estimate of fees and billing periods is provided to me so I can budget for the anticipated fees in advance.

(Enclosed Schedule "A" and Schedule "B," which form part of the within retainer agreement)

_____
Alfred Blake

_____
John Fink, lawyer

CLIENT ID # _____
c/o Gill St. John
20 Becca Drive, Orangeville
Ontario L6V 2N7
Tel: 905-534-6745
Email: gillstjohn@hotmail.com

Dated this __day of May 2018 at the City of Toronto, Ontario

2. Schedule "A": Waiver and Direction to Pay

Schedule "A"

Waiver and Direction to Pay

TO: John Fink
Barrister and Solicitor
c/o Fink Law
10 Denver Street, New Town
Ontario N2V 70D
Tel: 232-765-8976
Fax: 232-766-8790

I, Alfred Blake, hereby authorize and direct you, John Fink, Barrister and Solicitor, to share all the information in my detention review file and all my instructions to you as my lawyer to the persons named below:

Gill St. John and Tony St. John

I understand that by doing so, I have expressly waived solicitor-client privilege and confidentiality as the above-named persons will be privy to and will have knowledge of all matters, discussions and consultations between myself and you, my lawyer, John Fink. This waiver will operate and be of full force and effect unless later revoked by me in writing.

Furthermore, by this direction and authorization, I direct that you shall seek payment of your fee bills and disbursements from Gill St. John, who is responsible to make such payments for all the work that you will do on my file. This direction to pay will be effective unless later revoked by me in writing.

_____

Alfred Blake

_____

John Fink, lawyer

Dated this ___ day of May 2018 at the City of Toronto, Ontario

3. Schedule "B": Estimate of Fees

Estimate

Description of Work	Time in Hours
Initial telephone attendance:	0.5
Drafting retainer agreement and schedules:	1.0
Attendance at Rexdale IHC to execute retainer:	1.0
Correspondence to ID:	0.3
Review of detention review transcript or audio tape:	2.0
Interview of Alfred Blake at IHC to review detention review transcript and instructions:	1.5
Interviews and preparation of affidavits of Gill St. John and Tony St. John:	2.0
Preparation for the detention review hearing and any research on the law:	1.5
Attendance at the detention review at IHC:	3.0
Estimated hours:	12.8

Estimated cost:	$ 3,200.00
HST:	$416.00
Total estimated cost:	$ 3,616.00

Please sign below to evidence your acknowledgement and acceptance of the above estimate of fees. Note that this is only an estimate and may vary based on the caveat in the retainer agreement.

_____

Alfred Blake

_____

John Fink, lawyer

Dated this ___ day of May 2018 at the City of Toronto, Ontario

4. RCIC Retainer Agreement

Note: This template is provided by ICCRC for RCICs' consideration and use when drafting a Retainer Agreement. It is NOT meant to be used "as is." The template's suitability depends on a number of factors, such as the current state of the law and practice in the RCIC's jurisdiction, the category of representation, and the needs and preferences of the RCIC and Client. The Retainer Agreement must be completed with the actual terms and conditions of the business arrangement between a RCIC and his/her Client.

RCIC Retainer Agreement Template of the ICCRC

RCIC Membership Number: R_____
Client File Number: _____

This Retainer Agreement is made this ___ day of _____, 201_, between RCIC *[insert RCIC name]* (the "RCIC"), located at *[insert business address]* and Client *[insert Client name]* (the "Client"), located at *[insert address]*.

WHEREAS the RCIC and the Client wish to enter into a written agreement which contains the agreed upon terms and conditions upon which the RCIC will provide his/her services to the Client.

AND WHEREAS the RCIC is a member of Immigration Consultants of Canada Regulatory Council (the "Council"), the regulator in Canada for immigration consultants;

IN CONSIDERATION of the mutual covenants contained in this Agreement, the parties agree as follows:

1. DEFINITIONS
The terms "Client", "Council", "Disbursement" and "RCIC" shall have the meaning given to such terms in the Retainer Agreement Regulation of the Council.

2. RCIC RESPONSIBILITIES AND COMMITMENTS
The Client asked the RCIC, and the RCIC has agreed, to act for the Client in the matter of _____.

In consideration of the fees paid and the matter stated above, the RCIC agrees to do the following: *[describe in detail scope of services]*

Another RCIC will carry out the following: *[as applicable]*

3. CLIENT RESPONSIBILITIES AND COMMITMENTS
3.1 The Client must provide, upon request from the RCIC:

All necessary documentation in English or French, or if in another language with an English or French translation

3.2 The Client understands that he/she must be accurate and honest in the information he/she provides and that any inaccuracies may void this Agreement, or seriously affect the outcome of the application or the retention of any status he/she may obtain. The RCIC's obligations under the Retainer Agreement are null and void if the Client knowingly provides any inaccurate, misleading or false material information. The Client's financial obligations remain.

3.3 In the event Immigration, Refugees and Citizenship Canada (IRCC) or Employment and Social Development Canada (ESDC) should contact the Client directly, the Client is instructed to notify the RCIC immediately.

3.4 The Client is to immediately advise the RCIC of any change in the marital, family, or civil status or change of physical address or contact information for any person included in the application.

3.5 In the event of a Joint Retainer Agreement, the Clients agree that the RCIC may share information among all clients, as required. Furthermore, if a conflict develops that cannot be resolved, the RCIC cannot continue to act for both or all the Clients and may have to withdraw completely.

4. BILLING METHOD

The Client will be billed by *[insert billing method; by the hour or flat fee with payment by milestones or predetermined date]*.

The details of this billing method are as follows: *[list the hourly rate charged or the pertinent milestones or predetermined dates and amounts owing.]*

5. PAYMENT TERMS AND CONDITIONS

Professional fees: *[insert amount, including currency; e.g., C$, US$, etc.]*

Disbursements: *[describe in specific detail the disbursements on the file, such as immigration application fees to the government, courier costs, photocopies, etc.]*

Applicable taxes: *[include registered tax number]*

Total cost: *[insert amount, including currency; e.g., C$, US$, etc.]*

The above amount is to be paid by the Client and is subject to change upon mutual agreement of both parties.

6. PAYMENT SCHEDULE

Deposit: *[insert amount, including currency; e.g., C$, US$, etc.]*
(Paid at signing of contract)

Balance: *[insert amount, including currency; e.g., C$, US$, etc.]*
(Paid at time of filing)
Special arrangements mutually agreed upon by the Client and RCIC (e.g., payment by post-dated cheques, different currency, etc.): *[fill in as required]*

7. REFUND POLICY

The Client acknowledges that the granting of a visa or status and the time required for processing this application is at the sole discretion of the government and not the RCIC. Furthermore, the Client acknowledges that fees are not refundable in the event of an application refusal. If, however, the application is denied because of an error or omission on the part of the RCIC or professional staff, the RCIC will refund all professional fees collected.

The Client agrees that the fees paid are for services indicated above, and any refund is strictly limited to the amount of fees paid. Unused fees will be refunded in the following manner: *[describe the manner of refund, including method and timeframe]*.

In the event the Client is unable to contact the RCIC and has reason to believe the RCIC may be dead, incapacitated, etc., the Client should contact ICCRC.

8. DISPUTE RESOLUTION RELATED TO THE CODE OF PROFESSIONAL ETHICS

In the event of a dispute related to the Code of Professional Ethics, the Client and RCIC are to make every effort to resolve the matter between the two parties. In the event a resolution cannot be reached, the Client is to present the complaint in writing to the RCIC and allow the RCIC *[insert number of days]* days to respond to the Client. In the event the dispute is still unresolved, the Client may follow the complaint and discipline procedure outlined by the Council on their website under the heading "File a Complaint." *Note:* All complaint forms must be signed.

ICCRC Contact Information: Immigration Consultants of Canada Regulatory Council (ICCRC) 5500 North Service Rd., Suite 1002 Burlington, ON, L7L 6W6 Toll free: 1-877-836-7543

9. CONFIDENTIALITY

All information and documentation reviewed by the RCIC, required by IRCC and all other governing bodies, and used for the preparation of the application will not be divulged to any third party, other than agents and employees, without prior consent, except as demanded by law. The RCIC, and all agents and employees of the RCIC, are also bound by the confidentiality requirements of Article 8 of the Code of Professional Ethics. The Client agrees to the use of electronic communication and storage of confidential information. The RCIC will use his/her best efforts to maintain a high degree of security for electronic communication and information storage.

10. FORCE MAJEURE

The RCIC's failure to perform any term of this Retainer Agreement, as a result of conditions beyond his/her control such as, but not limited to, governmental restrictions or subsequent legislation, war, strikes, or acts of God, shall not be deemed a breach of this Agreement.

11. CHANGE POLICY

The Client acknowledges that if the RCIC is asked to act on the Client's behalf on matters other than those outlined above in this Agreement, or because of a material change in the Client's circumstances, or because of material facts not disclosed at the outset of the application, or because of a change in government legislation regarding the processing of immigration or citizenship related applications, the Agreement can be modified accordingly.

12. TERMINATION

12.1 This Agreement is considered terminated upon completion of tasks identified under section 2 of this agreement.

12.2 This Agreement is considered terminated if material changes occur to the Client's application or eligibility which make it impossible to proceed with services detailed in section 2 of this Agreement.

13. DISCHARGE OR WITHDRAWAL OF REPRESENTATION

13.1 The Client may discharge representation and terminate this Agreement, upon writing, at which time any outstanding fees or Disbursements will be refunded by the RCIC to the Client/any outstanding fees or Disbursements will be remitted by the Client to the RCIC.

13.2 Pursuant to Article 11 of the Code of Professional Ethics, the RCIC may withdraw representation and terminate this Agreement, upon writing, provided withdrawal does not cause prejudice to the Client, at which time any outstanding fees or Disbursements will be refunded by the RCIC to the Client/any outstanding fees or Disbursements will be remitted by the Client to the RCIC.

14. GOVERNING LAW

This Agreement shall be governed by the laws in effect in the Province/Territory of _____, and the federal laws of Canada applicable therein and except for disputes pursuant to Section 8 hereof, any dispute with respect to the terms of this Agreement shall be decided by a court of competent jurisdiction within the Province/Territory of _____.

15. MISCELLANEOUS

15.1 The Client expressly authorizes the RCIC to act on his/her behalf to the extent of the specific functions which the RCIC was retained to perform, as per section 2 hereof.

15.2 This Agreement constitutes the entire agreement between the parties with respect to the subject matter hereof and supersedes all prior agreements, understandings, warranties, representations, negotiations and discussions, whether oral or written, of the parties except as specifically set forth herein.

15.3 This Agreement shall be binding upon the parties hereto and their respective heirs, administrators, successors and permitted assigns.

15.4 This Agreement may only be altered or amended when such changes are made in writing and executed by the parties hereto.

15.5 The provisions of this Agreement shall be deemed severable. If any provision of this Agreement shall be held unenforceable by any court of competent jurisdiction, such provision shall be severed from this Agreement, and the remaining provisions shall remain in full force and effect.

15.6 The headings utilized in this Agreement are for convenience only and are not to be construed in any way as additions to or limitations of the covenants and agreements contained in this Agreement.

15.7 Each of the parties hereto shall do and execute or cause to be done or executed all such further and other things, acts, deeds, documents and assurances as may be necessary or reasonably required to carry out the intent and purpose of this Agreement fully and effectively.

15.8 The Client acknowledges that he/she has had sufficient time to review this Agreement and has been given an opportunity to obtain independent legal advice and translation prior to the execution and delivery of this Agreement.

In the event the Client did not seek independent legal advice prior to signing this Agreement, he/she did so voluntarily without any undue pressure and agrees that the failure to obtain independent legal advice shall not be used as a defence to the enforcement of obligations created by this Agreement.

15.9 Furthermore, the Client acknowledges that he/she has received a copy of this Agreement and agrees to be bound by its terms.

15.10 The Client acknowledges that he/she has requested that the Agreement be written in the English language; Les parties reconnaissent qu'elles ont exigé que ce qui précède soit rédigé en anglais. *[To be included in the*

English version of the Retainer Agreement drawn up by RCICs working in Quebec.]

16. CONTACT INFORMATION

Client Contact Information

Given name _____

Family name _____

Address _____ Telephone number _____

Cellphone number _____ Fax number _____

E-mail address _____

RCIC Contact Information

Given name _____

Family name _____

Address _____ Telephone number _____

Cellphone number _____ Fax number _____

E-mail address _____

IN WITNESS THEREOF this Agreement has been duly executed by the parties hereto on the date first above written.

_____

Signature of Client

_____

Signature of RCIC

17. ATTACHMENTS (IF APPLICABLE)

[examples: Initial Consultation Agreement/Agent Agreement/Designate authorization]

5. Correspondence to the Immigration Division in the Alfred Blake Case

John Fink
Barrister and Solicitor
10 Denver Street, New Town
Ontario N2V 70D
Tel: 232-765-8976
Fax: 232-766-8790

John Fink, L.L.B. (Hons.)
Barrister and Solicitor
Email: finklaw@gmail.com
LSUC #: 32161V

URGENT

SENT VIA FAX: 416-744-4274

May 3, 2018

The Immigration & Refugee Board
The Immigration Division
385 Rexdale Blvd.
Etobicoke, Ontario M9W 1R9

Attention: Registrar of the Immigration Division

Dear Sir/Madam:

Re: Alfred Blake
Client ID # 00087651
Date of Next Detention Review Hearing: May 9, 2018

Please be advised I have been retained by Alfred Blake who was detained by the CBSA and recently had his 48-hour detention review on May 2, 2018, at the Rexdale Holding Centre where he is being detained. I enclose the Counsel Contact Information Form to confirm my appointment as Mr. Blake's counsel. I will represent Mr. Blake at his next 7-day detention review at the Holding Centre on May 9, 2018.

In order to properly prepare for that review hearing, I ask that you provide me a copy of the detention review transcript of the hearing on May 2, 2018.

I also require a copy of Mr. Blake's GCMS notes. I will also make a separate request for these notes from the CBSA.

As the hearing is imminent, I would ask that this request be given urgent attention.

In the meantime, I thank you for your assistance.

Yours truly,

John Fink
Barrister and Solicitor
LSUC # 32161V

Enc: Counsel Contact Information Form

6. Correspondence to the Immigration Division under the Amended Chairperson's Guidelines on Detention, Effective April 1, 2019

John Fink
Barrister and Solicitor
10 Denver Street, New Town
Ontario N2V 70D
Tel: 232-765-8976
Fax: 232-766-8790

John Fink, L.L.B. (Hons.)
Barrister and Solicitor
Email: finklaw@gmail.com
LSUC #: 32161V

URGENT

April 25, 2019

SENT VIA FAX: 416-744-4274

The Immigration & Refugee Board
The Immigration Division
385 Rexdale Blvd.
Etobicoke, Ontario M9W 1R9

Attention: Registrar of the Immigration Division

SENT VIA FAX: 905-405-3526

The CBSA
Greater Toronto Enforcement Centre
6900 Airport Road, Station 2B
Mississauga, Ontario

Attention: CBSA Officer assigned to the detainee, Dustin Hoffer

Dear Sir/Madam:

Re: Dustin Hoffer
Client ID # 00093540
Date of Next Detention Review Hearing: April 30, 2019

Please be advised I have been retained by Dustin Hoffer, who was detained by the CBSA and recently had his 48-hour detention review on April 23, 2019, at the Rexdale Holding Centre where he is being detained. I enclose the Counsel Contact Information Form to confirm my appointment as Mr. Hoffer's counsel. I will represent Mr. Hoffer at his next 7-day detention review at the Holding Centre on April 30, 2019.

In order to properly prepare for that review hearing, I ask that you provide me a copy of the detention review transcript of the hearing on April 23, 2019.

Pursuant to paragraph *7.3.2* of the amended *Chairperson's Guidelines on Detention*, effective April 1, 2019, I require full disclosure of all the documents and information and evidence including exculpatory materials the Minister relied upon at the 48-hour and intends to rely upon at the forthcoming detention review hearing. Pursuant to the guidelines, I take the position that the Minister is not entitled to rely at the hearing on any information, evidence or documents that have not been disclosed to me. I also require the source of all the information, evidence and documents that the Minister provides so I can decide whether to summon to the hearing any officer who may have provided the Minister with the disclosed information for the purpose of cross-examination.

As the hearing is imminent, I would ask that this request be given urgent attention.

In the meantime, I thank you for your assistance.

Yours truly,

John Fink
Barrister and Solicitor
LSUC # 32161V

Enc: Counsel Contact Information Form

7. Affidavit of Gill St. John

IN THE IMMIGRATION DIVISION

IN THE DETENTION REVIEW HEARING OF ALFRED BLAKE

AFFIDAVIT OF GILL ST. JOHN

(SWORN MAY 7, 2018)

I, Gill St. John of the town of Orangeville in the county of Dufferin **MAKE OATH AND SAY AS FOLLOWS:**

1. I have direct knowledge of the matters to which I hereinafter depose.
2. I am a Canadian citizen and I have no criminal convictions or pending criminal charges against me. I have never had any trouble with the police or the authorities.

    Attached to this my affidavit marked exhibit "1" is a true copy of my citizenship card and the Bio page of my Canadian passport.

3. I have known Alfred Blake (Hereinafter referred to as Alfred) for nine months, having first met Alfred when I attended a church in Hamilton with friends and family sometime in September 2017. I came to know him as my brother, Tony St. John, knew Alfred's twin brother in our country of origin—Jamaica. I liked Alfred and soon we dated regularly. By the end of 2017, we both knew we loved each other and wanted to make a lifelong marital commitment with each other. I invited Alfred to come and live with me and Tony at my house in Orangeville. At the beginning of February 2018, he moved in with me. I asked him about his job at the Fresh Farmers Produce company in Hamilton and mentioned that it would be a long commute from my home to that farm. He told me he had to quit the job as one of his fellow employees was emotionally and physically abusive to him. I was shocked by the nasty behaviour of this fellow worker and could understand Alfred's reluctance to continue working there. He said he had arranged employment at a dairy farm in Grand Valley, which is a town that is a 20-minute drive from Orangeville. I knew there are many farms in that rural town and was pleased with his work plans.
4. During the time Alfred lived with me and Tony, he was always well behaved and obeyed the rules of our household. He contributed to the expenses of our home as he still had some savings. He told me he would contribute more money to our living expenses once he secured the job in Grand Valley. As he is quite skilled at carpentry, Tony, who is a licensed carpenter, gave Alfred occasional jobs to do until he could secure employment at the farm in Grand Valley at the beginning of May 2018. Things were going well with

Alfred and me, so much so that we planned to become engaged in the late summer this year.

5. On Monday, April 30, 2018, at about 11.00 a.m., while Tony and I were at work, I received a call from Alfred saying that immigration cops had come to my house and arrested him for speeding a few weeks ago. He told me he would call me in the evening, and he was about to talk more when I heard loud voices in the background, then Alfred hung up. Both Tony and I were distressed about Alfred's arrest and patiently waited for Alfred to call us. Later that evening, he called me and told me that he had been arrested because he was illegal in Canada as he was supposed to go back to Jamaica soon after he came to live with me in Canada but stayed on. During the call, I put Alfred on speaker-phone, so Tony could hear what Alfred was saying. Alfred told us he was being detained at Rexdale Holding Centre and wanted us to help him. Tony and I were upset that Alfred had lied to us, and I told Alfred we could not help him. However, the following morning I called an immigration lawyer, whom one of my friends recommended, to help me understand what was going on with Alfred. I was reluctant to provide a performance bond at that stage as I was worried about my student loan, even though the lawyer assured me my loan would not be affected by me standing as a bondsperson.

6. When I learned that Alfred's detention had continued after his 48-hour review, I decided to help Alfred as I knew he was a good person and always respected Tony and me, consistently following the rules of our household. I spoke to Tony, and he was also willing to help Alfred.

7. I've worked at the CIBC in Orangeville for the last three years. My gross income is $50,000 a year. After payment of all my statutory expenses, my net income is $38,000 per year. I own a 3-bedroom detached home at 20 Becca Drive in Orangeville. It is worth $350,000. I have a mortgage of $175,000 with annual mortgage payments of $12,000 per year. I can provide a performance bond of $3,000. However, if the member requires a higher bond then I am prepared to abide by such a decision.

Attached to this my affidavit marked exhibit "2" is a true copy of my notice of assessment for 2015-2017, a letter from my employer confirming my employment/income and the deed/mortgage documents of 20 Becca Drive, Orangeville, showing my ownership of the property and the mortgage that is owed on it.

8. Both Tony and I know Alfred's immigration history, and that he breached our immigration laws by fleeing from FFP where he was supposed to work in accordance with his work permit. Alfred also failed to leave Canada when he was required to do so on February 10, 2018 but decided to continue to live in Canada illegally as an overstayer. I understand these are serious breaches of the law. I have assessed the risk involved in being a bondsperson and I am confident that he will not imperil my bond and will appear for removal or any immigration proceedings. Since he has lived with Tony and

me, he has shown respect to us and obeyed our rules of the household. I do not believe he will jeopardize the trust we have placed in him.

9. I understand and appreciate the risk I face in being a bondsperson. I am fully aware that my performance bond will become payable if Alfred breaches any conditions of release that the member imposes on him. Both Tony and I will ensure that he is always supervised. I work day shifts and Tony usually works in his carpentry business in his workshop at our home during the day. Only occasionally, he visits his store during the day, and as Alfred is currently assisting Tony, he will be with Tony during the day and will accompany Tony to his store. Furthermore, we live in a quiet neighbourhood and we usually retire to bed at 11.00 p.m. When Alfred lived with us, he obeyed this bedtime household curfew and will continue to do so upon his release. I ask the Immigration Division to impose a condition of residence at my home in Orangeville, so Tony and I can exercise strict control and supervision over Alfred. Furthermore, I will check any mail to Alfred from the CBSA or the CIC [Citizenship and Immigration Canada] and ensure he complies with any directives in that mail. I intend to drive Alfred to the CBSA office on the dates and times he needs to report to them. Finally, I will make sure he reports for removal and any immigration proceedings, so he complies with his conditions of release.

10. I make this affidavit in support of Alfred's release on appropriate conditions and for no improper purpose.

SWORN BEFORE ME   )
This 7th day of May 2018)
at the City of Toronto   )

_____   _____
Commissioner for Oaths etc…,   Gill St. John

8. Affidavit of Tony St. John

IN THE IMMIGRATION DIVISION

IN THE DETENTION REVIEW HEARING OF ALFRED BLAKE

AFFIDAVIT OF TONY ST. JOHN

(SWORN MAY 7, 2018)

I, Tony St. John of the town of Orangeville in the county of Dufferin **MAKE OATH AND SAY AS FOLLOWS:**

1. I have direct knowledge of the matters to which I hereinafter depose.
2. I am a Canadian citizen and I have no criminal convictions or pending criminal charges against me. I have never had any trouble with the police or the authorities.

   Attached to this my affidavit marked exhibit "1" is a true copy of my citizenship card and the Bio page of my Canadian passport

3. I have known Alfred Blake (Hereinafter referred to as Alfred) for nine months. I first met Alfred at a church in Hamilton when I was visiting friends and family sometime in September 2017. I recognized Alfred as I knew his twin brother in Jamaica before I emigrated to Canada. At church I started to talk to him and then introduced Alfred to my sister, Gill St. John. I noticed that they soon started dating and, on some occasions, Alfred would come to our house in Orangeville and I got to know him better. At the beginning of February 2018, he moved in with Gill in our house in Orangeville. Gill told me that Alfred had left his job at the Fresh Farmers Produce (FFP) in Hamilton, as it would be a long commute from Orangeville. I believe he was looking for a job in a farm in a town near Orangeville.
4. When Alfred lived with us, he obeyed the rules of our household including an 11.00 p.m. bedtime curfew that Jill imposed on us because she did not want any noise after that time since we lived in a quiet and peaceful part of town. Alfred was always well behaved and respected the rules of our household. I know Alfred helped with some of the expenses of our household and intended to contribute more when he got a job.
5. I am a licensed carpenter, having worked in this industry for the last five years. I am self-employed. I have a workshop in our house where I do most of my work. I also have a shop in town, which I usually attend three times a week in the late morning until five in the evening. Alfred has some skills in carpentry, and the plan is that he will assist me in my business until he gets a full-time job. I intend to bring him to my shop when I go there if he

is released from detention so that I can supervise him during the day when Gill is at work.

Attached to this my affidavit are my CRA Notices of Assessment for the last 3 years marked exhibit "2", which shows I receive an annual net income of $30,000.00

6. On Monday, April 30, 2018, at about mid-day Gill called me at my shop in town and told me that Alfred had been arrested by the CBSA, Both Gill and I were distressed and wanted to know what was going on as Alfred did not tell her much. In the evening, Alfred called Gill to give her more information, and she put him on speakerphone. I was upset when he told us that he was illegal in Canada. He told us that he should have left Canada at the time he came to live with us. He also told us he was being detained at Rexdale Holding Centre and wanted us to help him. Both Gill and I were upset that Alfred lied to us, and we both told Alfred we couldn't help him. Furthermore, I didn't know what was involved in the detention review process and was reluctant to get involved in something that I did not know about.

7. A few days later when Gill told me Alfred's detention had continued after his 48-hour review, Gill and I decided to help Alfred as we knew he was a good person and always respected us and followed the rules of our household.

8. Gill and I know Alfred's immigration history. He disobeyed Canadian immigration law when he fled from the FFP when he was supposed to continue working there in accordance with his work permit. He did not leave Canada on February 10, 2018 as his work permit expired on that date. He continued to live in Canada illegally as an overstayer. I understand these are serious breaches of the law. I have assessed the risk involved in being a bondsperson and I am confident that he will not put my bond at risk and will appear for removal or any immigration proceedings. Since he lived with Gill and I, he respected us and demonstrated that he can follow the rules of the household. I do not believe he will risk losing the trust we have placed in him.

9. I am prepared to provide a cash deposit of $2,000.00. However, should the member believe a higher cash deposit is required, I am prepared to do this. I understand the risk I face in being a bondsperson. I know my cash deposit will be forfeited if Alfred breaches any conditions of release that the member imposes on him. Gill and I will ensure that he is always supervised. I attend my shop several times a week and as Alfred is assisting me in my carpentry business, he will attend the shop with me. I ask the immigration division to impose a condition that Alfred resides at our home in Orangeville, so Gill and I can supervise Alfred 24-7, which we are able to as he will be with me during the day. Furthermore, both Gill and I are at home after 5 p.m. in the evenings and the weekends. I will ensure he reports to the CBSA, attends any immigration proceedings and for his removal to Jamaica if that is required, so he complies with all the conditions of release.

10. I make this affidavit in support of Alfred's release on appropriate conditions and for no improper purpose.

SWORN BEFORE ME)
This 7th day of May 2018)
at the City of Toronto)

_____   _____
Commissioner for Oaths etc…,   Tony St. John

9. Counsel Contact Information Form

Immigration and Refugee Board of Canada
Commission de l'immigration et du statut de réfugié du Canada

Division(s): ☐ ID ☐ RPD ☐ IAD ☐ RAD

IRB File Number(s): _____

Counsel Contact Information

To be completed by counsel.
Providing the following information to the IRB will allow the divisions to verify that counsel is an authorized representative pursuant to the *Regulations Amending the Immigration and Refugee Protection Regulations*.

Given Name and Surname (Mr. Mrs. Ms.)

Law Firm or Company

Number and Street	Apt. #	City	Province	Postal Code

Telephone Number	Fax Number	Electronic Mail Address
( )	( )	

Membership of a professional organization
Check one

☐ Lawyer / Paralegal / Notary : _____
      Province

☐ Immigration Consultants of Canada Regulatory Council (ICCRC)   Membership Identification Number _____

Note : If there is any change to the information you have provided, please complete a new form and provide it to the IRB. **You must also inform us of any limitations on your retainer.**

Notice : The information provided is subject to disclosure under the *Privacy Act* and the *Immigration and Refugee Protection Regulations*.

Version française disponible en page 2

IRB / CISR 101.02 (12/2012)

10. Bondsperson Forms Issued by the IRB

Immigration and Refugee Board of Canada
Immigration Division

Commission de l'immigration et du statut de réfugié du Canada
Section de l'immigration

Bondsperson Information

DETAILS ABOUT THE DETAINED PERSON FOR WHOM A BOND IS BEING OFFERED

File No.: _____ Client ID No.: _____
Family / last name(s) / surname(s): _____
Given / first name(s): _____

DETAILS ABOUT THE PROPOSED BONDSPERSON

Family / Last name(s) / Surname(s): _____
Given / first name(s): _____
Status in Canada: ☐ Canadian Citizen ☐ Permanent Resident Other: _____
Home address: _____
City: _____ Province: _____ Postal Code: _____
Phone: Home: _____ Work: _____ Cell: _____

Financial Information

Name of employer: _____
Occupation: _____
Annual income: _____ Length of service: _____
Total amount of savings: _____

Property owned

Address: _____
Value of property: _____ Amount of mortgage owed: _____
Equity (value of property minus amount of mortgage owed): _____
What is the relationship of the proposed bondsperson to the detained person? _____
Will the detained person reside with the bondsperson? ☐ Yes ☐ No
If not, where would the detained person reside and how would the bondsperson supervise them?
_____
_____

Amount of bond offered

Cash deposit: _____ Performance bond (guarantee): _____

Note: For IRB purposes only. The information provided is subject to disclosure under the *Access to Information Act*, the *Privacy Act*, and the *Immigration and Refugee Protection Regulations*.

Disponible en français
ID/SI - 674 (Bondsperson Information) (04/13)

Immigration and Refugee Board of Canada
http://www.irb-cisr.gc.ca
Bondsperson Information

Canada

PRECEDENTS AND TEMPLATES • 249

11. Sample Release Order

Immigration and Refugee Board of Canada
Immigration Division

Commission de l'immigration et du statut de réfugié du Canada
Section de l'immigration

File No./N° de dossier : _____
Client ID No./N° ID client : _____

Order for release / Ordonnance de mise en liberté

In the matter of the Minister of Public Safety and Emergency Preparedness and
Dans l'affaire intéressant le ministre de la Sécurité publique et de la Protection civile et

_____
[name and given names of person concerned in block letters / nom et prénoms de l'intéressé en lettres moulées]

Before Devant : _____, Member of the Immigration Division
[name in block letters / nom en lettres moulées], commissaire de la Section de l'immigration

Pursuant to the *Immigration and Refugee Protection Act*, it is hereby ordered that the person concerned be released from detention subject to the following conditions:

Conformément à la *Loi sur l'immigration et la protection des réfugiés*, la Section de l'immigration ordonne par la présente la mise en liberté de l'intéressé sous réserve des conditions suivantes :

☒ _____
[name and given names of guarantor in block letters]
posts a guarantee (**performance bond**) in the amount of $ 2000 in the name of the Receiver General for Canada.

☐ _____
[nom et prénoms du garant en lettres moulées]
verse un cautionnement (**garantie d'exécution**) au nom du Receveur général du Canada au montant de _____ $.

☒ _____
[name and given names of depositor in block letters]
makes a **deposit** in the sum of $ 3000 in the name of the Receiver General for Canada.

☐ _____
[nom et prénoms du déposant en lettres moulées]
dépose au nom du Receveur général du Canada la **somme** de _____ $.

The person concerned shall:
☒ Present themselves at the date, time and place that a Canada Border Services Agency (CBSA) officer or the Immigration Division requires them to appear to comply with any obligation imposed on them under the Act, including removal, if necessary.

L'intéressé doit :
☒ se présenter aux dates, heure et lieu que fixe un agent de l'Agence des services frontaliers du Canada (ASFC) ou la Section de l'immigration pour se conformer à toute obligation qui lui est imposée sous le régime de la *Loi*, y compris le renvoi, si nécessaire.

☒ Provide CBSA, prior to release with their address and advise CBSA
 ☒ in person, or ☐ in writing of any change in address **prior to** the change being made.

☐ communiquer son adresse à l'ASFC préalablement à sa mise en liberté, et l'informer ☐ en personne, ou ☐ par écrit, de tout changement d'adresse **avant** la prise d'effet du changement.

☒ Report to an officer at the CBSA Office at: GTEC.
6900 Airport Road, Entrance 2B Mississauga, Ontario, L4V 1E8
on or before _TBA_
and (frequency) _once per week_
thereafter. A CBSA officer may, in writing, reduce the frequency or change the reporting location.
☐ confirm their departure with a CBSA officer prior to leaving Canada.

☐ se présenter devant un agent au bureau de l'ASFC à GTEC.
6900 Airport Road, Entrée 2B Mississauga, (Ontario) L4V 1E8
le ou avant le _____
et (fréquence) _____
par la suite. Un agent de l'ASFC peut, par écrit, réduire ou changer le lieu relatif à cette condition.
☐ confirmer son départ auprès d'un agent de l'ASFC avant de quitter le Canada.

☐ Reside at all times with _____
☐ _____

☐ résider en tout temps avec _____
☐ _____

I fully understand and agree to abide by the conditions imposed / Je comprends parfaitement et accepte de me conformer aux conditions imposées
☒ and the annex / et l'annexe : PC initials/initiales int. _____

AUG. 31 / 15
[dd/jj] [mm] [year/année]

_____
[dd/jj] [mm] [year/année]

_____
Signature of person concerned/signature de l'intéressé

_____
Signature of Interpreter / signature de l'interprète

You may apply in writing to the Immigration Division to change any of these conditions / Vous pouvez demander par écrit à la Section de l'immigration de modifier ces conditions.

If the person concerned is not released, the next detention review is scheduled for:
Si l'intéressé n'est pas mis en liberté, le prochain contrôle des motifs de détention aura lieu le : _SEPT 28/15_ at/à _9 AM_
                                                                                                            date   time/heure

Signed on / Signé le _AUG 31/15_ at / à _TORONTO_ _____
                    [dd/jj] [mm] [year/année]   [city/ville]   [Signature of member / signature du commissaire]

ID/SI–674T (09/08)   PERSON CONCERNED / INTÉRESSÉ   Canadä

Immigration and Refugee Board of Canada
Immigration Division

Commission de l'immigration et du statut de réfugié du Canada
Section de l'immigration

File No./N° de dossier : _____
Client ID No./N° ID client : _____

Annex to Order for Release: Additional conditions
Annexe à l'ordonnance de mise en liberté : conditions supplémentaires

In the matter of the Minister of Public Safety and Emergency Preparedness and
Dans l'affaire intéressant le ministre de la Sécurité publique et de la Protection civile et _____
[name and given names of person concerned / nom et prénoms de l'intéressé]

In addition to the conditions listed on the Order for Release, the person concerned shall:

☐ Fully cooperate with Canadian Border Services Agency (CBSA) with respect to obtaining travel documents.

☐ Be accepted as a client for supervision by the Toronto Bail Program and remain in good standing until such time as this condition is cancelled in writing by a CBSA officer.

☐ Not engage in any activity subsequent to release which results in a conviction under any Act of Parliament.

☐ Adhere to a curfew and be present always between the hours of _____ and _____ at the residential address provided to CBSA, except where specifically authorized in writing by a CBSA officer to engage in employment at the premises of a specific named employer and to travel directly to and from that place of employment. An officer may, in writing, reduce the hours that the person concerned must be present at his/her residence or authorize absence for a specific occasion.

En plus de respecter les conditions énoncées dans l'ordonnance de mise en liberté, l'intéressé doit :

☐ collaborer pleinement avec l'Agence des services frontaliers du Canada (ASFC) en ce qui a trait à l'obtention de titres de voyage.

☐ être accepté comme client du Programme de cautionnements de Toronto et demeurer en règle jusqu'à l'annulation de cette condition, par écrit, par un agent de l'ASFC.

☐ à la suite de sa mise en liberté, ne se livrer à aucune activité qui donne lieu à une déclaration de culpabilité en vertu d'une loi fédérale.

☐ respecter un couvre-feu et ne pas quitter l'adresse domiciliaire fournie à l'ASFC aux heures indiquées, soit de _____ à _____, sauf si un agent de l'ASFC l'y autorise expressément par écrit afin d'exercer un emploi dans un lieu de travail précis pour un employeur nommément désigné. L'intéressé est tenu de se rendre à ce lieu de travail et de rentrer chez lui directement. L'agent peut, par écrit, diminuer les heures auxquelles l'intéressé doit être présent à son domicile ou autoriser une absence pour une occasion particulière.

☒ Not authorized to work without a valid permit issued by CIC

☒ post a guarantee in the amount of $15,000 in the name of the receiver general for Canada.

Date : Aug. 31/15

Initials / initiales : Member / commissaire : _____
Interpreter / interprète : _____
Person concerned / intéressé : _____

PERSON CONCERNED / INTÉRESSÉ

Appendix G

IMPORTANT RESOURCES ON DETENTION

1. Chairperson's Guidelines effective June 2013 until amended on April 1, 2019:
   https://irb-cisr.gc.ca/en/legal-policy/policies/Documents/GuideDir02_e.pdf
2. The immigration manual on detention and enforcement, ENF 20, provides detailed instructions to CBSA officers on issues relating to enforcement, arrest and detention. It was updated November 2018 and contains information on the National Directive relating to the detention of children referred to in chapter 12.
   https://www.canada.ca/content/dam/ircc/migration/ircc/english/resources/manuals/enf/enf20-det-en.pdf
3. This immigration manual, ENF 8, provides detailed information about solvency tests for CBSA approval of performance bonds and cash deposits. This is the source for the extract referenced in chapter 13.
   https://www.canada.ca/content/dam/ircc/migration/ircc/english/resources/manuals/enf/enf08-eng.pdf
4. On June 22, 2018, an immigration manual was released that deals with alternatives to detention, including a Community Case Management and Supervision (CCMS) system and electronic monitoring. This is referred to in chapter 16 regarding recent developments.
   https://www.canada.ca/content/dam/ircc/migration/ircc/english/resources/manuals/enf/enf34-eng.pdf

5. The Laird Report is a recent and insightful study into the deficiencies in the detention review process, which influenced the amendment of the June 2013 Chairperson's Guidelines on Detention, effective April 1, 2019.
https://irb-cisr.gc.ca/en/transparency/reviews-audit-evaluations/Pages/ID-external-audit-1718.aspx
6. The University of Toronto publication of Hanna Gros and Yolanda Song, *No Life for a Child*, studies the plight and torment of children in detention.
https://ihrp.law.utoronto.ca/sites/default/files/PUBLICATIONS/Report-NoLifeForAChild.pdf

About the Author

Raj Napal practiced law as a defence trial lawyer in predominantly criminal cases in England for nearly fifteen years before he emigrated to Canada in 1996. There he continued the practice of criminal law but also developed an interest in immigration law. Over the years, his immigration practice became more focused on advocacy and appellate work in all divisions of the Immigration and Refugee Board and the Federal Court. Through this appellate work, he gained valuable practical insights into immigration law.

In August 2016, he began teaching an online immigration diploma course at Ashton College part time. During his online classes at the college, he wrote many case studies and articles to explain the practical aspects of immigration law and to teach how to be an effective advocate in the divisions of the Immigration and Refugee Board. Students enjoyed his practical, hands-on approach to the subject, and so Raj decided to write this book. He continues to combine an active immigration practice with his teaching.

Raj enjoys reading, boating, fishing, tennis and hiking. He loves being with his family and does not let the practice of law, teaching and writing interfere with the time he has with them. He is fortunate for their constant encouragement and support of his writing.